Khadduri, Majid,
1909-

Arab personali-
ties in politics

ARAB PERSONALITIES IN POLITICS

Dedicated
In Friendship
to
Mustafa Ben Halim
Eminent Statesman and Wise Counsellor

ARAB PERSONALITIES
IN POLITICS

By

Majid Khadduri

The Middle East Institute
Washington, D.C.
1981

Copyright 1981 by the Middle East Institute
Library of Congress Catalogue Card Number 81-82184
ISBN 0-916808-18-1
Printed in the United States of America

PREFACE

The revolutionary movement which swept the Arab world in the fifties and caused the downfall of several old regimes and dynasties has considerably altered the structure of Arab politics. Not only has new leadership begun to dominate the political scene, but also new ideas and ideals in politics have been discussed in my *Political Trends in the Arab World* (1970, 1972) and a selected number (twelve case-studies) of the new leaders that formed the subject-matter of my *Arab Contemporaries* (1973).

Since most of the twelve leaders scrutinized in the earlier book have passed away—only three are alive and no longer play a prominent role in politics—I decided that another book on Arab leaders might be useful to deepen our understanding of contemporary Arab politics. The aim of this work, however, is not only to present half a dozen case-studies of the *dramatis personae* who dominate the political scene today, but to inquire into the structure of politics in each country with regard to both the internal and inter-Arab relationships, from the perspective of the leader (or leaders) of each country and the ideas and ideals embodied in the national goals with which he is identified. In my view, inquiry into the interaction between the political leaders and challenging goals would be more illuminating for our understanding of Arab politics than an emphasis on shifting regimes which are not necessarily central in the present stage of political development.

This book is intended primarily for the general reader in Middle Eastern affairs and for readers in international affairs who have some background on the Arab world. It may also be useful for specialists on Arab affairs as it contains some of my thoughts and experiences in the Arab world and material obtained directly from Arab leaders which illuminates their ideas and character. Moreover, I have pursued in the preparation of this book the same method as in my earlier works which deal with the role of personalities in politics in terms of their interaction with ideas and ideals (goals) and with the manner in which these goals are carried out.

It is a pleasure to acknowledge the kindnesses of many friends and acquaintances who have readily given me assistance or counsel during the preparation of this work. Above all, I am grateful to the leaders who form the subject matter of this work and who all graciously agreed to grant me an audience—some more than once on different occasions—and provided me with material about their political roles and discussed some of the events, ideas and issues in which they were involved.

Some of the friends and acquaintances have read the work in part or as a whole and provided me with invaluable comments and suggestions. 'Abd al-'Aziz al-Khuwaytir, Minister of Education, Sulayman Sulaym, Minister of Commerce, and Ghazi al-Qusaybi, Minister of Industry (of the Saudi Government), have read the essay on the Saudi leadership. Ambassador L. Dean Brown, President of the Middle East Institute and former Ambassador to Jordan, read the essay on King Husayn. Ambassador Hermann F. Eilts, now University Distinguished Professor at Boston University and former Ambassador to Egypt, read the essay on President Sadat; and Ambassador Sadiq Jawad Sulayman, 'Uman's Ambassador to the United States, and Brigadier Colin C. Maxwell, Advisor to the Minister of Defense, read the essay on Sultan Qabus. William Sands, former Editor of the *Middle East Journal* and former Foreign Service Officer, and Ambassador Richard Parker, Editor of the *Middle East Journal*, read the entire work and offered many invaluable comments and suggestions. None is responsible for any error which the work may contain.

Majid Khadduri

CONTENTS

CHAPTER I

INTRODUCTION

According to the degree of the people
of resolution come the resolutions,
And according to the degree of noble
men, come noble actions.
al-Mutannabi (d. 965 A.D.)

The Arab countries that had adopted the parliamentary system as a form of government were looked upon by many contemporary writers in the early postwar years as having existed in a relatively "liberal age"; the other countries which were still governed by traditional or semi-tribal regimes were considered behind in political development and were expected to follow the path of the countries that had adopted parliamentary democracy in due time. In the wake of World War II, during which the regimes presided over by European dictators were swept away, there was an expectation in Arab liberal circles that parliamentary democracy would be consolidated and its prospects of improvement enhanced by the victory of democracy over authoritarianism.[1] Indeed, support for

---

[1] In the Arab World—indeed in several other lands—many liberal thinkers maintained that before the era of the Cold War even the Soviet Union was heading toward the democratization of its political system.

democracy was almost taken for granted, as political consciousness, aroused during the war by broadcasts and propaganda literature extolling the merits of a democratic way of life, created pressures urging the democratization of existing parliamentary systems. Above all, the new generation that began to grow up in the post-war years was imbued with liberal principles and hoped that Arab countries would achieve progress and development through democratic processes.

Following the war, when nationalist leaders were swept into power after the achievement of independence (Syria and Lebanon became fully sovereign and foreign influence was considerably reduced in Egypt, Iraq and Transjordan), the elder politicians who were presumably in favor of parliamentary democracy in principle betrayed authoritarian propensities and paid little or no attention to democratic procedures. The younger leaders, representing the new generation that began to exert an increasing influence in society after the war, aspired to play a role in the new regimes after independence and to pursue the cause of democratic freedoms. The majority of these, consisting essentially of intellectuals and professionals (lawyers, engineers, physicians, teachers and others), received their education in Western or national institutions organized on Western models and sought to achieve national goals (democracy, freedom and others) by participation in the political processes. They rendered professional services urgently needed and therefore their influence on the people as a whole could not be long ignored by rulers.[2]

---

[2]For a discussion of the role of the new generation and the influence

However, the older leaders, although they themselves had played the role of the generation that
was young after World War I and had advocated
liberal ideas in the name of which they began to
rule after independence, failed to recognize the legitimate aspirations of the new generation and refused to take its leaders into their confidence, least
of all to share authority with them, despite the fact
that they both sought at the outset to participate in
the political processes through peaceful methods.
Relying for support on landowners and the merchant community, the elder leaders were reluctant
to cooperate with the young leaders and thus appeared in the public eye as vain, self-seeking and
an obstacle to progress. They could no longer carry
the public behind them.

Very soon, the parliamentary system began to
appear meaningless and became so completely
dominated by an old generation that the younger
leaders despaired of any hope of its becoming an
instrument for progress. They had witnessed how
scandalously its processes could be misused by un-
scrupulous leaders and how no opposition was
permitted to check these trends. A crisis of parliamentary rule became apparent since the elder
leaders (the oligarchs) failed to share authority
with other groups or even secure the consent of
the public. Meanwhile, the right- and left-wing
groups (religious and radical elements) that had
long been opposed to the older leadership on the
grounds of its association with foreign influence
tacitly entered into an unholy alliance against the

---

of the young leaders in Arab politics, see my *Political Trends in the
Arab World* (Baltimore: The Johns Hopkins University Press, 1970),
pp. 129-32.

ruling oligarchs, despite their differing views about the form of government they envisioned and their disparate outlook toward society as a whole.

What gave all these elements an opportunity to combine and agitate against the elder leaders was, of course, the bankruptcy of the old regimes, when their weakness was first exposed during the Arab-Israeli war of 1948-49. Even before Israel was established, there was throughout the Arab World great concern about the Zionist threat. The public as a whole, not only younger men, was permitted to express its feelings by such means as street demonstrations, protests to foreign governments and organizations, and by free expressions in the press, on the ground that these nationalist activities were intended to influence the European and Western Powers to sympathize with their aspirations. The young leaders—indeed, leaders of all opposition groups—took an active part in organizing these demonstrations, which helped to strengthen their hold over the people. When the Arab Governments suffered the loss of their case at the United Nations and defeat in the war against Israel, the younger leaders joined hands with others to stir popular upheavals against the older leaders and were able to defy with impunity all those in power who failed in their national duty. The cry was that the Arab homeland was in danger.

The old generation (the oligarchs), though not unaware of the increasing influence of the new generation, failed to accommodate itself to the new force in society. They resorted to suppressing it by violent methods. Draconian measures brought only temporary respite, but the new generation was determined to resist the monopoly of power. Failure of the young civilian leaders to achieve power by

peaceful methods prompted the young officers to
intervene, as these officers (some had already been
in secret contact with civilian leaders) shared the
same views and aspirations as their civilian
contemporaries. They moved to achieve by the
weapons of their profession what the other young
leaders could not by protests and civil agitation.

No sooner had the *ancien régime* of the Arab
lands that had experienced revolutionary changes
been swept away than the unholy alliance among
the diverse groups combined against it came to an
end and each group sought to put forth its own
views and platforms, in contradistinction to others,
as the foundation for a new regime. Competition
and rivalry among the civilian leaders to whom the
young officers were expected to entrust power became so intense that the officers who seized power
were bound to remain in power. In time, the military regimes became self-perpetuating, because
each civilian group consciously tried to influence a
"faction" in the Army to seize power by force and
install a regime which would eventually give an
expression to one of the ideologies that had become fashionable in Arab society. This trend set in
motion a chain of military coups, as the precedent
set by one faction to achieve power by a short cut
through the Army inspired other leaders to use the
Army as a political ladder and thus the cycle of
military coups continued. Only when the Army
was brought under the control of a strong leader
who dominated the officers' corps did the spiral of
military coups come to a standstill.

However, the danger of its recurrence has not
yet disappeared. Even in the countries that have
not experienced military rule, the temptation that
an officer might seize power by a military uprising

is haunting civilian rulers and has prompted them
to provide security measures against contingencies.
Small wonder that in most Arab lands the question
of the survival of the regime has become a top pri-
ority and often the goals of reform and development have been subordinated to the requirements
of security.

Few Arab regimes are immune to sudden outbursts and possible downfall at any moment. Even
if it has at its disposal the potentialities for security,
none claims to possess all the requirements of continuity. Because of the Israeli dimension the confrontation regimes are in even more precarious
condition. Today, the immediate objective of all is
survival.

In the Arab countries that have not experienced
military rule, the leaders are seriously considering
reform plans intended either to overhaul or recast
the constitutional structures, hoping that in the
long run they might meet fundamental needs and
aspirations and take root in society. However, no
country claims to have yet reached such a stage.
Nor are the regimes that have been established by
revolutionary methods expected to endure, since
they are considered transitional, designed to
achieve social and economic development before
the envisioned permanent constitutional structures,
enshrining the goals in the name of which they
seized power, can be established.

In the circumstance, a study of the existing Arab
regimes as political "models" is not very illuminating, as these regimes are ephemeral and likely to
change at any moment. In almost all the so-called
revolutionary regimes, the leaders are preoccupied
not primarily with such issues as legitimacy and
political participation but with the more urgent

problems of security and survival. It seems, therefore, more meaningful if Arab politics were to be
studied in terms of the role of the *dramatis
personae*, who are grappling with the problems of
security on the one hand, and the set of ideas and
ideals (goals) with which the leaders are identified
and in the name of which they seized power, on
the other.

For a study of Arab politics from this perspective, I have already undertaken two separate
projects. The first, devoted to a study of the ideas
and ideals in politics, was designed to provide not
merely an exposition of the political ideas of a few
thinkers, but a critique of the major streams of
thought in their relationship to political movements.[3] The second, devoted to a few case-studies
of political leaders identified with one (or more)
major streams of thought and how they tried to
translate them into realities.[4] The study is confined
to twelve leaders, each of whom was consciously
selected to illustrate a category of political leadership and not merely an account of the major political leaders. Nor did that work deal with leadership
as it relates to the major problems and policies of
the particular country with which it was concerned. In this effort, the case-studies of Arab leadership is discussed in the context of political movements within each country concerned and in the
Arab World as a whole.

Since the beginning of the seventies, there has
been a shift in the trends of political thought as

---

[3]Readers who are interested in the scheme of the work might wish
to read the Preface as well as chapters 6 and 10 in my *Political
Trends in the Arab World*, before reading this book.
[4]See my *Arab Contemporaries: The Role of Personalities in Politics*
(Baltimore: The Johns Hopkins University Press, 1973).

well as in the kind of leadership which undertook to carry them out. Under Nasir's leadership, the stream of thought combining Arab nationalism with socialism, often called Arab Socialism—more specifically Nasirism—began to recede after Nasir's death in 1970 and a new brand of Arab Socialism, at first expounded by the Ba'th Party, began to reassert itself in Arab politics, especially following the Ba'th Party's seizure of power in Syria and Iraq, and a new blending of foreign and traditional concepts—cultural, political and economic—was set in motion under new conditions. After Nasir, Egypt's new leadership began to reexamine the relevance of Nasir's Arab Socialism and weigh it essentially on the scale of national interests and not on ideological premises. In Arabia, the present Saudi rulers are asserting their leadership in accordance with the religio-historical and geopolitical forces of the region rather than the ideological commitments of King Sa'ud, a contemporary of Nasir. King Husayn of Jordan, though his family was opposed by the Saudi dynasty, has followed a balancing policy of forces within and outside his country which found in the new Saudi leadership an ally supporting the role he had chosen to play in inter-regional relationships.

For a study of Arab politics from the perspective of this description, the two works published earlier, dealing with *ideas* and *personalities*, should either be revised and brought up to date or a sequel to each undertaken. Neither revision nor the provision of a sequel is considered practical, since the structure of each work, especially the one on personalities, needs to be recast. Perhaps a combination of the purposes of the two works in a single volume might prove to be more useful and illuminating to readers. An approach along this line is worth a try.

Furthermore, the categorization of Arab leaders as idealists, realists, or ideological, which was illuminating in *Arab Contemporaries*, is no longer necessary nor indeed relevant. The first generation of Arab leaders, the founding fathers of Arab nationalism, belonged to an essentially idealist school of thought. They were visionary and inspiring leaders whose goals consisted of promises that they could not fulfill. They entered the political scene with lofty ideas of establishing an independent and united Arab state, with the Arabic language and Arab culture as the new symbols of identity.

After World War I, when the Arab lands emerged neither united nor fully independent, the first generation of Arab leaders were divided into two schools of thought: the *idealist* and the *realist*. The latter, compromising with reality, accepted responsibility under foreign control and tried to the best of their abilities to achieve immediate objectives—mitigation of foreign influence, improvement of internal conditions, etc.—hoping that ultimate goals (full independence, Arab unity, etc.) would be realized in time. The former, the idealist school, asserting the ideas of the founding fathers of Arab nationalism, refused to compromise with reality. Some decided to withdraw from politics, but others preferred to play the role of a loyal opposition against foreign control. In taking such a line of action, they rendered an invaluable national service by criticizing the realists whenever they appeared weakening before foreign pressures.

During the interwar years, the idealists who played the role of loyal opposition were held high in the public eye, because they persisted in their

demand for full national freedom and often attacked the realists for compromises. Not identified
as idealists, they were known to the public under
the rubric of "nationalists," while the realists, almost always in the saddle, were often denigrated
by being labeled the "ally" of foreign influence.
Both, indeed, rendered invaluable services to their
countrymen, though often the realists, under foreign pressures, made decisions considered inconsistent with their country's interest for which they
were denounced as traitors and bitterly attacked in
the press. But that was the price of responsibility.[5]

After World War II, when almost all Arab countries achieved independence—indeed, all in time
became fully independent—the distinction between
idealists and realists on the basis of their cooperation with or opposition to foreign control became meaningless. Since foreign control no longer
remained the major bone of contention, both displayed a keen interest in public responsibility and
entered the political scene to achieve power. However, in their political rivalries and competition,
readiness or refusal to compromise with reality
was reflected essentially in their conflicting attitudes toward social problems. The idealists, perhaps more interested in abstract formulations, ei-

---

[5]Strictly speaking, both the idealists and the realists were in reality
"nationalists," as both were agreed on fundamental national objectives, such as independence and unity, but they disagreed on the
methods of achieving them. The idealists insisted on independence
as a matter of right and demanded withdrawal of foreign control
without having the power to provide them. The realists, aware of
Arab weakness, were prepared to wait until their people were ready
to achieve national goals. It was therefore unfair for the realists to
be labeled the "ally" of foreign influence, as they were as keen as
the idealists to bring foreign control to an end at the earliest possible
moment.

ther found in Islamic principles and values a source of inspiration or tended to fall under new radical winds. Both, the right and left, belonged subsequently to what might be called the ideological school.

From the early postwar years to the end of the Nasir era, the ideological leaders dominated the scene and the realists, faring not much better than during the period between the wars, were looked upon with disfavor and suspicion. After Nasir's departure in 1970, it became abundantly clear that the ideologues failed to achieve national goals—indeed, they brought disaster precisely because they had become out of touch with reality (a situation which brought in its train the Six-Day War)—and the realists began to come to the fore. Even the Ba'thist leaders who came to power in the post-Nasir era may be said to belong essentially to the realist school, though claiming to assert an ideology and often paying lip service to party slogans. President Hafiz al-Asad of Syria and President Ahmad Hasan al-Bakr (succeeded by President Saddam Husayn) of Iraq proved as realist as any other in the category. Today, the distinction between leaders on ideological or other grounds is meaningless. The pendulum has swung almost completely from the ideological to the realist position. The days when the masses used to applaud a Nasir with frenzy are perhaps over. The leaders who dominate the political scene today may be said to belong essentially to the realist school. Nor is there a leader who claims to be a Nasir or Qasim and styles himself as the "sole leader." Leadership in the Arab World today tends to be collective in the sense that no leader in the Arab World today can possibly make decisions alone without consultation with other groups or leaders working with him. Even under a military regime, the top leader is bound to share power with others and exercise it through the mechanism of a political party or other corollary organizations.

In this study, a different scale of categorization is proposed. The half dozen case-studies dealt with in this book are divided into three categories: the dynastic, military and centralizing leaderships. The first is entrusted not necessarily to a single leader but to a "House" which exercises power in accordance with the traditional pattern of authority tempered or amply qualified by new political concepts to accommodate changing conditions which might ultimately transform that leadership from a "traditional" (i.e. semi-tribal or dynastic) into a "modern," permitting the rise of leaders from outside the House in accordance with the emerging patterns of authority. In this category falls the Saudi and Hashimi leaderships of Saudi Arabia and Jordan. In the second category—the military leadership (Egypt, Syria, Iraq and others)[6]—while the Army may still have the final word in political decisions, the civilian leadership seems to re-assert itself and might ultimately bring the Army under its control. The third category, called the centralizing leadership, whose principal aim is to bring together under its command either diverse political entities, as in the United Arab Amirates, or decentralized, if not entirely fragmented, parts of the country as in 'Uman.

---

[6]A study of leadership in Iraq is not included in this work since a separate book on the Iraqi regime has already been published under the title *Socialist Iraq* (Washington, D.C., 1978), to which the reader may be referred.

In this work, which seeks to deepen our understanding of contemporary Arab politics, the method pursued is to relate ideas and ideals (goals), which provide guidance for leaders, to the circumstances and conditions of their respective countries. This method may strike the reader as essentially idealistic, since it stresses such intangible variables as values, legal norms and traditions, referred to collectively as "ideas and ideals"; these variables will not be studied in the abstract, however, but rather in relation to political movements and events in which the leaders have directly or indirectly been involved. The immediate objective of most leaders may or may not have been to translate ideas and ideals into realities by accommodation to conditions; but all Arab leaders who have been guided by ideals have not lost sight of the fact that once a certain set of ideas has been essentially translated into realities, they must move into another stage of realities in which they make a renewed effort to put the ideals into practice. This method, which I have called in an earlier work "empirical idealism," helps to illuminate in a more meaningful way the political development that is in progress now in the Arab World better than the method which stresses essentially tangible variables. Though I have made reference to this method only recently, (in the introductory chapter of my *Arab Contemporaries*), I have always tried to apply it in earlier studies on the contemporary Arab World.

Part One

MONARCHICAL LEADERSHIP

Whenever a chief of ours disappears,
another chief arises
One who speaks as noble men speak,
and acts as strong men act.

al-Samaw'al
(d. circa mid-sixth century A.D.)

CHAPTER II

THE SAUDI LEADERSHIP: KING KHALID AND CROWN PRINCE FAHD

> Let there be one nation of you calling
> for good, and bidding to honor, and
> forbidding dishonor, those are the pros-
> perers.
>
> *The Qur'an* III, 100.

No country has so suddenly emerged since World War II from relative obscurity to a prestigious position in world affairs as Saudi Arabia. Before 1973, it is true, Saudi Arabia was recognized as one of the major oil producers in the world; but it was only after the 1973-74 Arab oil embargo that her leadership began to attract the attention of the world and to be consulted by the Western Powers on major political questions affecting the Middle East as well as on oil and financial matters that have bearing on the world economy. In the Arab World, where Egypt had long asserted her leadership (reaching its height under President Nasir, who declared himself to be the spokesman of Pan-Arabism), this leadership passed to Saudi Arabia after Nasir's departure; indeed, the Saudi challenge to Egyptian leadership began soon after Egypt became involved in the revolutionary movement in Southern Arabia and the Saudi leadership assumed an increasing role in Arab affairs following Nasir's defeat in the Six-Day War of 1967. Yet no matter how important oil is in the modern age, its spiral influence is necessarily ephemeral—and even disastrous—unless this nature-given wealth is entrusted to competent hands guided by wisdom and experience which would provide stability and place the nation along the path of progress and development. Before a study of the Saudi leadership is attempted, a word on the significance of Arabia as a whole might be useful.

Before it became known for its oil deposits, the Arabian Peninsula had long been renowned for its historical-religious heritage and has always been held in Arab and Islamic eyes in the highest respect, owing to the fact that it was the cradle of Islam and the birthplace of the Prophet Muhammad. No less significant is the role Arabia had played in providing the initial dynamic forces that led to the expansion of Islam and the impact it had on the subsequent development of the Islamic Empire. According to modern scholarship and archeological evidence, Arabia was also the source of successive migrations of people who made their home beyond its desert borders and affected the course of history centuries before the rise of Islam.[1] In Arab tradition, Abraham went to the Hijaz, the western region of Arabia, where he built a temple known as the Ka'ba—later rebuilt by Ishmael—and which later the Prophet Muhammad

---

[1] For the view that Arabia was the source of migrations (*volkerwanderungen*) in the ancient Near East and the Arabs as its driving force, see Caetani, *Annali dell-Islam* (Milano, 1907), Vol. II, pp. 831ff; and C.H. Becker, "The Expansion of the Saracens," in H.M. Gwatkin and J.P. Whitney, *The Cambridge Medieval History* (New York, 1913), pp. 331ff. See also 'Abdullah H. Masry, "The Historic Legacy of Saudi Arabia," *Atlas*, Vol. I (1977), pp. 9-19.

turned into the Great Mosque. Makka, the place
where the Great Mosque was erected, and Madina,
the city in which the Prophet established his seat
of government, are the two holiest cities in Muslim
eyes.[2] Today the believers throughout the world
are reminded five times a day of the holy city of
Makka when they turn in prayers toward it (the
qibla, or the direction toward Makka) and, at least
once in a lifetime, to perform the *hajj* (the pilgrimage), and visitation of the Prophet's Mosque
(where he is buried) in Madina. This impressive
historical-religious heritage has become the focus
of attention of believers all over the world and a
source of inspiration for many reformers and
thinkers inside and outside the country.

No less important is Arabia's geopolitical position
as an "island"—indeed, it is called the *Jazirat al-
'Arab* (the Arab Island) by Arab geographers—surrounded by sea and desert which protected her
against foreign invasions and enabled her leaders
to play a significant role in regional and world affairs.[3] Had Arabia been under Roman or Persian
domination before the rise of Islam, conditions
would not have permitted the Prophet Muhammad
to embark on a political career and unify Arabia.
Arabia having been virtually a no-man's land beyond the reach of Roman or Persian authorities,
the Prophet was able to combine religious and po-

---

[2]According to Muslim geographers, who assume the Islamic world to
have the shape of a bird, Makka and Madina occupy the places of
the bird's eyes. See Ibn 'Abd al-Hakam, *Kitab Futuh Misr,* ed. Torrey
(New Haven, 1922), p. 1.

[3]The vast desert area to the north was an effective barrier against
foreign invasions, and conquests of the southern and eastern coasts
invariably proved transitory as native rulers were able eventually to
recover their lands from foreign invaders.

litical authorities, and Islam became the symbol of unity for Arabia.[4] In modern times, it would have been exceedingly difficult for the Wahhabi move ment or even the Arab Revolt of 1916 to material-ize had they not been initiated in areas where the Ottoman authorities had been least effective.[5] Since World War II, despite the overcoming of physical barriers by highly developed technology, most of the leaders of the Arabian Peninsula have been able to keep out of the ideological struggle between the Great Powers and to play a moderating, if not always a constructive, role in inter-regional con-flicts. Because of her control of the inland region, Saudi Arabia is potentially the most able among the Arab states to resist foreign pressures, notwith-standing the need for foreign technical know-how to develop the material resources of the country which has compelled her rulers to depend on the Western Powers and to cooperate with them. Ara-bia's geopolitical and geophysical potentials are likely to continue as important sources of wealth in the foreseeable future, unless nuclear power, or some other alternative sources of energy, competes with these regional resources.

The foregoing sources of power—historical, reli-gious, geopolitical and geophysical—are distributed unevenly among eight territorial sovereignties of the Arabian Peninsula. They all, however, in vary-ing degrees share their resources with other Arab

[4]For a somewhat different perspective on the role of Muhammad as Prophet and political leader, see A.J. Toynbee, *A Study of History* (London, 1934), Vol. III, pp. 469-70.
[5]The Sultan tried to suppress the Wahhabi movement but failed (see p. 24, n.[9] below). For remarks on the favorable location of Arabia for the Arab Revolt of 1916, see T.E. Lawrence, *Seven Pillars of Wisdom* (London, 1938), chs. 1-2.

countries to promote the welfare of the Arab people generally, directly or indirectly. This essay, though devoted primarily to a study of the Saudi leadership, also applies to the leadership of the other countries of Arabia.

II

The part of Arabia in which the future Saudi state was to emerge is the inland, known as the Najd, inhabited by tribal confederations almost invariably at war with one another. Some form of organized life has always existed around the coast since antiquity, but in the interior instability and natural anarchy reigned from time immemorial. The barren nature of the desert area, providing but meager resources, compelled the tribesmen always to be on the move in search of food and water and to make war for the acquisition of commodities— generally speaking, the tribes in the interior were always ready to attack their neighbors and these in turn would attack their next neighbors until the tribal wave reached the coasts and the urban communities of neighboring countries. These constant shifts of tribal warfare, described by T.E. Lawrence as the circulation of the Arabs in Arabia,[6] made it almost impossible to establish anything like a permanent organization.

So long as the tribes were engaged in such internecine warfare, no unity or order was expected to reign in the interior of Arabia. But whenever the attention of the tribes was focussed against an external enemy, they were ready to unite and to follow the leader who would guide them to achieve

---

[6]T.E. Lawrence, *op. cit.*, p. 37.

their objective. Such an opportunity presented itself when the Prophet's early successors embarked
on the wars of conquest outside Arabia and, provided with a sense of unity by their conversion to
Islam, they formed the conquering army of the
newly established Islamic state and were amply
compensated by the spoils of war. The *jihad*, a
war prescribed by religion, was the instrument
which diverted the stored energy of the tribes
from their inter-tribal warfare to an organized war
of conquest against the unbelievers.[7]

When the wars of conquest came to a standstill
and the Islamic Empire went on the defensive, the
Arabian tribes, no longer called upon to fight the
unbelievers, reverted to tribal warfare and to raids
against urban centers. For centuries, the principal
function of the provincial authorities around Arabia was reduced to raising taxes and organizing
mercenary armies in order to protect the urban
centers from periodic Arabian raids. It is true that
some paramount tribal chiefs often proved strong
enough to impose their authority on some portions
of Arabia, especially in the coastal areas, but those
dynasts were unable to establish permanent organizations, and when the paramount chief vanished,
insecurity recurred and inter-tribal warfare was
resumed.

This picture continued virtually unchanged until
the eighteenth century, when another opportunity
to unite the tribes arose under the leadership of a
paramount chief who, in the name of religious revival, took the field and launched campaigns
against rival tribes considered to have abandoned

---

[7]For the nature and drives of the *jihad*, see my *War and Peace in the
Law of Islam* (Baltimore, 1955), chs. 4 and 5.

the true teachings of Islam. The new Islamic resurgence took the form of a puritanical movement, which began first as a call to assert the fundamentals of Islam in accordance with the Hanbali school of law and theology, and a major politico-religious upheaval in Central Arabia. It is outside the scope of this essay to give an account of the rise and development of the Wahhabi movement, which may be found elsewhere;[8] but its impact on the assertion of Saudi leadership and the establishment of a permanent organization in Central Arabia call for an explanation.

The resurgence of Islam in the middle of the eighteenth century and its transformation into a political movement may be regarded as perhaps the most important event in Arabia since the rise of Islam. The two movements—the rise of Islam and the Wahhabi revival—though obviously not comparable in scope and objectives, have both united the tribes of Central Arabia by shifting their focus of attention from inter-tribal warfare to wars of conquest launched against their neighbors. However, since the expansion of Islam transferred the centers of power outside Arabia and took the form of a universal mission, the internal conditions of Arabia reverted to instability and chaos after the Islamic Empire began to decline and disintegrate. The Wahhabi movement, in contrast with the expansion of the Islamic state, focussed its attention essentially on Arabia and therefore may be said to

---

[8]See Husayn B. Ghannam, *Ta'rikh Najd* [History of Najd], (Cairo, 1949), Vol. I, pp. 25ff; and al-Shaykh 'Abd al-Rahman Ibn 'Abd al-Latif Ibn 'Abd-Allah Al al-Shaykh (ed.), *Kitab Lam' al-Shihab Fi Sirat Muhammad Ibn 'Abd al-Wahhab* (Riyad, 1394/1974). See also H. St. John Philby, *Saudi Arabia* (London, 2nd ed. 1950); and R.B. Winder, *Saudi Arabia in the Nineteenth Century* (New York, 1965).

have played the role of a "national" religion for Central Arabia. The identification of the Saudi House with the Wahhabi movement proved invaluable not only for the establishment of an organized authority in Central Arabia but also for its survival. The Wahhabi creed served as a watchword, if not an ideology, and the Saudi House, highly respected among its followers, provided leadership for the tribal community. The unity of civil and religious authority is not new in Islam, but it has often fallen into disuse. The marriage between Wahhabism and the Saudi leadership brought the duality of state and religion into active life again in Arabia. By providing a dynastic basis for the tribal community, the Saudi House helped to transform the chaotic conditions of Central Arabia into a permanent organization—a necessary stage for the establishment of a modern nation-state—before the Saudi state would reach its full development.

Though it emerged as a separate entity, the Wahhabi movement failed at the outset to establish an independent state. There were forces working from within and from outside Arabia that militated against the development of the state toward maturity. First, the Ottoman Porte, considering Central Arabia to fall under its jurisdiction, became concerned about the possible impact this religious resurgence might have on other Arab provinces, and tried not only to suppress the Wahhabi movement as a heresy, but also to bring the Saudi House under its control. For this reason, the Ottoman authorities instructed the provincial governors of Cairo and Baghdad to dispatch forces that would reduce the Saudi state to the provincial level.[9] Sec-

---

[9]Only Muhammad 'Ali, Viceroy of Egypt, who had just organized an army on a European model, responded to the Sultan's appeal in 1811, but despite almost three decades of campaigns which carried

ond, competition and rivalry among the Saudi pretenders to rulership, which reached its height in the mid-nineteenth century, led to a civil war which undermined the Saudi House and prepared the way for the rise of the rival House of Rashid at Ha'il. For a while Central Arabia was torn by two rival houses. In 1891, Ibn Rashid finally drove 'Abd al-Rahman Ibn Sa'ud, head of the Saudi dynasty, from Riyad and entered into an alliance with the Ottoman Porte. Meanwhile the Ottoman authorities had grown in strength in Arabia and were able to extend their control to Western Arabia and the northern part of Eastern Arabia. By the turn of the twentieth century, most of Arabia passed under Ottoman domination.[10]

But Ottoman control of Arabia, though seemingly secure, proved shortlived, because the Ottoman Empire as a whole was on the decline and its destruction was soon to be completed during World War I. The new forces that were in the making for the emergence of a new political structure in the Arab World after World War I gave the Saudi state an opportunity to reemerge under a new leadership. 'Abd al-'Aziz Ibn Sa'ud, later to be known as Ibn Sa'ud, had already assumed leadership of the Saudi House ever since he captured Riyad from Ibn Rashid in 1902.[11] So long as the

---

the Egyptian army to the heart of Arabia, the Viceroy of Egypt finally ordered his army to withdraw from Arabia in 1840. For a brief account of the Egyptian campaigns, see Henry Dodwell, *The Founder of Modern Egypt* (Cambridge, 1931), ch. 2.

[10]For a brief account of Ottoman penetration into Arabia and the decline of their power, see D.G. Hogarth, *Arabia* (Oxford, 1922), pp. 93-99, 113-131.

[11]The story of how Ibn Sa'ud set out from his exile in Kuwayt with hardly more than a handful of followers (later to become some 40 men) and captured the former seat of power from his rival Ibn Rashid has often been told in several works. For Ibn Sa'ud's own version of the story, see Fu'ad Hamza, *al-Bilad al-'Arabiya al Su'udiya* [The Saudi Arabian Lands] (Riyad, 2nd ed., 1948), pp. 20-26.

two houses of Ibn Rashid and Ibn Sa'ud competed for leadership, Central Arabia remained divided. However, the fall of the Ottoman Porte, Ibn Rashid's principal source of power, signaled the end of Ibn Rashid's leadership. That end came sooner than it was expected, as Ibn Sa'ud's forces, strengthened and reorganized after World War I, were able to unify Northern Arabia within less than a decade. From that time, Ibn Sa'ud emerged as the founder of the new Saudi state. Would he be able to provide it with a permanent foundation?

III

"He may well be the big man you represent him to be," said D.G. Hogarth[12] in a conversation with Philby, "But after all what is he? A great Badawin chief of outstanding ability like the old Muhammad Ibn Rashid and others who have passed across the Arabian stage, having their mark on history certainly, but nothing like a permanent organization. We know what has invariably happened on their deaths—a wild reversion to the natural chaos and anarchy of Arabia. Now Ibn Sa'ud is human after all, and what will happen when he dies? The same old anarchy again!"[13]

After World War I, three Arab personages—the Sharif Husayn in the Hijaz, Ibn Sa'ud in Riyad, and Ibn Rashid in Ha'il—had already made their ap-

---

[12]A noted scholar at Oxford University who served as a counsellor at the British Residency in Cairo during World War I. See T.E. Lawrence, *Seven Pillars of Wisdom* (London, 1938), p. 48.

[13]See H. St. J. Philby, *Arabian Days: An Autobiography* (London, 1948), p. 159.

pearance on the Northern Arabian stage as the great rival leaders contending for power and whose ambitions obviously extended beyond their respective boundaries. As noted before, Ibn Rashid's rule, which was dependent on Ottoman support, was first reduced and then overthrown by Ibn Sa'ud, not without difficulty, after World War I. There remained in Northern Arabia only two rival leaders—the Sharif Husayn and Ibn Sa'ud.

Since she was the ally of both the Sharif Husayn and Ibn Sa'ud, Great Britain was confronted with an exceedingly awkward and difficult situation. She tried at the outset to reconcile their conflicting ambitions by focussing their attention on two different directions; but since the two great dynasts had their eyes fixed on future control over the whole of Northern Arabia, Britain was bound to decide sooner or later on whom she had to depend—and consequently to support—as the principal ally if the two leaders were to come into irreconcilable conflict.

Though Ibn Sa'ud had already demonstrated his ability and great courage in war and diplomacy and received the support of a number of Britain's proconsuls in Arabia, there were others in London who seem to have been looking for the future leadership of Arabia in other directions. The Colonial and the Foreign Offices had divergent views on the matter—each represented a school of thought which looked on Arabia from a different perspective. Before World War I, the viewpoint of the Indian and Colonial Offices prevailed and their advisors in the field—Sir Percy Cox, Arnold Wilson, Shakespear and others—urged His Majesty's Government to depend for the protection of British interests in the Indian Ocean on Arab rulers of the

Gulf and Central Arabia. For this reason, Britain extended her protection to the rulers of Kuwayt, Bahrayn and the Trucial Coast, and came to a tacit understanding with Ibn Sa'ud to the south of Kuwayt, although formal recognition of independence and support for his regime was not extended until 1915.[14]

After the outbreak of the war, however, the Foreign Office advisors in the field—Sir Henry Mac-Mahon, Gilbert Clayton, Hogarth and others—began to view the situation from a different angle. They argued that the growing British influence in the Eastern Mediterranean and the Red Sea required the support of leaders in areas where Arab nationalism had already begun to develop and saw in the Sharif Husayn and his sons the potential rulers who would provide leadership for the Arab nationalist movement as the new ally of Britain. Since Sir Percy Cox had been transferred to Persia before the outbreak of hostilities and Shakespear died in action in Central Arabia (in one of Ibn Sa'ud's campaigns against Ibn Rashid in 1915) it fell to less influential men like Sir Arnold Wilson and Philby to plead the support of Eastern Arabia's rulers as the most able and dependable allies for Britain.

More specifically, the controversy between the two schools was narrowed down to a choice between Sharif Husayn and Ibn Sa'ud as the future

---

[14]In the so-called 'Uqayr Treaty, Ibn Sa'ud's independence was recognized provided that no dealings with another Power were to be undertaken without consultation with Britain. For this arrangement, Ibn Sa'ud was granted political, military and financial assistance. For text of the treaty, see Hafiz Wahba, *Jazirat al-'Arab* [The Arab Island] (Cairo, 1935), pp. 350-51; and J.C. Hurewitz, *The Middle East and North Africa In World Politics: A Documentary Record* (New Haven, 1979), Vol. II, pp. 57-58.

ruler of Northern Arabia. Because Sharif Husayn
was the descendant of the Prophet and the guardian of the holy sanctuaries in Western Arabia, the
British Government sought by these symbols to
gain Arab and Islamic support against the Ottoman
Empire during the war.

It was to this religio-his-
torical heritage that Hogarth referred in this conversation with Philby, calling it the "permanent organization," as the reason for British preference
for Husayn's leadership over that of Ibn Sa'ud.

Despite the lack of agreement with Sharif
Husayn over several issues—later developing into
sharp disagreement on fundamentals—the British
Government sided with Sharif Husayn whenever
there was a conflict between him and Ibn Sa'ud.
Invoking the British commitments of 1916—embodied in the so-called MacMahon Correspon-
dence—Sharif Husayn went as far as to claim sovereignty over all Arabia except South Arabia and
the Gulf principalities which had been under British protection. Ibn Sa'ud rejected Sharif Husayn's
claims and the conflict between the two leaders,
beginning at the outset on frontier issues which
Britain could not resolve, led eventually to war
(1924) and the incorporation of the whole of the
Hijaz in Ibn Sa'ud's kingdom. Thus Husayn's rule
came to an end.

Though Ibn Sa'ud challenged Sharif Husayn despite British support for his leadership, he proved
in the long run to be a man of greater insight and
dependability than his rivals. Becoming more difficult to deal with as he grew older, Husayn gradually lost control even over his countrymen, while
Ibn Sa'ud, proceeding to consolidate his position
step by step, unified the country as it expanded
from coast to coast. It soon became abundantly

clear that his hold over a large portion of Arabia
was the culmination of a long career of industry
and good judgment and not merely the product of
coincidental events and auspicious circumstances.
From the time he captured Riyad in 1902 to his
death in 1953, Ibn Sa'ud spared no time in consolidating his rule and laying down the foundation of
a new political structure which would ensure the
survival of the Saudi state. No reversion to the
"natural chaos and anarchy" upon his death occurred; on the contrary, the new political structure
he had founded continued to develop after him as
a permanent institution and no longer dependent
on one particular ruler or another. In retrospect,
one might well refer to the life-long pattern of his
political behavior as the political testament of Ibn
Sa'ud, but its elements were not laid down as a
logical plan; they can be reconstructed from the
steps and actions that he took during his governance.

Ibn Sa'ud's political ideas were derived not from
fanciful ideas or abstract notions about state and
society, but from his own experiences in public life
extending over half a century. From childhood, he
was more interested in outside activities than in in-
door studies, though he managed to learn the
Qur'an when he was eleven years old and to receive instructions in religion and law (the Shari'a)
from a private tutor. It was, however, from his association and experiences with men of action of
his day—his great rival Ibn Rashid of Ha'il and his
renowned friend Shaykh Mubarak al-Sabah of
Kuwayt, not to speak of many visitors and representatives of foreign governments—that he learned
not only the manners and customs of great men

but, perhaps more important, how to tackle difficult problems and resolve them.[15] From his country's history and traditions—indeed, from the history and traditions of Islam as a whole—he carried the tradition that state and religion must be united. In Central Arabia, this unity had been achieved when Muhammad Ibn Sa'ud and Muhammad Ibn 'Abd al-Wahhab came to an agreement to unite the sword with the creed and establish the Saudi state—Islam and the Wahhabi teachings were to indicate the goals and the state was to be the instrument with which to achieve those goals in accordance with changing circumstances. Ibn Sa'ud appealed to the religious feeling of a tribal force known as the Ikhwan (Brothers), who provided the Army with which he was able to consolidate his power. But the Ikhwan, essentially a puritanical group, were opposed to change. Since they became an obstacle to progress, Ibn Sa'ud began to encourage them to settle and engage in agriculture in order to divert them from public life and reduce their influence. In place of the Ikhwan, a new Army, modeled on Western patterns, was organized to insure unity and provide security.[16]

Aware of the fact that he was the ruler of an essentially tribal society, he was convinced that if that society were to live in peace, its authority would have to be exercised by strong leadership.

---

[15]For Ibn Sa'ud's visits to Kuwayt to consult with Shaykh Mubarak, see Amin al-Rayhani [Rihani], *Ta'rikh Najd al-Hadith wa Mulhaqatih* [The Modern History of Najd and Its Dependencies] (Bayrut, 1928), pp. 103-6, 107-8, 114-18, 135-37, 165-70, 177-206.

[16]For a study of the Ikhwan, see John S. Habib, *Ibn Sa'ud's Warriors of Islam: The Ikhwan of Najd and Their Role in the Creation of the Saudi Kingdom, 1910-1930* (London, 1978).

He seems to have concluded that in order to insure continuity authority must be entrusted to an established house or dynasty that would provide strong leadership. Perhaps pride induced him to think that the dynasty which his great grandfather had established over a century and a half ago was the one which would provide the requisite leadership; indeed, the record of the dynasty demonstrated that his judgment was sound.

However, Ibn Sa'ud did not pretend that his House was in perfect order. Twice before him the Saudi state had been shattered by dissension, as noted before. Authority, in Ibn Sa'ud's eyes, was in the last analysis identical with the ruling House, and was ultimately derived not from the people but from religion and the state, united within the framework of the sacred law—the Shari'a.

Needless to say, Ibn Sa'ud did not himself prescribe that his House should provide leadership for the country—the precedent had already been set by his ancestors. He had, however, laid down the rule that his successors should be from among his own sons in accordance with seniority. Recalling the disaster that befell his House because of quarrels among pretenders and the rise of a rival house that ruled Central Arabia half a century before, he admonished his sons that such a quarrel should never again be repeated. It was no secret that in the last few years before his death Ibn Sa'ud had doubts about his eldest son's ability to succeed him, but he was not in favor of changing the rule of seniority because such a precedent might lead again to quarrels among pretenders and undermine the prestige and leadership of his House. Shortly before his death, he gathered the leading members of his House and impressed upon them

the need to respect the seniority rule. It is reported
that all promised to abide by the rule and in his
presence took an oath to be loyal to Sa'ud upon his
assumption of authority as king, even if he or anyone else after him proved less than qualified in
their eyes.[17]

With regard to foreign policy, Ibn Sa'ud made it
clear once and again that Saudi Arabia should always maintain peaceful relations with the outside
world. More specifically, he stressed that as far as
the other Arab countries were concerned, Saudi
Arabia should not interfere in their domestic affairs. True, Ibn Sa'ud had come into conflict with
Sharif Husayn of the Hijaz, but his relations with
the Sharif's sons—Faysal and 'Abd-Allah, rulers of
Iraq and Trans-Jordan—were correct, and even
friendly, after the Hashimi House had given up its
claim to the Hijaz.

These broad points, reflecting Ibn Sa'ud's
thought and actions, were to serve as guidelines
for his successors, but they were not intended to
be applied without consideration to changing circumstances. The Saudi leaders have, indeed, considered these guidelines subject to modification,
though they have on the whole followed them con-
sistently, especially in their relations with other
Arab countries. Thus, when King Sa'ud was unwittingly drawn into Arab conflicts, the other Saudi
leaders—Faysal, Khalid, Fahd and others—seem to

---

[17]I have it on the authority of some of my informants from the Saudi
family and senior Saudi Advisors that Ibn Sa'ud had some reservations about Sa'ud's fitness to be a ruler and he may have preferred
Faysal to be the Crown Prince, but he seems to have thought that
the danger of breaking the rule of seniority would be greater than
allowing Sa'ud to rise to the throne.

have objected to this departure and tried to assert
a foreign policy consistent with their father's goals.

IV

"Ibn Sa'ud," said Rashad Fir'awn, "was endowed with unique qualities; none of his sons
claims to possess all his qualities, though each one
has indeed inherited some but not all of them." [18]
Both physically and mentally he stood head and
shoulder above all the men around him. In physical stature and courage, though not in wisdom
and good judgment, his son Sa'ud, who ruled from
1953 to 1964, was almost equal to him; his son
Faysal, who replaced Sa'ud as ruler from 1964 to
1975, inherited his father's wisdom and good judgment, though not his physical stature and drive;
King Khalid, who succeeded Faysal in 1975, possesses his father's excellences in integrity and fair-
mindedness but has shown no great ambition to
pursue power or to be involved in the detailed
business of government as Chief Executive. The
Amir Fahd, the Crown Prince and the next in line
for succession, perhaps comes nearest to his father
in outlook and general qualities—he is reputed to
possess wisdom, ambition and the will-power to
achieve the goals for which the Saudi House
stands. The Amir 'Abd-Allah, Commander of the
National Guard, and the Amir Sultan, Minister of
Defense, have distinguished themselves as very

---

[18]Rashad Fir'awn (Pharaon), the first Minister of Health under Ibn
Sa'ud's regime and now advisor to King Khalid, came originally
from Syria and has been over 40 years in the service of the Saudi
House. He served in a number of offices on the Cabinet level and
had other functions at the Royal Palace (the writer's interview with
Rashad Fir'awn, Riyad, January 11, 1979, and January 1, 1980).

ambitious and courageous and both might live long enough to ascend the throne. The thirty-five sons—not to mention those who died in infancy— form the first generation of the Saudi House after Ibn Sa'ud's departure; but each of these offspring, as well as each of Ibn Sa'ud's half a dozen brothers, has his own family. It is exceedingly difficult to cite the number of the members of the Saudi House who are alive, consisting of all Ibn Sa'ud's descendants and the descendants of his brothers. It is said that they exceed two thousand princes.[19]

However, not all the members of the Saudi House have entered service of the state and those who hold public offices do not enjoy equal voice in public affairs. Indeed most of the princes today lead private lives and look after their own personal affairs. Some, who are interested in public affairs, participate in organizations and public activities, as it is considered their duty to encourage the public in the service of society. The majority, however, seem to be content in their rather prestigious and comfortable lives, pursuing their own social or business enterprises. As a princely class, they tend to inter-marry within the family though their males often married female commoners and have not shied from fraternizing with them.

Nor did all who have entered service of the state hold high political posts. True, under Ibn Sa'ud's regime most top offices, including Cabinet portfolios, command of the Army and provincial governorships, were entrusted to members of his family, but today this is no longer the rule, as an increas-

---

[19]This figure would become over five thousand if we consider the families that have been associated and inter-married with the Saudis (like the Sudayris, the Jilawis, the Thunayyans and others) as princely members of the Saudi House.

ing number of the new generation of Saudi citizens who received higher education abroad have entered service of the state and have risen to Cabinet rank and high offices. Because of the country's potential and the increasing opportunities for work outside the Government, not only the patrician Saudi clan but also plebeians prefer to work in the private rather than in the public sector.

All members of the Saudi House, however, whether in public or private capacities, possess a high sense of moral responsibility, stemming partly from the historical-religious heritage that the founders of the Saudi state have bequeathed and partly from a feeling that the survival of the Saudi regime is not only the responsibility of a few Saudi leaders but the responsibility of all. Considering themselves as guardians of the regime, members of the Saudi House have developed the practice of holding informal meetings, attended not necessarily by all but by some, to discuss both public and private affairs *in camera*. It is said that they often speak frankly on family affairs whenever something has gone amiss and they admonish—they even move to deprive from his post or privileges— anyone of their number if they feel he has acted contrary to family, let alone public interests. In these meetings, the rule of seniority prevails not only as a matter of procedure but also in deference to the wisdom and experience of elder members.

In their public behavior pattern, the members of the Saudi House conduct themselves as if they form an organization equivalent to a political group or a party which provides leadership and acts as a link between society and state. Not only do the members who hold positions in the state receive private citizens in their offices—indeed, the

King today observes the tradition of holding daily councils which are open to all who wish to see him, and a weekly council to meet the ulama (religious scholars) and tribal leaders—but also others who are not in the service of the state often receive visitors who talk openly about public and private affairs. Thus the leading members of the Saudi House keep themselves, directly or indirectly, well informed about public affairs and communicate their information and personal views to those who hold public offices. In their relations with compatriots, whether in public or private capacities, the members of the Saudi House have shown on the whole sympathy, magnanimity and understanding. Scarcely has any of them seemed to have displayed vengeance, as they prefer to give concessions and waive personal privileges rather than arouse reproach and discontent. True, occasional criticism has been leveled against some, but the Saudi House as a whole has been held in high respect and the loyalty of all has never been questioned.

As the ruling elite, the Saudi leaders are quite aware that unless they maintain solidarity and cooperation in the governance of the country, all may suffer disrespect and a possible fall from power. Thus, it is for valid reason that whenever they appear in public they observe strictly their family's mores and display deep respect to one another—indeed, the younger in particular defer to the older and when they sit in a public gathering they follow the rule of seniority in the order in which they take their places. Nor do they criticize one another in public. Indeed, even when they meet *in camera*, though they speak their minds openly, they seldom level sharp criticism against one another; they seem merely to present differing opinions and viewpoints for discussion, and the views of the older members, considered to reflect wisdom and experience, often prevail.

Because of his prestige, power and the relatively limited income of the country, Ibn Sa'ud's pattern of monocratic rule was considered highly advantageous, especially in the early years when the country had just been separated from the Ottoman Empire and was indeed in need of strong leadership. But after his departure none of his sons was able to follow in his footsteps and impose his will on others. Defying advice, King Sa'ud tried and failed. So disastrous were the consequences of his arbitrary rule—his squandering of public money, interference in the domestic affairs of other Arab countries and others—that the position of the whole Saudi House seemed to have been undermined, which prompted the leading members of the family to force him first to relinquish some of his powers to the Council of Ministers, headed by his brother Faysal, and then to abdicate in favor of Faysal.[20] In order to repair the situation, Faysal repudiated Sa'ud's reckless individual rule and consciously tried to follow the country's traditions and the guidelines laid down by his father, Ibn Sa'ud.[21]

After Ibn Sa'ud's departure, the Saudi House seems to have come to the conclusion that power

---

[20]For an account of the abdication of Sa'ud and of Faysal's pattern of leadership, see my *Arab Contemporaries* (Baltimore, 1973), ch. 6.

[21]In an interview with King Faysal in 1966, and earlier with King Sa'ud in 1955, it became clear to me that Sa'ud tried to avoid references to his father while Faysal asserted his own personal views demonstrating his intention to conform to family traditions, practices and guidelines. This impression was confirmed in the course of my talks with some of my informants during recent visits to Saudi Arabia.

must be shared not only with an increasing number of other houses but also with the new generation that has arisen since the war and has shown an interest in the governance of the country. The tendency to share power with the new generation has become even more apparent since Faysal's departure. Accordingly, the higher echelon of the bureaucracy has been filled with young men who received higher education abroad, of whom several have reached Cabinet rank and been allowed to participate in the decision-making process. These young men have been recruited to represent various sections of the country and given a share of the responsibility to carry out decisions in which they participated. The Saudi leaders today may well be said to be satisfied with presiding over the state and providing guidance and direction rather than in monopolizing power and isolating themselves from the public. Only the Heads of State and Government and a handful of high offices, including some Cabinet posts, are being held today by members of the Saudi House, while a larger number of high positions in an expanding structure of the state have been filled with personnel who seem to be quite prepared to cooperate with the Saudi leaders in their endeavors to create a modern nation-state. Before a discussion of the emerging structure of polity is attempted, a study of the personality and character of the leading members of the Saudi House might be illuminating.

V

King Khalid, the fifth son of Ibn Sa'ud, was born in 1331/1912 in Riyad when his father went to war with the Ottoman authorities in Eastern Arabia in an effort to capture al-Ihsa' (al-Hasa), the coastal area of the Gulf lying between Kuwayt and Qatar, considered by Saudi rulers to have been part of the territory under their control before it passed under Ottoman domination almost a century before. Upon his triumphant return to Riyad, Ibn Sa'ud was delighted to meet his newly-born son on the occasion of the annexation of the eastern province to his kingdom.

From childhood, Khalid received attention from his father and even greater attention from his mother (d. 1963), who was close to her husband, and when he grew up he often accompanied his father and witnessed some of his desert exploits at first hand. Not inclined to stay home, he paid greater attention to outdoor activities and spent most of his early years in the desert which he seems to have loved. His early experiences in the desert made him quite knowledgeable about the tribal way of life and he came to know many tribal chiefs with whom he kept a life-long friendship. But he managed in his spare time to acquire basic knowledge about religion and the Shari'a and to recite some parts of the Qur'an from memory. Asked by the writer about the book that had the greatest influence on him, he had no hesitation in replying that it was the Qur'an. Deeply influenced by his early religious instruction, he grew up a man to whom moral principles became overriding, and his father was quick to note the impact of morality on his son's conduct. For this reason he seems to have enjoyed very high respect within the family—this and other good-mannered qualities compelled all to listen to young Khalid. Even his father, it is said, who often paid no attention to personal requests, was prepared to listen to him, because the father realized that his son possessed a fair-minded disposition and rose above personal gains.

Growing up in a home where he received full parental attention and relative comfort, Khalid suffered no personal insecurity or deprivation. Faysal, Ibn Sa'ud's third son, who suffered the loss of his mother soon after he was born, grew up in his mother's family and saw very little of his father until he was old enough to realize that he had to trade on his talent in order to attract his father's attention and make his way up in the Saudi House. Appreciating Faysal's good judgment, his father began to pay attention to him and entrusted him with important missions which aroused the jealousy of his older brother Sa'ud, who might have suspected that Faysal's ambition was to gain precedence over him in the Saudi House. From childhood Khalid harbored no such feeling—he grew up confident and found that not only father and mother gave him love and attention but also brothers and friends showered him with high praise and great attention. His greatest assets were, and still are, his integrity and straightforwardness. As a result, he found everything he desired within reach and all paid attention and readiness to offer assistance. Fully content, he displayed no great ambition and feared no competition from brothers. On the contrary, his congeniality and disinterestedness induced his brothers to offer him privileges denied to others.

Aloof and not destined to be in the line of succession, as he was preceded by three older living brothers, young Khalid did not even seek a public office and spent most of his early years in the desert. Nor was he inclined to be drawn into active social life; he preferred to stay within his own family circle and was married rather early in life. Until World War II, his travels were confined to the Gulf and Egypt; but during and after the war, he visited Europe and the United States on more than one occasion. His first visit to the United States via West Africa and Brazil in 1943 gave him an opportunity to get acquainted with several foreign countries and observe the Western way of life at first hand. In 1945 he accompanied the Amir Faysal, then Foreign Minister, to the San Francisco Conference, which laid down the United Nations Charter, and participated for the first time in an international conference—in the first conference he attended in 1939, the Palestine Round-Table Conference in London, he went as an observer in the company of the Amir Faysal. These and other short-term official functions provided him with varied experiences in foreign and domestic affairs which proved invaluable for the exercise of his responsibility when he rose to the throne.

His turn to become the second in the line of succession came when the Amir Faysal suddenly succeeded his brother Sa'ud as King in 1964. In accordance with the Sa'udi rule of succession, the Amir Muhammad, second in seniority to Faysal, was in line to become the Crown Prince. Three months after he came to the throne, King Faysal dispatched Rashad Fir'awn, his personal advisor, to sound out Muhammad's preparedness to become the Crown Prince. The Amir Muhammad, according to Fir'awn, replied that he was not interested in the throne and that he would relinquish his seniority right to his full brother (from the same mother), the Amir Khalid, next in line to him.[22] Indeed, it is public knowledge that the Amir Muhammad, though he keeps himself well-informed on public affairs, had no desire to be burdened with responsibility and regal paraphernalia and preferred to lead his own way of life and exercise personal influence outside rather than inside official circles. But he is keenly interested in public affairs and he is reputed to express his views freely to other members of the Saudi House.[23] Thereupon, King Faysal approached the Amir Khalid, who showed no great enthusiasm at first to become the second in the line of succession, but accepted the offer as a matter of duty. King Faysal appointed him officially as the Crown Prince and deputy Prime Minister on March 29, 1965. In 1968, the Amir Fahd, Minister of the Interior, was appointed as second deputy Prime Minister. It was then taken for granted that the Amir Fahd was destined to become the Crown Prince, should the Amir Khalid rise to the throne, as the Amirs Nasir and Sa'd, who precede the Amir Fahd in seniority, have shown no interest in public affairs nor did their Saudi brothers seem to have been inclined to entrust them with public responsibility.

From 1965 to 1975, during the period he served as Crown Prince, the Amir Khalid was not in the best of health, as he suffered a heart attack and had to undergo surgery. Nonetheless, he continued to attend to public functions and, upon the assassi-

---

[22]The writer's interview with Rashad Fir'awn (Riyad, January 11, 1979). See also Khayr al-Din al Zirikli, *Shibh al-Jazira Fi 'Ahd al-Malik 'Abd al-Aziz* [The Peninsula During the Reign of King 'Abd al-Aziz (Ibn Sa'ud)] (Bayrut, 1970), Vol. IV, p. 1046.

[23]In their private gatherings, I have been told, the Amir Muhammad assumes his position of seniority whenever the Saudi Amirs meet for informal talks.

nation of King Faysal on March 25, 1975, he succeeded him to the throne. On the same day, the
Amir Fahd, second deputy Prime Minister, was
proclaimed Crown Prince and became the deputy
Prime Minister. Because of the heart condition of
King Khalid, Crown Prince Fahd has undertaken
not only the responsibility of running the business
of government as deputy Prime Minister, but also
in providing guidance and inspiring confidence for
a country in need of strong leadership. Except on
special occasions when the King presides over the
Cabinet, the Amir Fahd ordinarily chairs Cabinet
meetings. In his absence, the Amir 'Abd-Allah, who
became second deputy Prime Minister and Commander of the National Guard, chairs the meetings.
The Amir Sultan, next in official rank (though not
in seniority) who served shortly as Governor of Riyad, continued as Minister of Defense; the Amir
Na'if, former Governor of Riyad and deputy Minister of Interior, became Minister of Interior; and the
Amir Salman, deputy Governor of Riyad, succeeded the Amir Sultan as Governor of Riyad. The
Amir Sa'ud, son of King Faysal, became Minister
for Foreign Affairs, partly in deference to his father, who had long served as Foreign Minister before he became King, and partly because of his
own competence and experience in the Department of Petroleum and Minerals.

Amir Fahd's background and personality throw
light on his role as a leading member of the Saudi
House and the public figure to whom all essential
powers have been delegated. Second in line of succession to the throne, he was born in Riyad on October 24, 1920. His mother, Hissa, the fifth wife of
Ibn Sa'ud, was a Sudayri—one of the established
houses with which the Saudi House was closely
connected by marriage. Hissa gave birth to over a

dozen children, collectively known as the Al Fahd, after the name of the senior child, the Amir Fahd, in accordance with traditions.[24] Hissa was a remarkable woman who took a special interest in the upbringing of her children and inspired them with a sense of family solidarity. She insisted, it is said, that her children should get together at least once a day at lunch or dinner and that she see them before they retired to bed in the evening. This tradition of getting together, providing an occasion to talk about family affairs, was observed after her death in 1969—the Al Fahd often met to dine at the house of the eldest sister, Lu'lu'.[25]

Though Ibn Sa'ud was too preoccupied with public affairs, he often visited the house of Hissa and talked with the children. "He was very kind to us," said the Amir Fahd to the present writer, "but he was also very strict and often applied discipline." The Amir Fahd recalled an incident which prompted his father to lock him in a room for over two hours because of a quarrel with a neighbor's son. Ibn Sa'ud punished his own son in order to prove his strictness and impartiality, although the quarrel seems to have been initiated by the neighbor's son.

From childhood, the Amir Fahd showed an interest in learning and studied in the newly established Palace School for the training not only of

---

[24]Seven members of Al Fahd are male and have held important offices in the state. They are as follows: Fahd, the Crown Prince; Sultan, Minister of Defense; Na'if, Minister of Interior; Salman, Governor of Riyad; and Ahmad, Deputy Minister of Interior. See Zirikli, *op. cit.*, Vol. III, p. 995.

[25]In an interview with the writer, the Amir Fahd paid a high tribute to his mother who seems to have inspired her children not only with love and solidarity but also with ambition and taught them good manners (the writer's interview with the Amir Fahd, Riyad, December 29, 1979).

Saudi princes but also children in the neighborhood who desired to study in that school.[26] In addition to formal training at the Palace School, the
Amir Fahd pursued his learning by private tutoring
and reading, and showed an interest in Arab history and literature. Later he became interested in
Arab and foreign affairs, and he is known today to
be one of the best informed among the Saudi
princes on world affairs.

"Where did you go for further study after the
Palace School?" I asked the Amir Fahd. "I attended
my father's seminars," he replied. Noting that his
father was in the habit of meeting often with his
advisors to discuss affairs of state, he saw that if
he were to sit and listen to what went on, he
would improve his education and acquaint himself
with public affairs in which he was keenly interested. He used to wait for the advisors outside his
father's office and to join them in meetings in
which they discussed all kinds of questions relating
to domestic and foreign affairs. Fahd, sitting in silence in a corner, kept attending the meetings of
the Advisory Board for years.[27] One day (shortly
after World War II), his father called him to his office. Either to examine him on what he had
learned or to question him about his future plans,
his father began the interrogation by asking him
what the purpose of his attendance of the Advisory

---

[26]Owing to scarcity of schools, Ibn Sa'ud assigned one of the Royal
Palaces to be used as a school to set a precedent for others to encourage the spread of education in the country—(The writer's interview with 'Abd al-Aziz al-Khuwaytar, Minister of Education, December 31, 1979). See also Zirikli, op. cit., Vol. II, pp. 644-45.

[27]In answer to a question about how often he attended those meetings, the Amir Fahd replied "for almost ten years," and went on to
say that he learned not only information about the country but how
his father made decisions.

Board was. Fahd explained how fascinating in his eyes those meetings were and how much they had improved his education. Impressed by his son's answers and satisfied that he was genuinely interested in the Advisory Board, Ibn Sa'ud told him to attend its meetings regularly and participate in the discussion, presumably because he was satisfied that his son had passed the examination and had become ready for public service.

Before he was entrusted with an office, the Amir Fahd continued his apprenticeship as a member of the Advisory Board for another six or seven years. Meanwhile, his travels abroad and his meetings with Arab and Western leaders gave him further insights into public and human affairs. In 1945, he visited Egypt and attended the United Nations Conference at San Francisco as a member of the Saudi delegation, headed by the Amir Faysal, Foreign Minister of Saudi Arabia. After he rose to a Cabinet post, he made many visits to Europe and the United States, and talked with a number of Arab leaders with whom he later developed personal friendships. He also seems to have established a good working relationship with Faysal ever since he accompanied him to the United States in 1945. In 1946, the Amir Fahd recalls, he paid a visit to Faysal in the desert and had a long conversation with him on public affairs. After talking about his own personal experiences, Faysal intimated to Fahd that his remarks might be useful to him when the time came to assume responsibility.

In 1953, when Crown Prince Sa'ud became Prime Minister, the Amir Fahd was appointed Minister of Education. In that position, he launched an elaborate program to establish schools in all parts of the country and was credited with being the first Minister who encouraged girls to enter public schools. In 1961 he became Minister of Interior, when the Amir Faysal, then Crown Prince, formed his second Cabinet. Both as Minister of Education and Minister of Interior, Fahd distinguished himself as an able administrator and enlightened public servant. He remained as Minister of Interior after Faysal rose to the throne and devoted much of his time to domestic affairs. He supported Faysal in his rivalry with King Sa'ud and was instrumental in the movement culminating in the abdication of Sa'ud in favor of Faysal in 1964.[28]

Upon the accession of King Khalid to the throne, the Amir Fahd became Crown Prince and deputy Prime Minister, as noted earlier. For health reasons, King Khalid delegated the actual conduct of the business of government to the Crown Prince. But it would be misleading to draw the conclusion that the Amir Fahd makes all decisions independently. In all important matters, he obtains the prior authorization of the King before he carries them out. Nor does the Amir Fahd ignore the opinions of other interested parties, least of all the senior members of the Saudi House and the country's principal dignitaries.

Unlike King Sa'ud, who displayed a tendency to assert personal rule, the Amir Fahd, following the pattern set by King Faysal, prefers to delegate power to the Council of Ministers, over which he or the Amir 'Abd-Allah presides, and correlates the work of the various departments.[29] In an attempt

---

[28]For an account of this movement, see Gerald deGaury, *Faisal* (London, 1966), chs. 13-14.
[29]More recently, the Council of Ministers, owing to pressure of work, has delegated some of its functions to the various departments to decide independently on matters of purely technical character.

to govern through the instrumentality of the highest executive organ, it is possible that the Cabinet would not only serve as a check on the powers of the Head of State, but also as a step for the development of the Saudi political structure toward a democratic system.

VI

Cabinet government began to evolve long before Ibn Sa'ud died in 1953. It may be regarded as an offshoot of the Hijazi system of government; for, before the Hijaz was incorporated by Ibn Sa'ud into his kingdom, it had a form of government composed of legislative and executive branches modelled on the Ottoman system of which it was part before World War I.[30] Upon its separation from the Ottoman Empire, a legislative body called *Majlis al-Shura* (Consultative Assembly) and a Cabinet, headed by a Premier, had been established. The Cabinet was responsible to Sharif Husayn himself.[31]

Relatively more advanced than Central Arabia, which was governed by Ibn Sa'ud as an essentially tribal community, the Hijaz enjoyed separate self-governing institutions and its system operated under a Viceroy, representing Ibn Sa'ud as Head of the State. For a short while, following his being proclaimed King of the Hijaz by its Consultative

---

[30]The Sharif Husayn, before he declared his independence from the Ottoman authorities in 1916, was the Viceroy of the Hijaz and the provinces under his control were represented in the Ottoman Parliament. His sons, 'Abd-Allah and Faysal, with a few others, were members of Parliament in Istanbul before World War I.

[31]For a brief account of the composition and work of the Consultative Assembly under Sharif Husayn, see Zirikli, *op. cit.*, Vol. II, pp. 569-80.

Assembly, Ibn Sa'ud ruled the Hijaz and Najd as a dual monarchy, a form of *Ausgleich*. He had already been proclaimed the Sultan of Najd in 1919. In 1932, by a decree unifying the two countries into one state, he became the King of a united state, officially called the Kingdom of Saudi Arabia.

The unity of two countries possessing different political systems might be advantageous to one and disadvantageous to the other until an accommodation is achieved by both and the country as a whole is placed on the same level of progress and development. By its incorporation with Najd, the Consultative Assembly and the Cabinet of the Hijaz, though never abolished in theory, fell into disuse. The Ministry of Foreign Affairs in particular continued to function under the jurisdiction of the Viceroy of the Hijaz—the Amir Faysal—as Foreign Minister for the whole kingdom. This Ministry, especially after it was reorganized in 1931, set the precedent for others to develop as the basis for the future Council of Ministers. In 1932 a Ministry of Finance was established to reorganize the financial affairs of the country under one department. In 1944, a Ministry of Defense was established. In 1951 it was deemed necessary to bring the various provinces which had been directly controlled by the King under the jurisdiction of the newly established Ministry of Interior. In 1953 three new departments were created to deal with Education, Agriculture and Communications. In 1954, a year after Ibn Sa'ud's death, two more departments were created—Commerce and Health and later several others.[32]

---

[32]For an account of the origins and structure of the various departments of government, see Fuad Hamza, *al Bilad al-'Arabiya al-Su'udiya*, p. 114ff.

The immediate cause for the creation of a Council of Ministers which helped to coordinate the work of the various departments and supervise their actions was Ibn Sa'ud's failure in health which necessitated the delegation of his powers to Crown Prince Sa'ud in 1953. Even before Ibn Sa'ud's illness, the heads of the then existing departments began to act more independently as the country was developing and the pressure of work in each department required quick actions without prior authorization of the Head of State. In a broader sense, therefore, the creation of a Council of Ministers was in response to a widely felt growing need as well as to the immediate cause or circumstance that had given rise to its birth.

When the Council was first established on October 9, 1953, it was presided over by Crown Prince Sa'ud as Prime Minister, because the ailing old King could not himself preside, but after Sa'ud ascended the throne he continued to preside and appointed Crown Prince Faysal as Prime Minister without much power.[33] This raised the fundamental question whether the King should be his own Prime Minister, combining the functions of the Heads of State and Government. Very soon, however, when King Sa'ud displayed a propensity for individual rule with the consequent deterioration of financial conditions, the Saudi House seems to have impressed upon King Sa'ud the need to entrust the Premiership to Crown Prince Faysal in 1958. But when Faysal succeeded Sa'ud in 1964, as King, he continued to preside over the Council of

---

[33]For text of the decree to establish the Council of Ministers, see H. St. J.B. Philby, "The New Statute of the Council of Ministers," *The Middle East Journal*, Vol. 12 (1958), pp. 318-23. See also Charles W. Harrington, "The Saudi Arabian Council of Ministers," *The Middle East Journal*, Vol. 12, (1958), pp. 1-19.

Ministers as King and Premier. King Khalid, perhaps mainly for health reasons, has delegated his powers as Premier to Crown Prince Fahd, though remaining in theory as his own Premier and presiding only over meetings devoted to important matters. Thus, no clear distinction has yet been drawn between the functions of King and Premier, although the trend is toward ultimate separation of the two offices. Until such separation becomes complete the King may resume his role as Premier at any moment and the Crown Prince would attend as a member of the Council. In the event an elected Assembly is set up, the King would perhaps be bound to give up his function as Premier, relieved of responsibility, since the Cabinet would presumably become responsible to the Assembly.

Today, the Council of Ministers may be regarded as the core of the political system, as it is the central body that correlates the work of all departments and enacts statutes in conformity with Islamic law and supervises their implementation. It is composed of some twenty-four Ministers, each heading a department—or a Ministry[34]—selected on the basis of competence and experience and appointed by the King.[35] The Council meets ordinarily once a week, presided over by the Crown Prince as

[34]If the Minister is appointed as a Minister without portfolio, he would be a Minister of State entrusted with a specific function. In 1978 there were three Ministers without portfolio, one of whom resigned.

[35]Apart from the senior princes, who represent the Saudi House, there are some seven or eight Ministers who hold Ph.D. degrees, each in his field of specialization. They are as follows: 91) 'Abd al-'Aziz al-Khuwaytir, Minister of Education; (2) Ghazi 'Abd al-Rahman al-Qusaybi, Minister of Industry; (3) Sulayman 'Abd al-'Aziz Sulaym, Minister of Commerce; (4) Muhammad Abduh Yamani, Minister of Information; (5) 'Abd al-Rahman Ibn 'Abd al-Aziz Al al-Shaykh, Min-

first deputy Premier (the Amir Fahd) and, in his absence, the second deputy Premier (the Amir 'Abd-Allah). In the meeting for the budget, the King, in his capacity as Premier, ordinarily presides and all questions of policy relating to foreign, financial, defense affairs and others are open for discussion before the budget is approved. It finally becomes law upon approval by the King. A special committee, composed of a few Ministers, is set up by the Council to supervise implementation of the projects laid down under the Five-Year Plan.[36]

Since 1973, in consequence of the sudden increase in income from oil, the Council of Ministers has become very active and has begun to meet more often to discuss projects considered necessary to speed up development. There were two schools of thought concerning the expenditure of surplus income—one school argued in favor of the distribution of the surplus among the people through additional projects of development while the other school, though agreed on speeding up development, counselled moderation. At the outset, the first school prevailed and a large volume of currency appeared in the market with the consequent rise in prices and fall in the purchasing power of money. Four of the Ministers—the Ministers of Finance, Commerce, Industry and Planning—raised the question of inflation and persua-

---

ister of Agriculture; (6) Muhammad 'Abd al-Latif al-Mulhim, Minister of State; (7) Husayn 'Abd al-Razzaq al-Jaza'iri, Minister of Health; (8) 'Abd-Allah Muhammad 'Umran, Minister of State (resigned in 1978); and 'Alawi Kayyal, Minister of State.

[36]Two Five-Year Plans have so far been laid down—the first in 1970 and the second in 1975. For a study of the latter, see Ministry of Planning (Saudi Arabia), *Second Development Plan, 1395-1400/1975-1980* (Riyad, 1976), prepared under the direction of Hisham M. Nazir, Minister of Planning. A third plan is in preparation.

sively argued in favor of the slowing down of the process of expenditure. Upon consultation with foreign experts, the Cabinet finally decided in 1976 to decelerate development and save the surplus for investment.

Despite a ceiling, the budget has often been adjusted to meet exigencies and political pressures. Nor have the Ministers, especially the technocrats, been able to overhaul the administrative system, since they have constantly been confronted with bureaucratic obstructions and the reality of the inadequate training of personnel which rendered it difficult to inspire efficiency and high morale in the system. Above all, the corrupt practices, which still prevail in most traditional societies, proved exceedingly difficult to control, for these are inherited traits from the past with which only time and sound education can cope.[37]

But the country, despite inertia and bureaucratic deficiencies, is committed to reforms as the Saudi leaders have often declared. The public, especially the new generation, has become increasingly critical and has demanded complete change of the political system. Most of them, however, prefer the evolutionary rather than revolutionary methods of change.

What are the ultimate goals of change? Although it is difficult to be specific on what the outcome would be, the majority seems to agree that the

---

[37]See the Amir Fahd's statements about the bureaucracy and administrative reform (al-Hawadith, January 11, 1980, pp. 17-21), and the writer's interviews with Sulayman 'Abd al-'Aziz al-Sulaym, Minister of Commerce (Riyad, January 5, 1979) and Ghazi al-Qusaybi, Minister of Industry (Riyad, December 30, 1979). See also Ghazi 'Abd al-Rahman al-Qusaybi, al-Wazir wa al-Tahadiyat al-Idariya [The Minister and Administrative Challenges]—a lecture given at the Faysal University at al-Dammam in January 1979 (mimeographed).

emerging political system should develop on democratic models.

Though the reform process is by its very nature
tedious and slow, a beginning to overhaul the system is deemed necessary. Until now only a modest
step has been undertaken since the Council of Ministers had been set up—the creation of a High
Committee, composed of three members and a
rapporteur, designed to operate as a steering committee to speed up the work of the Council of Ministers by preparing specific proposals and memo-
randa on pending issues for discussion.[38] There are
also a number of Cabinet Commissions set up to
implement development projects designed to speed
up the work of reconstruction, such as the Petroleum Commission, headed by the Amir Fahd and
administered by Shaykh Ahmad Zaki Yamani; the
Royal Commission for Jubayl and Yanbu', set up
specifically for reconstruction and development
projects in the two cities of Jubayl and Yanbu',
headed by Hisham Nazir, the Minister of Planning,
and assisted by Faruq Khidr, Secretary of the
Commission; and the Higher Education Commission, entrusted with the task of formulating educational policy and making proposals for implementation by the Ministry of Education and the
Ministry of Higher Education. These Commissions,
especially the Royal Commission for Jubayl and
Yanbu', are standing committees and operate as almost independent departments, designed to relieve
the Council of Ministers of the pressure of work.
There are also temporary and *ad hoc* committees,

---

[38]Today the High Committee is composed of Crown Prince Fahd,
who presides, and the Amir 'Abd-Allah, Commander of the National
Guard, and the Amir Sultan, Minister of Defense. Rashad Fir'awn is
its Rapporteur.

set up to prepare proposals and reports on specific matters for the Council of Ministers, but they vary considerably in nature and scope depending on the task for which they were set up.

But if the emerging political system is ever to arouse public interest and endure, it must be integrated within the larger social structure and allow participation by an increasing number of the people. Thinking along these lines in higher Saudi circles has been going on for a while. Indeed, there is a pressure from the politically conscious segment of society demanding some form of political participation. As a first step to enlist participation, it has been suggested that the Consultative Assembly, a representative body which still exists in name but has fallen into disuse, might perhaps be reactivated. Initially, the Assembly might be composed either of half-elected and half-appointed members, or perhaps a fully elected Assembly, representing both the tribal and urban communities, might be established. Such a step would not only strengthen the Cabinet system, but might also advance the system as a whole a step further toward democracy.

Once the step to call a National Assembly is taken, the process of enlisting political participation is likely to follow. If public response would be favorable and no serious conservative reaction stirred to obstruct it, democracy should be on its way to take root in the country.[39]

---

[39]During his last visit to Saudi Arabia in 1979-80, the writer has learned that a decision to call the Consultative Assembly had already been taken, but that the promulgation of a Constitution and an electoral law would have to await the provincial reorganization of the country which is now under way.

VII

Today the Saudi leaders are no less concerned
with foreign policy than with domestic affairs,
partly because of the need for protecting the country from foreign pressures and partly because of
the country's emergence as a major factor in the
regional balance of power. In a broad sense, Saudi
foreign policy may be said to have been shaped by
two sets of forces—its perennial religio-historical
heritage and its shifting geopolitical position. These
forces had affected the region as a whole before
Arabia and the other Arab successor states
emerged as independent states.

Before World War I, when Arabia was part of
the Ottoman Empire, the Sultan as Caliph and
spokesman of Islam exercised his powers to protect the holy sanctuaries and other symbols of
Islamic identity. After the disintegration of the
Ottoman Empire and the abolition of the Caliphate,
the Islamic functions of the State were reduced
and distributed among the successor states in varying degrees. For a short while, Sharif Husayn (and
subsequently his sons), supported by Britain, tried
to play the role of the Ottoman Porte in Arab lands
by virtue of his position as guardian of the holy
sanctuaries in the Hijaz and of his leadership of the
Arab nationalist movement. After he took possession of the Hijaz, Ibn Saʻud became the custodian
of the holy sanctuaries.

Before World War I the Ottoman Sultan was
able to maintain on the whole peace within his do-
minions and provide regional security. In domestic
affairs, he invoked the sacred law and religious authority to secure loyalty of his subjects. He also
maintained forces in key positions to keep order in

the provinces. In foreign affairs, he resorted to the game of playing off one Great Power against another to protect the integrity of the Empire until World War I. However, after the war, the task of keeping peace and regional security devolved upon the successor states which sought security and peace by resort to the maintenance of a regional balance of power within the larger global balancing system.

In Arabia, Ibn Sa'ud, concerned not only about the security of his country but the region as a whole, provided certain guidelines for his House to be followed in accordance with changing circumstances. Aware of the general forces that had always affected Arabia's foreign relations—the religio-historical and geopolitical forces—he laid down a broad outline of foreign policy which might be summed up as follows:

To begin with, in principle the world might still be considered as it was viewed during earlier periods, as being divided into Islamic and non-Islamic lands, perhaps reminiscent of the division of the world into the *Dar al-Islam* and *Dar al-Harb*, in accordance with the teachings of the early Muslim jurists, and Saudi Arabia, as part of the first, would be in theory in a state of war (the *jihad*) with the other. However, since the concept of the *jihad* has undergone considerable changes in modern times and since Saudi Arabia is a member of the United Nations and other international organizations which prescribe peace as the basis of relationships among nations, the traditional concept of the state of war has been replaced by the concept of peace as the basis of relationships among nations.[40] Yet

---

[40]For the concept of the *jihad* and its changing meaning, see my *War and Peace in the Law of Islam* (Baltimore, 1955), chs. 5 and 13; and the *Islamic Law of Nations* (Baltimore, 1966), p. 60ff.

the tradition of dividing nations on ideological grounds seems to have persisted, as Saudi Arabia views the so-called socialist countries as a threat to Islamic countries on the grounds that socialism (and, of course, Communism) and Islam are incompatible ideologies. For this reason, Saudi Arabia has maintained no diplomatic relations with the Soviet Union and other socialist countries, though she has recognized them as states, and considers their outlook in foreign affairs as opposed to the Islamic outlook. More specifically, Soviet activities in the Arab World have been considered a direct threat to Saudi Arabia. Thus, the Saudi leaders sought, by cultivating friendly relations with countries opposed to the Soviet Union, to restrain communist penetration into Arab lands. Moreover, Saudi Arabia has tried, by offering economic assistance, to encourage countries that have already been exposed to Soviet influence (Egypt and the Sudan a few years ago and more recently South Yaman) to reduce their dependence on Soviet support and cooperate with Western countries for their progress and development.

Before World War II, Ibn Sa'ud looked to Britain as the Great Power which would support him against rival Powers—Italy, Germany and the Soviet Union. As to the other countries, it became almost a traditional policy for each to look to one of the Great Powers as an ally in the regional balancing system. Some, like Turkey and Iran, were able to assert their independence because of the rivalry between one Great Power and another; but most of them, after they achieved independence, began to vacillate between one Great Power or another depending on the ideological wind of change. Saudi Arabia may well be regarded as the country that followed a consistent foreign policy and tried to maintain in particular friendly relations with Western countries.

After World War II, when the United States began to champion the cause of democracy against Communism, Saudi Arabia began to look to the United States as the natural ally in the East-West conflict. In a broad sense, this conflict is construed by Saudi Arabia as a contest between Communism and Islam. Agreement between Saudi Arabia and the United States on world affairs has been augmented by economic and technological cooperation. In technology and oil exploration, American-Saudi cooperation, beginning in the mid-thirties when oil exploration started, led to extensive oil exploitation by American oil interests (ARAMCO). After the war, oil exploitation laid the ground for other forms of cooperation—cultural, economic and otherwise—which established what might be called the emergence of a traditional friendship between the two countries. American support for Israel, especially in the Six-Day War of 1967, has been looked upon by Saudi Arabia, let alone other Arab countries, with disfavor and contrary to Arab interests. Because of American delivery of arms to Israel in the October War of 1973, in which the Arabs won initial victory, American support of Israel provoked an Arab oil embargo in which Saudi Arabia was bound to participate—perhaps the only step taken by the Saudi leaders against the United States in the history of Saudi-American relations. American support for Israel apart, no step has been taken by either country which might be considered contrary to the interests of the other. On the contrary, the Saudi leaders have done their best endeavors in the periodic meetings of the Organization of Petroleum Exporting Countries

(OPEC) to restrain the trend of raising the price of oil and to keep oil production higher than Saudi needs to relieve the energy crisis. In 1979-80, when the energy crisis in the United States became so serious, Saudi Arabia increased its oil production by a million barrels a day in response to American appeals, despite Saudi dissatisfaction with American proposals to settle the Arab-Israeli conflict as laid down at Camp David in 1978 without prior consultation with Saudi leaders.

In her relations with other Arab countries, Saudi Arabia has followed on the whole the guidelines laid down by Ibn Sa'ud. Peace and friendly relationships, Ibn Sa'ud is reported to have reiterated, should be the primary objective of Saudi foreign policy toward all Arab lands. Secondly, Saudi leaders have been warned against interference in the domestic affairs of the Arab countries, presumably on the grounds that other Arab countries themselves should not interfere in Saudi domestic affairs, since each Arab country had chosen its own form of government and wished to maintain its independence within the collective system established under the Arab League in 1945. Thirdly, if a conflict should arise between one Arab country and another (or between one and several others), Saudi leaders were advised to take a neutral position—never to take sides with one against the other, regardless of their personal feelings—and to seek reconciliation of their differences by offering Saudi good offices to resolve them.

Despite Ibn Sa'ud's normalization of his relations with the Hashimi House, Saudi suspicion of Hashimi intentions to recover the Hijaz continued to exist until the downfall of Hashimi rule in Iraq in 1958. Since the death of his grandfather in 1952,

King Husayn of Jordan, the principal spokesman for the Hashimi House today, has kept friendly relations with Saudi Arabia. Indeed, the Saudi leaders became great supporters of Husayn's regime after the fall of the monarchy in Egypt and Iraq, as the Hashimi House is no longer a threat to their rule and proved to be a supporter of moderate over radical and revolutionary regimes.

Since World War II, Saudi-Egyptian relations have become friendly and often very intimate, despite the legacy of the Egyptian campaigns against the rise of the first Wahhabi-Saudi state in the early nineteenth century and the subsequent strained relations over Egyptian pilgrimage privileges and other matters.[41] However, shortly after the Egyptian Revolution of 1952, Saudi relations with Egypt's military rulers became strained largely because of their military intervention in Southern Arabia after the 1962 overthrow of the Imamate in the Yaman.

Because Egypt is considered an important member in the Arab family, Saudi Arabia has always recognized the significance of her role in inter-Arab relations. Even under Nasir, despite frequent strains, the Saudi leaders tried to maintain correct relations with Egypt. After the Six-Day War (1967), they supported her politically and economically and Sadat's policy of dissociating Egypt from Soviet influence and seeking American support to put an end to wars with Israel has been welcomed by the Saudi leaders. But while Sadat's objectives were considered sound, his means have been ques-

---

[41]For a brief account of Saudi-Egyptian relations, see Zirikli, *op. cit.*, Vol. II, pp. 661-713, and A.J. Toynbee, *The Islamic World Since the Peace Settlement* (Survey of International Affairs, 1925) (London, 1927), pp. 289-93.

tioned, especially some of the steps—his visit to Jerusalem in 1977 and the subsequent signing of the Camp David agreements of 1978-79—which were undertaken without prior consultations with other Arab leaders. On the whole, however, the Saudi leaders have taken a moderate position among the supporters and critics of Sadat in Arab Summit meetings. No matter how Egypt's leaders choose to act, Saudi Arabia cannot afford to let them fall under radical influences or turn toward the Soviet Union because of failure to provide them with economic assistance. Despite occasional strained relations, Saudi Arabia may well prove in the long run to be Egypt's greatest supporter, as her attitude after Camp David demonstrated.

Though the Iraqi Revolution of 1958 may have eliminated one possible reason—the pretensions of the Hashimi House—for strained relations between Iraq and Saudi Arabia, it introduced new elements, mainly ideological and foreign policy differences, that initially strained relations. However, after consolidation of their regime, the Iraqi leaders have demonstrated their emphasis on the country's independence and their readiness to resist Communist activities irrespective of their alliance with the Soviet Union. It is indeed to the credit of the two principal Saudi and Iraqi leaders—the Amir Fahd and Saddam Husayn—that the two countries have been brought closer than ever before to correlate their regional policies to the mutual advantages of both countries. Saudi Arabia has sided with Iraq in its drive to re-assert its sovereignty over the Shatt al-Arab.[42]

---

[42]For a background of Iraqi-Saudi relations, see my *Socialist Iraq* (Washington, D.C., 1978), pp. 159-61.

Like other Arab countries, Saudi Arabia considers Israel a threat not only to the four countries surrounding it but to the Arab world as a whole. In line with other Arab countries, she has maintained a state of war with Israel and supported the confrontation Arab countries whenever hostilities with Israel broke out; her participation in military operations has been largely symbolic, but in the economic and political spheres it has been quite substantial. Since the Six-Day War, and especially since the indecisive war of 1973, Saudi Arabia has supported the movement to settle the Arab-Israeli conflict by peaceful rather than by violent means on the grounds that war proved ineffective as a means to force Israel to withdraw from the territory it occupied in 1967. For this reason, Saudi leaders have supported all endeavors to make peace with Israel, provided the settlement would include the establishment of a "homeland" for the Palestinians. Saudi Arabia maintains that peace with Israel cannot possibly be achieved if the Palestinians are not given a homeland in the remaining portion of Palestine—the West Bank and Ghazza—to which the Palestinian émigrés (if they so wished) could return. Saudi Arabia has welcomed American participation in the settlement of the conflict and has urged recognition of the Palestine Liberation Organization (PLO) as representative of the Palestinian people on the understanding that the PLO will eventually recognize the existence of Israel as provided in the Security Council Resolutions 242 and 338. Since the PLO has not yet publicly accepted the existence of Israel—although it tacitly accepted Resolution 242 at the Arab Summit meeting in Baghdad (1978)—the Saudi leaders have yet to persuade the parties concerned to bring the PLO into the peace process.[43]

VIII

In the foregoing discussion of the Saudi leadership, we have indicated how the progress and development of the country have created new demands that affected the structure of politics and perhaps foreign policy. It is perhaps in order at this stage to ask whether the people as a whole are satisfied with the regime over which the Saudi leaders preside. While the survival of the regime is not necessarily in question, there have existed in the country groups and individuals holding differing views stemming from varied sources and motivations which might be considered opponents whether loyal or hostile. Who are they?

There are three categories of opponents. They are: (1) Persons within the Royal House who hold differing views; (2) Religious elements who demand in the main a greater emphasis on fundamentalism, some of whom are opposed to change and development in principle; (3) Radical elements, some who are opposed to the regime, and others who advocate the overthrow of the Royal House in favor of a secular regime. Let us begin with the latter.

---

[43]For official statements on foreign policy, see Ministry of Information, *Addresses by King Khalid at the Pilgrimages in 1975 and 1977* (Jidda, 1975 and 1977); and *Address by Crown Prince Fahd in 1978* (Jidda, 1978). See also al-Shaykh Manna al-Qattan, *Faysal Ibn 'Abd al-'Aziz wa Da'wat al-Tadamun al-Islami* [Faysal and the Islamic Solidarity] (Riyad, 1976); and Bakr 'Umar al-'Amri, "al-Fahd wa al-'Alaqat al'Alamiya" [Fahd and International Relations], *al-Bilad* (Jidda, January 28, 1978).

First, the radical elements have been in existence
since the reign of King Ibn Sa'ud, but some have
become more active over the past two decades.
These have varied from those holding radical left-
ist views to those holding moderate liberal principles. They have been so isolated and scattered in
the country, however, that they can hardly be ac-
curately identified and information about them is
both scanty and often exaggerated. Some have
been identified and known to have existed in Jidda
and Riyad and in the coastal areas in the east and
in the south near the borders of Yaman. Their
clandestine activities varied in intensity from time
to time depending on the events in the region and
conditions in the country. Some, it is said, have
been inspired by families in the Hijaz and Najd like
the Utayba tribes who were long in conflict with
the Saudi House.[44] Others, especially younger men,
were inspired by radical and revolutionary movements that have swept neighboring Arab countries
in recent years. They have neither been able to be
consistent nor to survive very long, as the Saudi security forces have closely pursued them and have
arrested a few and brought them to trial. They
were either expelled or thrown into prison whenever the evidence was sufficient to condemn them.
It is exceedingly difficult to know the names or the
identity of their leaders, as they have always been
under cover and scattered in the country. As a result, they have never existed as serious organizations and their recurring activities have never
really constituted a danger to the regime.

Second, there have always existed religious leaders since the reign of Ibn Sa'ud who opposed

---

[44] See Jonathan Aitken, "For the Saudis, A Shift From Theocracy,"
The Washington Post, November 28, 1979.

changes considered in their eyes to be inconsistent with the pristine teachings of Islam. In the thirties, the *Ikhwan* (Brothers), it will be recalled, protested against the importation of foreign technological instruments and reproached the authorities for allowing them to be imported. Considering these elements an obstacles to progress, Ibn Sa'ud dealt with them in a constructive manner and arranged their resettlement in rural areas.

Since Islam is considered one of the basic pillars of the regime, the Saudi leaders have been tolerant of religious elements which have shown concern about Islam on the grounds that their teachings were not considered inconsistent with the Saudi policy of upholding religion as a foundation of the regime. But so long as reconstruction and development are not considered in conflict with Islam's religious and ethical values, the protests of extremists against change were often considered beneficial as a means to counteract the demands of progressive elements calling for more rapid changes.

However, the sudden capture of the Great Mosque in Makka by religious elements resorting to violence came as a surprise to the Saudi leadership since they appeared to have the objective of not only asserting Islamic fundamentalism but also confronting the regime. They sought to entrust power to the Mahdi, a Messiah who claimed to derive his authority from God. In accordance with Islamic (Sunni) traditions, a reformer from the house of the Prophet will appear at the turn of every century and will set upright everything that has gone amiss in Islamic society and establish the rule of divine law. Since the fourteenth century (according to the Islamic era) was drawing to a close, many a religious thinker in Islamic lands must have been reminded of the possibility of the coming of the Mahdi at such a crucial time. Muslims have never been subjected to greater threats: the threats of Communism, Zionism and the neo-imperialism of the West which is exporting to Islamic lands technological innovations and commodities which have radically changed the fabric of Islamic society and undermined its spiritual and moral values. In some Islamic lands outside Arabia, these changes have long been taking place despite the protests of religious leaders; but in the cradle of Islam, these changes cannot be tolerated, in the view of religious dissidents. Since the Saudi leaders have been permitting—indeed sponsoring—these changes, they must be held accountable for them. In this sense, the religious activities that culminated in the capture of the Great Mosque in Makka on the first day of the Fifteenth Century (November 20, 1979) constituted a serious threat to the regime.

The Saudi reaction to this threat was prompt and exemplary. Armed by a *fatwa* (opinion of the 'Ulama), signed by thirty religious scholars, they were permitted to use force to recapture the Great Mosque and to cope with this religious upheaval in a crushing manner, since the leaders of the movement had been arrested before on more than one occasion and pardoned on the grounds that religious activities constituted no threat to the regime. Muhammad Bin 'Abd-Allah al-Qahtani, who declared himself the Mahdi, was killed in action; the leader of the movement, Juhayman, and his supporters, were captured and condemned to death by a religious court on the grounds of sedition and violation of Islamic law.[45]

---

[45]Juhayman Bin Muhammad Bin Sayf (1944-80), of the Utayba tribe, began his movement in Makka and tried to spread it both inside and

The significance of the Juhayman uprising is that it shows that discontent with the existing regime is not only confined to liberal groups urging reform and modernization but also includes religious and extremist leaders who were taken for granted as potential supporters of the Wahhabi-Saudi establishment. The Saudi House, it is said, was tolerant of criticism in religious circles, because their call for religious revival was considered devoid of political ambition. Since Juhayman resorted to force and called for a change of the regime, religious activities can no longer always be identified with the official Wahhabi creed. The Saudi approach to reform, though moderate in nature in deference to the country's traditions, can become a source of danger if religious elements are not reconciled to it.

The third category, which may be called the loyal opposition, is from within the Royal House. Despite their solidarity and cooperation, some members of the Saudi House, when they have met in the closed family sessions, have often given views on public affairs different from those they give while in office. Because the principle of primogeniture is not in question, they feel confident about discussing their differences. Self-criticism within the family—indeed, within any group—is a healthy sign indicative of strength rather than weakness. Unless members of the family speak frankly on public affairs, the position of all may be undermined. But rumors of differing views have

outside Saudi Arabia. It is said that he had several hundred followers outside the country when he launched his attack on the Great Mosque in 1979. An extreme Sunni Fundamentalist, he rejected other heterodox creeds, including Shiʻism, and repudiated any association with other non-Muslim communities.

often been interpreted as manifestations of a struggle for power among contending members of the Saudi House. Whenever these differences have focussed on foreign policy, the allies and adversaries of the Saudi House seem to suspect that a struggle for power must have been taking place behind the scenes, the outcome of which might be the fall of one senior member and the rise of another. In 1978 and 1979, a lively debate about the Sadat peace initiative raged in the country—indeed, throughout the Arab World—and led to differences of opinion among members of the Saudi House, especially after the Saudi delegation, headed by the Amir Fahd, had attended the Summit meeting in Baghdad in 1978.[46]

As a great friend of Saudi Arabia, the United States seems to have expected the Saudi leaders to exert a greater influence on the Arab countries that met in Baghdad than they did. Since the Saudi leaders, on their part, expected the United States to obtain commitments from Israel permitting the Palestinians to establish a homeland on the West Bank and in Ghazza—not to speak of the Saudi special interest in East (Arab) Jerusalem—which were not reflected in the Camp David agreement, they felt they were bound to support the Arab position taken at the Baghdad Summit rather than the position the United States had taken at Camp David.[47]

---

[46]In Western circles, the Amir Fahd was expected to counsel moderation and prevent actions intended to isolate Egypt from the Arab World. Though he was not expected to stop the application of collective sanctions against Egypt, he was able to prevent the expulsion of Egypt from the Arab League—her membership was only suspended—and influenced Iraq to accept the position of the confrontation states concerning peaceful settlement with Israel. Without Saudi intervention, Egypt would have been dealt with more harshly.
[47]For the view that the Saudi House is divided into two camps, the

Rumors of differing views among the Saudi leaders vis-à-vis their relations with the United States naturally aroused conflicting concern among the two rival Great Powers—the United States and the Soviet Union. The latter, in an effort to exploit a possible Saudi rift with the United States, proposed to establish diplomatic relations and purchase large quantities of Saudi oil. The American press, in reporting the rumors of differing views among the Saudi leaders (which was not unnaturally taken in Saudi Arabia to reflect the views of high American officials),[48] gave the impression that the Amir Fahd, because of his support of the Baghdad resolutions, was losing his leadership in a struggle for power with other rival members of his House. To dispel any doubt about dissension, King Khalid and the Amir 'Abd-Allah, second in line to the throne, made a statement in early April 1979 in which they gave strong verbal support to the Amir Fahd and the position he had taken at the Baghdad Summit meetings. These statements seem to have prompted the American government to dissociate itself from the rumors reflected in the press and declare that it was against American interests to foster dissension among the Saudi leaders. By their firm stand on foreign policy objectives, the Saudi leaders demonstrated the primacy of solidarity over differing views and made it clear that they were not prepared to compromise their obligations

---

pro-Western and the pro-Arab, with the Amir Fahd holding the balance between the two, see Don N. DeMarino, "Royal Functionalism and Saudi Foreign Policy," *Foreign Affairs* (Autumn, 1979), pp. 181-84.

[48]See Jim Hoagland, "U.S. Sees Signs Saudi Leadership May be Shifting," *Washington Post* (April 15, 1979); cf. Cord Meyer, "The Vital, and Ticklish U.S.-Saudi Balance," *Washington Star* (May 4, 1979).

toward the other Arab countries. Disagreement on Camp David and Sadat's peace initiative with Israel apart, the Saudi leaders reasserted in no uncertain terms their traditional friendship and cooperation with the US in the areas of mutual interest.

In viewing its leadership in retrospect, the Saudi House has performed its functions with a relatively high degree of prudence and competence. It is the oldest ruling house in Arabia. Its claim to survival depends partly on its readiness to assume responsibility and partly on its ability to serve as a link between the various sections of the people— the tribal chiefs, the 'Ulama (religious leaders) and the business community—and coordinate their activities and create cohesion and social solidarity. However, aware that its survival does not depend only on the old generation, it has sought to enlist the cooperation of an increasing number of young men who received modern education abroad (and more recently in the country's new educational institutions) by entrusting to them responsible positions and sharing authority with them. In pursuing such a policy, it has in fact been preparing young men from both the Saudi House and the public as a whole to become the future leaders of the country. The next step, as noted before, is to enlist the public to participate in political decisions through representative institutions. This step has yet to be taken. By its endeavors to hold the country together and place it along the path of progress and development, the Saudi House seems to be prepared to fulfill the promise of its leadership. Few leaders in the Arab world could claim a similar record of achievements.

CHAPTER III

THE HASHIMI HOUSE: KING HUSAYN OF JORDAN

> The story of Jordan is the epic of a desert which is being transformed into an oasis that has just begun to fulfill the promise of its hard-working people.
>
> King Husayn

Dislodged by the Saudi House from its rule over the Hijaz in the mid-twenties, the Hashimi family tried to build its kingdom in the northern Arab lands of Iraq and Transjordan, but the revolutionary movement that swept the Arab world after World War II and sought to achieve Pan-Arab unity went contrary to Hashimi designs and frustrated the efforts to achieve Arab aspirations under its leadership. In Syria, Hashimi rule was short-lived (1918-1920); in Iraq, after a decade and a half, the Hashimi Monarchy was overthrown by a military uprising and replaced by a republic in 1958.

Only in Jordan did the Hashimi House find a relatively secure throne. However, it was not King 'Abd-Allah, who entered Transjordan (as the country was then called) to establish a base from which he would extend Hashimi control over other Arab lands, but his grandson—King Husayn—who succeeded in consolidating Hashimi rule and identify-

ing his leadership with the country's destiny. The throne he inherited, however, hardly seemed secure at first, and only a few well-wishers expected it to last long. Yet few Arab leaders have been able to survive as long as King Husayn or match the power he wielded over his country. Compared with its neighbors, Jordan enjoys today perhaps greater stability than most of them.

It is proposed in this essay to inquire into the sources of King Husayn's power and the events and circumstances that helped him to survive and hold the country together. In a broader sense, this essay is a study of the forces that prescribed a role for Jordan to play in the Arab world and of the leadership qualities of the man to whose destiny the country is entrusted.

II

Although created to meet immediate needs and exigencies in 1920, Transjordan (the region lying to the east of the River Jordan), possessed certain qualities and potentials which have permitted it to achieve more than merely transient purposes. At the outset, very few envisaged the country as outliving its founder, the Amir (later King) 'Abd-Allah, who seems to have considered his rise to the throne of the country not the fulfillment of personal ambition but as a stepping stone to extend his family's rule, which had first been reduced and then eliminated from Arabia, to northern Arab lands and perhaps eventually to recover its lost territory in Arabia.

'Abd-Allah's dream of bringing northern Arab lands under his family's control was not realized, but neither did Jordan (the new name of the country after the annexation of the West Bank in 1950) cease to exist after its founder's departure. King Husayn, its new ruler (following the brief rule of King Talal, who succeeded 'Abd-Allah), perceived in the country's separate existence the unfolding of certain national and historical purposes beyond those envisioned by his grandfather and seems to have been determined to reorganize and consolidate the regime over which he presided and identify the country's national interests with his own personal interests. For this reason he may well be regarded as the second founder of Jordan and, in recognition of his services, his people today seem to owe him more than the ordinary allegiance to a Head of State. What are these purposes and how did King Husayn bring them into meaningful operation and place the country along the path of progress and development? Three underlying forces might be identified to account for Jordan's separate and continuing existence. They may be called the geopolitical, the dynastic and the demographic factors. A fourth, a combination of two or three of the foregoing forces, might be called the ideological.

From antiquity, the region that forms the Kingdom of Jordan today had either been an autonomous (or semi-autonomous) appendage of a great empire that dominated the eastern Mediterranean or a buffer state playing the role of an honest broker whenever that empire disintegrated into a set of successor states. In either case, Jordan's rulers, whether they were fully sovereign or proconsuls appointed by a higher authority, played with great success their historical role among neighbors whenever they were independent rulers and rendered valuable services to the higher authorities by maintaining public order and protecting the empire of which the country was a part against periodic tribal raids from the vast open desert that lay across its frontiers. In ancient times, it served as a buffer zone first between Egypt and the Assyrian-Babylonian empires and then between Rome and Persia. In medieval times, it played a similar role between Iraq (under the 'Abbasids) on the one hand and Egypt (under the Fatimids and their successors) on the other. As part of those great empires, Jordan asserted some form of local autonomy (political or administrative), often implied in the special label of "al-Urdun" as a separate unit which meant more than a geographical expression.[1]

After World War I, following the destruction of the Ottoman Empire—the last of the great empires that dominated the eastern Mediterranean—the stage for a possible role to be played by Jordan among the successor states was set. To become an independent state and play the role of a buffer, Jordan awaited the rise of a ruler who would lead the country to play its historic role. The Amir 'Abd-Allah, who witnessed with a keen eye his brother's expulsion by France from Syria, of which the southern province of al-Urdun was a part, moved with a small force from the Hijaz into that province and presided over its destiny as a separate state when the French forces took control of Syria in 1920.

---

[1]The special name of al-Urdun, a sub-division of Syria consisting of both sides of the River Jordan, may be traced to the Umayyad period under the Islamic Empire, and its importance as a separate administrative unit is reflected in its privileges to mint its own coins (some of these coins may be seen today in 'Amman's museum) and other functions of local character. For the historical significance of Jordan, see Ann Dearden, *Jordan* (London, 1958), ch. 2.

However, when 'Abd-Allah entered al-Urdun and established his rule over the country, he was not content to play merely the historic role of a ruler over a buffer state; he intended to use his newly acquired throne as a stepping stone to extend his Hashimi family's domination from the Hijaz over northern Arab lands. France's insistence on dominating the Levant States and British support of Zionist claims to Palestine restricted Hashimi ambition to govern northern Arab lands to Transjordan and Iraq, and the rise of Ibn Sa'ud as a rival not only undermined but later eliminated Hashimi rule in the Hijaz, while Egyptian rivalry to any ruler desiring to dominate the Arab Crescent restricted Hashimi control to only a small portion of that area. Despite King 'Abd-Allah's lifelong endeavors to create a union between his newly adopted kingdom and Iraq and extend his rule to Syria and Palestine, he succeeded only in the annexation of the West Bank—the remnant of the portion assigned by the UN Partition Plan of 1947 to Palestinians to form a state—and in the reestablishment of the historic al-Urdun (Jordan) in 1950. He was assassinated in 1951 for his alleged tacit compromises with Israel in order to establish his rule over the West Bank and for his attempts at entering into a peace agreement with Israel, because his actions were considered to compromise Arab interests and serve his personal ambition.[2]

King Husayn, upon whose shoulders fell the mantle of Hashimi leadership, has shown no ambi-

---

[2]If it served Arab interests, King 'Abd-Allah saw no harm in entering into negotiations with all sides; but he was not prepared to make peace with Israel if it did not serve Arab interests (see Sir Alec Kirkbride, *From the Wings: Amman Memoirs 1947-1951* [London, 1978], pp. 3-5, 21-22).

tion to pursue Hashimi objectives beyond Jordan, even after Hashimi rule in Iraq was overthrown in 1958. As the legitimate successor to King Faysal II, head of the Arab Federation, he could have challenged the Iraqi revolutionary regime.[3] But in reality he has disclaimed any pretension to extend his rule or influence beyond Jordan. In order to survive, he followed a moderate and a neutralist policy toward his neighbors, and never took an extreme position on foreign policy issues. If he ever found himself drawn into an alliance with one neighbor or joining a coalition of one bloc against another, he sooner or later reverted to Jordan's traditional neutrality and normal—if not friendly—relations with all neighbors. In a word, he seems to be determined to continue the historic role of Jordan as a buffer state and to insure the survival of the country with whose destiny he is entrusted.

Next to the historical and dynastic factors that influenced the role of Husayn as an Arab leader, the demographic structure of the country, especially after the annexation of the West Bank, seems to be no less important. Before the annexation of the West Bank, Transjordan was made up of East Bankers who were essentially homogeneous, notwithstanding the existence of small non-Arab minorities (Circassians, Kurds, Turks and others) in the country. Given all the rights of Jordanian citizenship, the Palestinians of the West Bank as a whole might have been able to play a constructive role in the development of the country, as both Palestinians and Jordanians share the same cultural and historical heritage. But many Palestin-

---

[3]The Arab Federation, consisting of Iraq and Jordan, was created early in 1958. King Husayn was to succeed King Faysal in the event the throne of the Union was vacated.

ians, having lost the greater portion of their homeland to Israel, agreed to become Jordanian citizens
only as a means to use Jordan as a base of operation to recover their lost territory. Since King
Husayn felt unprepared to risk a war with Israel,
the Palestinians looked to other Arab rulers, especially to President Nasir of Egypt, who was advocating a Pan-Arab union under his leadership, to
achieve the goal of recovering their homeland. Palestinian support of Nasir's Pan-Arab policy, however, came into direct conflict with King Husayn's
policy which asserted Jordan's independence,
while Palestinian aspirations to recover their
homeland prompted them to support the drive to
include Jordan in an Arab union under Nasir's
leadership. Furthermore, Husayn's policy of moderation and friendship with the Western Powers,
who were considered by the Arabs to have been
responsible for the creation and survival of Israel,
was confronted with Nasir's defiance of the West
and his policy of positive neutrality, presumably
designed to free the Arabs from dependence on the
Great Powers. Although Husayn was no less concerned than Nasir about Israel, Nasir's rhetorical
denunciation of Western support for Israel aroused
a greater excitement among Palestinians and
gained their support for his leadership over that of
Husayn. This may well explain the reluctance of
the Palestinians to be integrated with the Jordanians, who displayed no great enthusiasm for Nasir's
policy and asserted their country's independence
from foreign control. No less important is the fact
that the Palestinians, more highly educated and
skilled than the Jordanians, especially those from
the tribal and semi-tribal portions of the country,
tended to take advantage of their qualifications

and experiences and to enrich themselves at the expense of native Jordanians. Resenting these Palestinian propensities, the Jordanians denounced the Palestinians as foreign elements who had no roots in Jordanian society.

This disenchantment between the two peoples became more pronounced after the Six-Day War, partly because the number of Palestinians on the East Bank was increased by those who fled the West Bank in panic after the Israeli occupation, and partly because the Palestinian Liberation Organization (PLO) used Jordan as a base for its periodic raids into Israel, with consequent indiscriminate Israeli retaliations against Jordanians as a whole. Unable to reconcile Jordan's security requirements with PLO demands, King Husayn felt compelled at least to expel the PLO from his kingdom in 1970, permitting to remain only those who agreed to obey his orders. Despite their willingness to accommodate to Jordan's security requirements, most Palestinians in Jordan are still hopeful that the time will come when they can return to their homeland and have not completely resigned themselves to being assimilated and forming a cohesive part of Jordanian society. Although he has always been ready to plead the Palestinian case in international councils, King Husayn was bound to look first after Jordanian interests as Jordan forms the basis of his operation and the source of his power.[4]

Finally, King Husayn, whether influenced by the winds of ideology that began to spread in the Arab world or by his own experiences since he came to the throne, has developed a set of views and a ra-

---

[4]For the role of Palestinians in Jordan, see Clinton Bailey, *The Participation of the Palestinians in the Politics of Jordan* (Ann Arbor, 1969).

tionale that govern his policies and actions. These views, which will be discussed at a later stage, may be called Husayn's goals and ideals, derived partly from the collectivist doctrines that have become fashionable in several Arab countries and partly from Western liberal principles and values. Some of his ideas are also derived from Islamic teachings and family traditions. His goals and ideals have not yet been reformulated into an official ideology for Jordan, but there is no doubt that they provide guidelines for Jordan's domestic and foreign policies and have inspired a sense of unity among people who have not yet formed a nation-state in the modern sense. Husayn's own upbringing and attachment to the country in which he was born throw light on the role he was to play as its leader.

III

Born in 'Amman (November 14, 1935) fifteen years after his grandfather had established a throne on the East Bank of the River Jordan, King Husayn has a good reason to consider his birthplace as his native land, to which indeed he has always been attached. This fact, in contrast with his grandfather's nostalgic feeling towards the Hijaz—his birthplace—made King Husayn look at Jordan not merely as a kingdom which he inherited from father and grandfather, but as the country with which his whole life has been identified. Unlike his grandfather, at no time in his career did he ever use Jordan as a stepping stone for another throne or as a base for a larger kingdom.[5]

[5]King Husayn's agreement to establish the union between Jordan and Iraq was primarily intended to counteract a rival Arab union to

The second important fact was his father's tragic mental illness and abdication before Husayn finished school. Husayn's parents—Talal and Zayn—were first cousins but the two were entirely different characters. The father, though usually gentle and retiring, was mentally ill and came into conflict with his father, King 'Abd-Allah, who pronounced him unfit for the throne. This conflict, it is said, had a damaging effect on the son and may have accentuated the illness beyond recovery. The mother, possessing a strong personality, became the central figure and took special care in the upbringing of her son, hoping he would rise to the throne if his father failed to do so. King 'Abd-Allah's disappointment with his son's inability to comprehend his ideas and to learn in preparation for his future career grieved his family. Husayn, fond of his father, sympathized with his condition, which made him quite conscious at a tender age of his responsibilities—a feeling which his mother seems to have aroused, and she encouraged him to keep close to his grandfather for parental sympathy and guidance.[6]

King 'Abd-Allah on his part noticed Husayn's alertness and readiness to learn. He used to take him in his arms and inspire him with stories and anecdotes about his ancestors and Arab history with which he had great familiarity. Husayn, fascinated with his grandfather's accounts, listened

Hashimi rule rather than to enable one partner of the union to annex the other, although the Iraqi leaders hoped that they might eventually achieve annexation of Jordan by Iraq.

[6]See Faridun Sahib Jam, ed., *al-Husayn: Mihnati Kamalik, Ahadith Malakiya* [al-Husayn: My Profession As King, the King's interviews], translated and up-dated by Ghalib 'Arif Tuqan ('Amman, 1978), pp. 21-2, 25-6. (Hereafter cited as Tuqan, *The King's Interviews*). See also Sir Alec Kirkbride, *op. cit.*, pp. 120-126.

with admiration. He also watched how his grand-father talked with his Ministers and with visitors, and learned at first hand the manners of courtly life and how to handle men. "Most days," says Husayn, "I returned to the Palace before evening prayers and dined with him [his grandfather], and over the evening meal I would listen to him talking about the subtleties and pitfalls of the hazardous profession of being a king."[7] This close association between grandfather and grandson created deep affection between them and, as Husayn said in his autobiography, had "the most profound influence on my life."[8] Disappointed with his son Talal, King 'Abd-Allah began to think of his grandson as the more suitable successor than his son and made no secret of his thought to some of his Ministers, though Talal remained officially the Crown Prince to the end of 'Abd-Allah's life.[9] In the light of Husayn's subsequent handling of his country's affairs, he demonstrated that he had already learned quite a bit from frequenting his grandfather's court before he rose to the throne.

Husayn's education at schools had been hectic. Because of war conditions he received his early education at 'Amman and at Victoria College in Alexandria before he went to England for further study. At Victoria College, where he spent two years (1949-51), he seems to have done rather well, but his learning was confined to language and history and he excelled in extracurricular activities. It

---

[7] See King Husayn's autobiography, entitled *Uneasy Lies the Head* (London, 1962), p. 16 (Hereafter cited as Husayn's *Autobiography*).
[8] Husayn, *op. cit.*, p. 10.
[9] The writer's interviews with Zayd al-Rifa'i ('Amman, June 12, 1977). See also Hazza' al-Majali, *Mudhakkirati* ('Amman, 1960), pp. 105-106.

was, however, at Harrow, where he spent a year, that he began to receive a more thorough education. He took his work very seriously and maintained a high standard, despite initial difficulties. His education at Harrow was cut short, however, when, after only one year, he was proclaimed King on August 11, 1952, at the age of seventeen and had to leave the College.

Since Husayn was still a minor, Parliament appointed a Regency Council to exercise his constitutional powers until he came of age a year later. This short span—from 1952 to 1953—gave him an opportunity for further training abroad. He returned to England to enter Sandhurst where he was given a short course. At Sandhurst, he worked very hard, proved that he was able to maintain the high standard of the College and showed an ability in outdoor training that he had never done before in classrooms. His training at Sandhurst taught him discipline, self-control and a stress on duty.[10] In April 1953, he returned to 'Amman, and on May 2, he appeared before Parliament to take the constitutional oath and began to exercise his constitutional powers.

Husayn's accession to the throne put an end to a number of schemes concerning the future status of Jordan. More specifically, there were then two schools of thought. One, which might be called the Jordanian school, composed in the main of native Jordanian leaders, asserted the country's independence and advocated the succession of one of 'Abd-Allah's descendants. The other school, con-

---

[10]The fact that he often calls all persons older than himself "sir" reflects the impact of that training. In his speeches, he often refers to the notions of honor, duty, country and God, which are indeed Arab notions, but are also in accord with his training in England.

sisting of leaders who held Pan-Arab ideas, advocated union with Iraq on the grounds that the two countries were ruled by the same Royal House and that the future stability of Jordan and her needs for foreign economic assistance would be insured if the two countries were to form one kingdom. King 'Abd-Allah is said to have proposed such a plan to Iraq shortly before he was assassinated as he was concerned about the country's future stability if his son Talal were to succeed him.[11]

Jordan's neighbors and allies, especially Saudi Arabia and Britain, watched the course of events within Jordan with keen interest. Opposed to consolidation of Hashimi rule, Saudi Arabia was against Jordan's unity with Iraq and is said to have influenced Tawfiq Abu al-Huda, Jordan's Prime Minister, who seems to have been at first in favor of unity with Iraq, but changed his mind and supported Talal's succession.[12] Britain, on friendly terms with both Jordan and Iraq, may have been indifferent on the issue in principle, but saw grave dangers in the succession of Talal owing to his mental instability and his outspoken views about British domination. Accordingly, Britain supported the Jordanian school, provided Husayn was to be in the line of succession.

At the outset the Jordanian leaders who advocated Jordan's independence were divided as to who should be 'Abd-Allah's successor, as Talal was obviously ill and unsuitable for the throne. Some were in favor of Husayn, Talal's son, who was 'Abd-Allah's own favorite candidate; others argued in favor of Nayif, Talal's brother. They finally

---

[11]The writer's interviews with several Jordanian and Iraqi leaders.
[12]Majali's *Memoirs*, pp. 10-12.

came to the conclusion that Talal, officially the Crown Prince, should at first succeed in accordance with the terms of the Constitution, as his exclusion might be construed to have been done under British pressure, owing to his critical views of British domination rather than his illness. They argued that if Talal, after his accession to the throne, proved incapable of exercising his powers, he would then be deposed by Parliament and Husayn would succeed in accordance with the line of succession provided by the Constitution. According to this argument, Nayif, without constitutional revision, would have no claim to the throne, and Husayn, though still a minor, would succeed without difficulty. Because he was a minor, a Regency Council would exercise Husayn's constitutional powers until he came of age. By this arrangement, which proved satisfactory to all, the Jordanian leaders acted with prudence and saved the country from internal conflict.[13]

While the controversy over succession was going on, Husayn was still in school in England, but he was not completely unaware of the internal struggle and he seems to have been in touch with those who were working for his succession. Circumstances were indeed favorable for him, but what helped him above all were his own personal qualities which encouraged those working for him to support him against rival candidates.

IV

Though the obstacles in Husayn's way to the throne were overcome without much difficulty, there were conflicting forces in the country with

---

[13]This arrangement seems to have been agreeable to the British Gov-

which he had to deal, if his throne were to survive. Some of these forces were in the main the legacy of traditional personal rule, but it was aggravated by King 'Abd-Allah's propensity to concentrate all power in his hands and gather around him only men who were ready to obey him in his drive to achieve his ambition of creating a larger kingdom than Jordan under Hashimi rule. After his departure, leadership devolved upon a set of figures who could not agree on common objectives. Indulging in a struggle for power, they became very active and began to organize political parties and groups which rendered conflict and competition among them more intense. What intensified the struggle was the upsurge of Arab nationalism in the postwar years and the increasing activities of socialist and radical groups—the Ba'th and Communist parties in particular—vying for power, with the consequent threat not only to the Monarchy, but to the security and independence of the country itself. How did Husayn respond to the challenge and what did he do to survive?

At the outset, Husayn sympathized with the elements that desired a change along liberal and nationalist reform measures, being himself young and imbued with lofty ideas. From the time he had studied in England, he kept in touch with a number of young men, some in high diplomatic posts— Fawzi al-Mulqi in London, 'Ali Abu Nuwar in Paris and others—who used to fraternize with him and to take him to places of entertainment where they

---

ernment. "His Majesty's Government," says Sir Alec Kirkbride (the British Ambassador to Jordan) "who were not directly concerned with the problem, made it clear in their instructions to me that they were anxious that there should be no flaw in the legitimacy of the new monarch" (Sir Alec Kirkbride, *op. cit.*, 142).

could talk to him freely. Among other things, they
discussed public affairs with him and called his attention in particular to restrictions on the freedom
of the press, domination of Jordan by the British
military and diplomatic missions and the need to
entrust the Army Command, then under General
Glubb and other British officers, to Jordanian officers. Husayn listened to them with great interest,
perhaps mainly because he wanted to learn about
the state of affairs in the country, but he seems to
have also shared some of their views and promised
to carry them out after he had returned to the
country and assumed his constitutional powers.[14]

Fawzi al-Mulqi, Jordan's Ambassador to the
United Kingdom, whom I had known as a classmate at the American University of Bayrut in the
early thirties, was a perceptive and highly gifted
young man who went back to serve his country in
a junior post. After further study, he entered politics and then went to England to represent his
country at the Court of St. James.[15] While in England, Husayn was highly impressed with his ideas
and personality and he seems to have decided to
entrust him with the seals of power upon his return to Jordan. He was Husayn's first-picked Premier. Mulqi promised to introduce reforms and remove the shackles that impeded progress and
development. During his tenure of office, from
May 1953 to May 1954, he provided the country
with a number of legislative acts which permitted
freedom of the press, released persons detained for
political reasons, and allowed political parties to be

---

[14]Tuqan, *The King's Interviews*, pp. 47-48.

[15]He became first a veterinary surgeon, but very soon he abandoned
his work and entered public service (cf. Sir Alec Kirkbride, *op. cit.*,
pp. 87-88).

organized. Other laws dealt with economic, social
and municipal reforms. But these measures,
though hailed with almost universal acclaim,
aroused the concern of older leaders and vested interests who saw power slipping from their hands
and warned that unless freedom of the press and
political parties were checked the regime might
collapse and the Monarchy itself might be swept
away.[16] Under pressure, Mulqi resigned for reasons
which had nothing to do with internal security.[17]

For over two years, from his accession to the
throne in 1953 to 1955, King Husayn tried to
strengthen his regime by refocussing attention
from domestic to foreign affairs. He appealed to
his Arab neighbors—Saudi Arabia, Egypt and others—to support him against increasing Israeli
threats. Since his regime was under attack by the
Arab press on the grounds that it was dominated
by Great Britain, he declared that he was prepared
to reduce British influence if his Arab neighbors
would promise to replace foreign financial assistance by Arab assistance; but his efforts came to
naught because there was a widespread suspicion
in the Arab World that British influence in Jordan
was so entrenched that it was beyond Husayn's
ability to cope with it.

In 1955 the ensuing conflict between the so-
called revolutionary and traditional (often referred
to in the press as reactionary) countries reached a

---

[16]The writer's interviews with Fawzi al-Mulqi in 1955 and 1958.

[17]In April, 1954, Parliament passed a resolution to dispatch a cable to
Vishinsky, the Soviet delegate to the UN, thanking him for his defense of Arab rights at a recent meeting of the General Assembly.
This action, considered by the Government's opponents as another
sign of its weakness, prompted the King to ask for the resignation of
the Government (May 2, 1954) and Mulqi tendered his letter of resignation on the same day.

high pitch when Iraq joined Turkey in organizing a
defense system known as the Baghdad Pact (February 28, 1955) and to which Britain (and indirectly the United States) adhered, promising substantial military assistance. The revolutionary
countries, led by Egypt, advocated a policy of
"positive neutrality" which was then construed to
mean no commitment to either side in East-West
conflict, though Egypt depended on the Soviet
Union for military assistance. While King Sa'ud of
Saudi Arabia wavered at first between the two
camps, King Husayn began to realize that his country's independence and security depended on
Western goodwill rather than on the support of
Arab revolutionary leaders. Persuaded by the advantages of the Baghdad defense system to his
country, Husayn sought to receive economic and
military assistance by joining it. But Nasir, contending that Egypt would be outflanked by this
alliance, called on all Pan-Arab leaders to oppose it
on the grounds that the system was a Western im-
perialist scheme designed to divert attention from
the Arab enemy—Israel—to the Communist threat,
despite Soviet support of the Arabs against Israel.

In Iraq, where the Monarchy was still strong, the
Baghdad Pact became a cornerstone of foreign
policy; but in Jordan, where Husayn's hold over
the country had not yet been consolidated, the pact
was rejected under the attack of opposition leaders
and mob outbursts allegedly stimulated by Pan-
Arab broadcasts. In retrospect, Husayn's action in
Jordan proved in the long run more prudent than
that of the Iraqi branch of his House; for, though
the Iraqi Monarchical regime succeeded in erecting
the Baghdad defense system, the Monarchy itself
was overthrown three years later—at least in part

for forging that system—by the military establishment when it rose in revolt against the Monarchy, while in Jordan Husayn's repudiation of the Baghdad Pact gave the opportunity to consolidate his rule over a country that later became the supporter of a policy of cooperation with the West.[18]

For over a decade and a half, from the repudiation of the Bagdad Pact in 1955 to the expulsion of the Palestine Liberation Organization from Jordan in 1970, King Husayn addressed himself to the basic problem of the stability of his regime; for, he rightly held, no matter how sound his foreign policy was he could not safely pursue it if his regime were not supported by his subjects. For this reason he sought to eliminate the causes of disaffection between him and the public on the one hand and pursue a policy of reform on the other which would place the country on the path of progress and development. Four basic steps were deemed necessary if these objectives were to be achieved.

To begin with, Husayn was often under the attack of the Arab press for his friendly relations with the West, though he firmly asserted his country's independence and national interests. But, no matter how keen he was about national freedom and independence, the legacy of British influence from pre-independence years and the existence of British missions in the country, though highly exaggerated in the press, were telling against him. He was, therefore, bound in the long run to reduce British influence if he were to win popular support and consolidate his regime.

---

[18]For an account of Husayn's dealings with the Baghdad Pact, see Majali, *op. cit.*, pp. 153-155.

However, Britain, since his grandfather's days, had paid generously for Jordan's army and air force and made up the deficit in annual budgets. Owing to increasing criticism of British influence and failure of Britain to support Jordan against several Israeli incursions into its territory, Husayn demanded that Britain either provide Jordan with further military assistance or give up some of the privileges granted to her under the Anglo-Jordanian treaty of 1948. Negotiations in 1954 resulted in no agreement, as Jordan needed British military and financial assistance and Britain would not give up the privileges provided by the treaty. In 1955 Husayn tried to replace the treaty with Britain by joining the Baghdad Pact, but failure to adhere to the pact, as noted before, postponed action on the treaty. In 1956, following the tripartite attack on Egypt, negotiations between Jordan and Britain were resumed. Realizing the futility of keeping her military mission in Jordan against hostile popular feeling, Britain decided to withdraw it and give up all her privileges and obligations. The abrogation of the treaty in 1957, to the great satisfaction of Jordanian nationalists, opened a new chapter of friendship and goodwill between the two countries.[19]

The act that had perhaps given even greater satisfaction to popular demands was the King's decision to dismiss General John Bagot Glubb, Commander of the Arab Legion, early in 1956, while negotiations for the termination of the treaty were underway. The King and the General have both provided us with their versions of the affair—the

---

[19]For the steps taken to terminate the treaty, see Munib al-Madi and S. Musa, *Ta'rikh al-Urdun* ('Amman, 1959), pp. 606-610, 651-660.

King giving disagreement on strategy and British control of his Army as his reasons, and the General, insisting that he always acted as an official of the Jordanian Government and not of Britain, contended that the issue between him and the King had arisen because of the difference of age[20]—but the whole affair cannot be understood save within the general framework of events of the time. King Husayn, as noted before, was under attack by opponents for his country's subordination to British influence. If the King were ever to reduce British influence and gain public confidence, he was bound to dismiss Glubb. Neither the British Government, which was not unaware of the King's feeling about General Glubb, nor the General, to whom a hint that he should retire had been made, heeded.[21] It was indeed unfortunate that General Glubb, who served Jordan with integrity and devotion, should be dismissed in circumstances of high emotions rather than retired in an atmosphere of gratitude and recognition of long service.[22]

No less significant than Husayn's attempt at reconciling Western goodwill with the assertion of his country's independence was the coincidental cooperation between Pan-Arabs and Communists in

---

[20]King Husayn's *Autobiography*, Chap. 9; General J.B. Glubb, *A Soldier With the Arabs* (London, 1957), p. 26.

[21]King Husayn's *Autobiography*, p. 115; General Glubb, *op. cit.*, p. 366, "I had already told the King that," says General Glubb, "if he did not want me, I was ready at any time to resign." (Ibid, p. 386); but he seems to have been advised to do nothing (Ibid, p. 367).

[22]In a conversation about General Glubb with Sir Alec Kirkbride, British Ambassador to Jordan, in 1960, Sir Alec told me that after Jordan achieved independence, he suggested to General Glubb that both he (Sir Alec) and Glubb should retire from service in Jordan to give evidence that Jordan no longer remained under British influence; Sir Alec said he retired and later went to Libya, but General Glubb refused to retire. Years later I asked General Glubb, during

the postwar years, which rendered the task of denouncing Soviet penetration into Arab lands as a
threat to Arab interests more difficult for leaders
like Husayn. In Jordan, Pan-Arab ideas were
strongly held by elements that resented British influence and by young men and Army officers who
aspired to play a role in politics. Since freedom for
the expression of political opinion was allowed
after Husayn's accession to the throne, the Pan-
Arabs and the new political parties in Jordan supported the revolutionary movement led by President Nasir against the West which came into
conflict with King Husayn's regime. Two prominent leaders—Sulayman al-Nabulsi, a civilian, and
'Ali Abu-Nuwar, an officer—dominated the political scene and almost brought the Monarchy to the
verge of destruction. Nabulsi, another classmate of
mine at the American University of Bayrut, was an
outspoken critic of British influence in Arab lands
since his college days and became deeply involved
in politics after he returned to Jordan. Riding the
crest of the Pan-Arab wave in his country in the
mid-fifties, he became Prime Minister and sought
to bring Jordan into close cooperation with Nasir's
Pan-Arab drive against Western influence. Abu-
Nuwar, whom Husayn picked up as successor to
Glubb's command of the Army, worked hand-in-

one of his visits to us in Washington as a friend, about Sir Alec's
suggestion that he should have retired from Jordan after independence. General Glubb replied that Sir Alec Kirkbride was in fact in
the service of the British Government and was under obligation to
carry out British policy in Jordan while he (Glubb) was not in the
service of the British but of the Jordanian Government. In his *Soldier With the Arabs*, Glubb says that he often reminded Jordanians
that he, in the service of the Jordan Government, was under obligation to carry out the orders of the Jordanian and not of the British
Government. (See General Glubb, *A Soldier With the Arabs*, p. 72). Cf.
Gerald Sparrow, *Hussein of Jordan* (London, 1960), chap. 3.

hand with Nabulsi and tried by a military coup to overthrow the regime, as Husayn was considered opposed to Nasir's scheme of Pan-Arab unity. But Husayn, supported by Jordanian elements concerned about the destruction of his regime, stood up to the challenge and defeated the elements opposed to him. He appealed to the tribal elements in the Army, reflecting Jordanian reaction against the incorporation of Jordan in a Pan-Arab union, foiled Abu-Nuwar's coup and brought the Armed Forces under his control.[23] Encouraged by the Army's support, Husayn made it clear to civilian leaders that he was opposed to parties that espoused radical doctrines and issued a letter to Nabulsi warning in no uncertain terms that he would no longer tolerate Communist propaganda.[24] Alienated from the Army, Nabulsi saw the futility of remaining in power and tendered his resignation to the King without resistance (April 10, 1957). The collapse of the Nabulsi-Abu-Nuwar plot marked the decline of Pan-Arab activities in Jordan, but sporadic assaults on pro-Western leaders, including attempts on Husayn's life, have continued unabated to the present.

Radical Palestinian elements, frustrated by Arab inability to recover their homeland from Israel, presented perhaps the greatest threat to King Husayn's throne. Ever since Israel was established, the Palestinians have considered Jordan, having the largest common frontiers with Israel, the country from which they could attack Israel most ef-

---

[23]For Abu-Nuwar's abortive coup and the events leading up to it, see King Husayn's *Autobiography*, chaps. 10-11; and Madi and Musa, *op. cit.*, pp. 661-680. See also Peter Snow, *Hussein* (Washington, 1972), chaps. 5-15.

[24]See text of the letter in Madi and Musa, *op. cit.*, pp. 666-67.

fectively. Like his grandfather, Husayn held that
both he and the Palestinians were incapable of
launching a frontal attack on Israel, and cautioned
against acts of violence which often resulted in unnecessary destruction of Jordanian towns and villages through Israeli retaliation. He maintained that
until Arabs as a whole became strong enough to go
to war with Israel, Jordan should avoid single-
handed confrontation, as its contiguous lands were
the most exposed to Israeli forces.

Although many Palestinian leaders have sided
with King Husayn and have seen the futility of
confrontation without adequate preparation, the
radical elements have always urged the use of war
and violence even if their incursions into Israel
proved suicidal. They argued that relaxation of
violent activities, giving the impression that Palestinians have acquiesced to existing conditions,
might eventually lead to the acceptance of Israel
by the Arabs and the Palestinian cause would be
lost forever. For this reason, Husayn's argument
against war with Israel was unacceptable—and
even denounced by radicals as betrayal—as it revealed his personal insecurity and concern about
his throne rather than anxiety about Israeli attacks
against Arab lands. Some extremists, exasperated
by his policy, called for his assassination; most of
them saw in his regime an obstacle in the way of
achieving their goal and sought to overthrow it at
the earliest possible moment.

Like his grandfather, Husayn welcomed the Palestinians and extended to them all the privileges
that other subjects enjoyed in his country. He was
indeed not unsympathetic with their grievances; he
seized every possible opportunity on the national
and international levels to plead their case and de-

fend their rights. He has, however, genuinely believed that peaceful rather than violent methods were more effective in arousing Western support for legitimate Palestinian demands as long as the Arabs as a whole were unable to stand up to Israeli might. On the contrary, he believed that violence and sporadic attacks on innocent individuals in airports, schools and other public places have often antagonized potential friends and supporters.

Nevertheless, Husayn did not shrink from supporting the Arab forces directly or indirectly whenever they were involved in fighting with Israel, as the conflicts of 1967 and 1973 demonstrated, even though he realized that Arab forces were not adequately equipped militarily. Despite Husayn's First Minister's warning against quick action, he went to war in 1967 under Nasir's influence and gave partial support in 1973 because he felt that inaction, when other Arab rulers were at war with Israel, would weigh very heavily on his conscience.[25]

Moreover, in an agreement with Nasir, he promised to allow Palestinian guerilla activities in his territory as a means to influence Israel to withdraw from occupied Arab lands.[26] At the outset the Palestinians were appreciative of Husayn as well

---

[25]The writer's interview with Sa'd Jum'a, Jordan's Prime Minister in 1967 ('Amman, June 10, 1977). See also Jum'a's *al-Mu'amara wa Ma'rakat al-Masir* [Conspiracy and the Battle of Destiny] (Bayrut, 1968). However, Zayd al-Rifa'i, another Prime Minister, felt that the entry of Jordan in the war, resulting in the loss of the West Bank, was a mistake and Husayn could have survived without participation in the war (the writer's interview with Rifa'i in 'Amman, June 12, 1977). Cf. Vick Lance and Pierre Lauer, *Hussein of Jordan: My War With Israel*, tr. J.P. Wilson and W.B. Michael (New York, 1969).
[26]After the Six-Day War, Nasir seems to have considered the closure of the Suez Canal to European shipping and Palestinian guerilla activities as possible means to support the political pressure to influ-

as of other Arab support. But the Palestinian activities which started as warfare directed against Israel gradually began to change their focus from Israel to Jordan and then to other Arab countries on
the grounds that regimes of these countries were
not fully cooperating with them and therefore unworthy of survival. This brought the Palestinian
leaders into conflict with Jordan—later with other
countries—and the ensuing civil war resulted in
the expulsion of Palestinian guerillas from Jordan
in 1970 because their leaders consciously sought to
replace the regime in Jordan by another, friendly
or subordinate to them. What aggravated the situation was the division of the Palestinian leaders into
factions each falling under the influence of one rival Arab country or another, each of which tried
to use the faction under its influence (by virtue of
the economic and military assistance being given to
it) against other rival countries. Since most of the
leaders had received assistance from countries unfriendly to the Jordanian regime, the majority of
the Palestinians engaged in guerilla activities in Jordan became opposed to Husayn and came into direct conflict with him.

Matters came to a head in 1970. For four years,
the guerillas who began their incursions into Israel
from Jordanian borders gradually retreated into
the interior because of crushing Israeli counter-at-
tacks and bombing of their sanctuaries. They
found shelters first in agricultural settlements and
towns and finally moved into the big towns and
cities, including 'Amman, the capital of Jordan.
Frustrations with the enemy necessarily prompted

---

ence Israel to withdraw from the lands occupied in 1967. King
Husayn seems to have promised Nasir to give him support for this
plan.

the guerillas to find a safety valve for their anger
in encroachments on civilians—it is said that some
became arrogant and aggressive—and when the
authorities intervened to stop them, they clashed
first with the police and then with the armed
forces. The Ba'th leaders, for ideological if not for
other reasons, had for long been opposed to
Husayn, and after they achieved power in Iraq in
1968, they began to increase their activities against
his regime by extending economic and military assistance to the guerillas. Since there had already
been an Iraqi force[27] in Jordan to support her
against possible Israeli attack after the Six-Day
War, the Iraqi force indirectly encouraged the
guerilla leaders to oppose the Jordanian regime
shortly after the Ba'th Party came to power in
Iraq. In September 1970, when the relations between the Palestinian guerillas and King Husayn
were strained, the Iraqi government seems to have
informed the Palestinian guerillas that if they were
ever to come into an open conflict with the Jordanian authorities, they could count on Iraqi military
support. Some Arab countries, including Egypt,
urged the guerilla leaders to come to an understanding with Husayn and to divert their activities
to the common enemy, but the radical elements
were so exasperated with Husayn that they were
determined to overthrow his regime before they
could concentrate on the enemy. Yasir Arafat,
head of the Central Committee of the PLO, assumed direct control of the guerilla forces in their
struggle against the regime. He seemed to have obtained Syrian and Iraqi assurances of support on

---

[27]Estimated at about 15,000 soldiers (See Tuqan, *The King's Interviews*, p. 230).

the grounds that Husayn was obstructing the Palestinian operations against Israel. Fighting lasted almost a week. The Palestinians, despite the participation of Syrian volunteers, were unable to win, because Husayn, by an appeal to the nation and to his loyal Jordanian Army, was able to resist with determination and vigor.[28] On September 20, a Syrian force, consisting of some 200 tanks, crossed the frontiers deep into Jordanian territory and occupied the town of Irbid, and the Iraqi force, presumably on the basis of instructions from Bagdad, was prepared to join in the drive to overthrow the regime.

Faced with this threat, Husayn naturally felt bound to defend not only his own regime but also the country against a Syro-Iraqi intervention. He appealed to the Arab heads of state and government, then meeting in Cairo, as well as to the Western Powers for support.[29] Warnings from these Powers—including an exchange of notes between the United States and the Soviet Union on the situation—seem to have induced Syria to withdraw her tanks and to have discouraged the Iraqi garrison in Jordan from joining the Syrian and Palestinian forces. Israel, claiming to have joined the Western Powers in their support of Jordan, prompted King Husayn to reject the claim, though Henry Kissinger, the American Secretary of State, may have personally encouraged Israel to join in

---

[28]On September 15, 1970, a Military Government, headed by Lieutenant Muhammad Dawud, Chief of the Jordanian forces, was formed and entrusted with the task of coping with the internal situation. For the events leading up to the conflict between the Palestinian guerillas and the Jordanian forces, see the Ministry of Information, *al-'Amal al-Fida'i Fi al-Urdun* [The Guerilla Operations in Jordan] ('Amman, 1970), pp. 82ff.

[29]*Ibid*, p. 97.

the warning without Husayn's prior authorization
or approval.[30] The crisis was finally resolved by an
agreement among the Arab states, signed in Cairo
on September 27, 1970, by virtue of which the Palestinian guerillas agreed to terminate their operations and most of them voluntarily withdrew
from Jordan.[31]

In the foregoing struggle among competing
groups, King Husayn emerged, though not entirely
unscathed, as the leader who succeeded in reducing or superseding nearly all the Palestinian forces
operating within the regime over which he presided. Step by step, he was able to eliminate rival
army officers, ideological elements and guerilla
leaders—steps which he had undertaken not necessarily by design but which were dictated by the coincidental sequence of events and which enabled
him to emerge as the unrivalled leader who could
at times of danger stand up to the challenge.
Though still a constitutional Monarch in theory, he

---

[30]The writer's interviews with the late al-Sharif 'Abd al-Hamid
Sharaf, former Jordanian Ambassador to the United States and later
Chief of the Royal Palace; and 'Abd-Allah Salah, former Minister of
Foreign Affairs and now Jordan's Ambassador to the United States.
The story of Kissinger's possible arrangement with Israel to participate in Western warnings to Syria and Iraq was first published in
Marvin and Bernard Kalb, *Kissinger* (Boston, 1974), chap. 8. Ambassador Sharaf, having been personally involved in the exchange of
notes between Jordan and the United States, wrote letters to the editors of the *New York Times* taking exception to Kalb's account. For a
full account of American involvement in the Jordanian crisis of
1970, see William B. Quandt, *Decade of Decisions: American Policy
Toward the Arab-Israeli War, 1967-1976* (Berkeley, 1977), chap. 4. In
late 1980, while an Arab Summit was in session in 'Amman, Syria
again concentrated a force (estimated at about 30,000) on Jordan's
borders intended to influence King Husayn to postpone the meetings
which Syria had boycotted. As in 1970, Husayn made it clear that he
was not prepared to capitulate under Syrian threats.

[31]In addition to the interviews with 'Abd al-Hamid Sharaf and 'Abd-
Allah Salah, the writer was given a full account of the Palestinian

concentrated all powers in his hands and emerged
as the sovereign who could call and dismiss Cabi-
nets at his pleasure and carry the country with
him by a careful balancing of forces. Before we inquire into the methods he pursued to achieve objectives, it is appropriate to discuss first his political
views and aspirations which directly or indirectly
define his goals and objectives.

V

Even before he went to school, young Husayn
learned from his grandfather that he belonged to
the noblest of Arab families, the Prophet's family,
and that he was descendant in direct line from the
Prophet's daughter Fatima, married to 'Ali, cousin
of the Prophet and the head of the line of Imams
who claimed to rule by legitimate right. A deep respect for his House, called the Hashimi House, because of its descent from Hashim (the Prophet's
uncle), and a driving sense of mission to restore the
glory of the Arab past governed both King 'Abd-
Allah and his father, the Sharif Husayn of Makka
(later King Husayn of the Hijaz), who led the Arab
Revolt in 1916 against the Ottoman Empire to enable the Arabs to gain their independence, presumably in the belief that the Hashimi family was destined to rule over the modern Arab World. The
Hashimi destiny, however, was never realized, because of a shift of fortune and unfavorable circumstances which eventually reduced its leadership only to Jordan.

The Hashimi misfortune is another familiar sub-

---

operations in Jordan by 'Adnan Abu 'Awda, Minister of Information,
during his visits to Jordan in 1975 and 1976. For Iraq's involvement
in the crisis, see my *Socialist Iraq* (Washington, 1978), pp. 59, 60-61.

ject on which King 'Abd-Allah lectured his grandson and admonished him to understand its significance. Because they were denied their alleged right
to succeed the Prophet after his death in A.D. 632,
the Prophet's descendants—*Al al-Bayt*—often suffered persecution and even death and a legend developed that the *Al al-Bayt,* the House of the
Prophet, had become the Family of Sorrow owing
to the persecution suffered by its leading members
ever since the Prophet departed from the scene.
Indeed, persecution has become an obsession in
the minds of almost all members of this family. Although King Husayn suffers no persecution complex, he and his grandfather have, in moments of
weakness, voiced the Hashimi sorrow, either because they sought consolation by resort to fatalism
or because they felt they were in need of public
sympathy.[32]

Outside family influences, Husayn was exposed
to secular education, and in the era of the upsurge
of Arab nationalism, he was bound to adopt Arab
nationalism as one of his goals and sympathize
with Arab nationalists who called for full
independence, Arab unity and opposition to Israel
and Zionist pressures. But as the only surviving
ruler of the Hashimi House, his Arab nationalism
was naturally influenced by the Hashimi conception of Arab nationalism and he rejected the views
of rival leaders who advocated other variants of
Arab nationalism.

---

[32]See Tuqan, *The King's Interviews,* p. 216. It has been reported that
King 'Abd-Allah once said to Samir al-Rifa'i, a former Premier, that
the Hashimi Monarchy which his father, the Sharif of Makka, had
founded in the Hijaz in 1916 might well end in Jordan with the rise
of his grandson Husayn to the throne (the writer's interview with
Zayd al-Rifa'i, 'Amman, June 12, 1977).

Husayn's idea of nationalism stems first from Islam—a force, he says, which embraces tolerance, love of God, love of good deeds, and a deep-rooted sense of justice—which led to the establishment of the Islamic Empire.[33] In the modern age, after the Arab nation had lost its independence, the Hashimi House championed the cause of the Arab revival and rose in revolt against Ottoman domination during World War I. But after that war the Arabs' allies denied the unity and independence, which the Hashimi House had championed, and set up not a single Arab state, but separate states as well as Israel. Instead of meeting this challenge by a unity of purpose and concerted action, the Arabs responded by "the forces of negativism, disarray and selfishness," and the lack of understanding of the nature of the forces that led to the loss of Palestine to Jewish colonial endeavors.[34]

What should the salvation be for the Arab World, Husayn asked? Most Arab leaders have advocated nationalism and Arab unity as the salvation. Husayn, while agreeing in principle on nationalism and Arab unity, calls for "true nationalism" and "Arab unity." What is true Arab nationalism? It is, he says, as follows:

---

[33] The force of Islam, Husayn says, was embodied in the word *taqwa* which combined a moral and political content. Morally it was based on faith in God and politically on the concept of equality among individuals, irrespective of ethnic or social differentials. See Husayn, "How to Unite Arab World," *Life International* (May 23, 1960), p. 30; and *Autobiography*, p. 69.

[34] "It is often said," Husayn adds, "that the Palestine question is a chronicle of missed opportunities . . . The tragic undoing and dismantling of the Palestine people, to which their leadership unwittingly contributed, was that they adamantly refused to understand or accept this unpleasant but elementary fact of life" (Husayn's foreword to King Abdullah's *My Memoirs Completed* [London, 1978], p. xiv).

Nationalism properly means the ultimate loyalty of the individual to the Arab World as a whole; it demands that a Jordanian be an Arab first and a Jordanian second, an Iraqi an Arab first and an Iraqi second. Loyalties to lesser concepts have seriously weakened our ability to pursue constructive policies.

My own concept of Arab nationalism, for example, is quite different from what I understand President Nasser's to be. If I interpret his aims properly, he believes that political unity and Arab nationalism are synonymous. Evidently he also believes that Arab nationalism can only be identified by a particular brand of political unity. If this is his belief, I disagree. It can only lead, as it has in the past, to more disunity. The seeking of popular support for one point of view or one form of leadership in countries other than one's own has fostered factionalism to a dangerous degree, splitting countries to the point of revolution. It is nothing but a new form of imperialism, the domination of one state by another. It makes no difference if both are Arab states. Arab nationalism can survive only through complete equality.

It is in our power as Arabs to unite on all important issues, to organize in every respect and to dispel the frictions between us .... But we have as yet been unable to unite properly against our two most potent enemies: Communism and Zionism.[35]

As to Arab unity, he calls for a debate on the practical steps to be undertaken, as the principle of unity has already been agreed upon. There are, he said, four natural units in the Arab-speaking world: the Fertile Crescent, the Arabian Peninsula, the Nile Valley, and the Maghrib. As to the practical steps, he suggested the following:

---

[35]*Life International,* pp. 82-83; *Autobiography,* pp. 74-76.

Let the countries in these natural units associate themselves in whatever way they choose as a step toward the great goal of an Arab nation. Let their association be voluntary, and let it embrace only what the people of each country want to embrace—whether it be culture, economics or defence. Let political alliance, if it is desirable at all, be the last step . . . .

To such a proposal Jordan pledges the full weight of its power and strength—It would subscribe immediately to any practical step designed to realize it. Our only plea is for well considered action.[36]

In principle, Husayn is in favor of democracy and opposed to Communism, but his views about both are too general and vague perhaps because he is not too sure that the Arabs are yet ready for democracy as it exists today in the West and he is almost certain that Communism is destructive to Arab values and traditions. "There are in the free world," he says, "different interpretations of the term democracy." To copy one system of government or another completely and to apply it to a new state with a different culture is obviously impractical and even dangerous, in his opinion. Western democracies themselves, he rightly maintains, have continually discovered that they must make adjustments to deal with changing times. In the Arab world, many political parties have adopted the slogan of democracy, but these parties or groups have identified themselves with elements outside their country. For this reason, he denounces the parties and groups that identify themselves with the reverse of democracy. Communism, he maintains, entered the Arab World under

---

[36]*Life International*, pp. 85-86; *Autobiography*, p. 80.

the guise of nationalism. But he does not fully explain his objection to it save that it is contrary to Islamic principles and that it is a divisive force among the Arabs.[37] His objection to other radical parties, especially the Ba'th Party, is based on the same grounds that they advocate vague slogans such as freedom, socialism and Arab unity, but that they developed no real reform programs. Their slogans, he holds, are merely means by which they hope to achieve power. For this reason, he warns that "we do not feel we can yet afford the luxury of these parties in our democratic process."[38] Not only has Communism been banned in Jordan since 1953, in accordance with the Combatting Communism Act, but also all political groups. Above all, Husayn objects to the revolutionary method with which radical parties seek reform and development. In his view, the use of violence is a negative method of reform; progress and development should be carried out by peaceful and not by violent means. He has pursued this method in Jordan and hopes that his country will become a model of reform for other Arab lands. As early as 1960—he still holds the same view today—he said:

> Jordan seeks to play one role, that of a model state. It is our aim to set an example for our Arab brethren, not one that they need follow but one that will inspire them to seek a higher, happier destiny within their own borders. We propose to devote, without ever losing sight of the ultimate goal of a united Arab nation, our full time and energy to

[37]See Husayn's *Autobiography*, pp. 68-69.
[38]See Foreign Office, *al-Urdun wa al-Qadiya al-Filastiniya wa al-Alaqat al-'Arabiya* [Jordan and the Palestine Question and Arab Relations] ('Amman, n.d.) pp. 10-11.

the creation of a way of life that we hope in time all Arabs will achieve. We are supposed to be an underdeveloped country. But we are not underdeveloped in those attributes that will eventually make us great—pride, dignity, determination, courage, confidence, and the knowledge that nothing can be achieved without work.[39]

VI

Husayn's foreign policy, differing from his grandfather's objective of using Jordan as a stepping stone, fitted well with Jordan's historical role as a buffer state. In order to survive, Husayn was bound to keep a balance among rival neighbors and to follow a moderate and neutralist policy toward them. If he ever found himself drawn into an alliance with one neighbor or joining a coalition of one bloc against another, he very soon reverted to traditional neutrality and normal relations. Husayn's foreign policy consisted in the main of asserting Jordan's independence, pursuing a neutralist policy with neighbors, and coming to an understanding (formal or informal) with a Great Power that would protect that independence.

As an Arab country, Jordan was naturally prepared to support other Arab countries whenever one (or more) of them was attacked by another country. Not only did she give diplomatic support at UN meetings and at other international councils, but was also prepared to go to war even if she were to suffer defeat at the hands of the enemy.

[39]See *Life International* p. 86. See also Husayn's speech at a meeting of Jordan's Provincial Governors and Mayors on April 13, 1977, in Ministry of Information, *al-Khitabat al-Malakiya Fi 'Am al-Yubil al-Fiddi* [The King's Speeches in the year of the Silver Jubilee] ('Amman, 1977), pp. 33-35.

No Government in Jordan, perhaps not even King Husayn himself, could remain in power if Jordan failed to support an Arab country that became the subject of an attack by Israel. Jordan was also prepared to support an Arab neighbor whenever it became involved in a conflict with a non-Arab neighbor, as shown in her effort to offer good offices in the Perso-Iraqi dispute over Shatt al-Arab, or in a conflict with a Great Power, as evidenced in the conflict between Egypt and Britain over Suez and between Algeria and France. But Jordan consciously followed a neutralist policy if a conflict ensued between two or more Arab countries—as the conflicts between Egypt and Libya, and Syria and Iraq, to mention only two examples, have demonstrated—although her ruler's sympathy may well be known to have been with one side against the other.[40]

As an Arab country whose rulers have always professed Arab nationalism, Jordan was and is still in favor of Pan-Arabism and Arab unity, but as a buffer state Jordan has refused to be completely dissolved in any plan of unity. Jordan's rulers, although accepting Arab cooperation in principle, have always been jealous of their own powers and have indeed refused to be dominated by any Arab leader who sought to call for Arab unity over the heads of Arab rulers. In 1958, when Jordan joined Iraq in an Arab Federation to counteract Nasir's grand design of Arab unity, Husayn remained the *de facto* sovereign of Jordan. Jordan's intent to

---

[40]In the case of the conflict between the two Arab countries of 'Uman (Oman) and South Yaman, and the conflict between North and South Yaman, Husayn had no hesitation into supporting 'Uman and North Yaman on the grounds that Communist infiltration into South Yaman justified his intervention on behalf of 'Uman and North Yaman.

maintain her identity is partly determined by her role as a buffer state from antiquity and partly by domestic and regional conditions of the modern age.

In the global conflict between East and West, Husayn has no hesitation in declaring himself to be on the side of the West. Because of initial British support, Husayn's grandfather chose Britain as the Great Power to support Jordan's independence. Husayn's dependence on the goodwill and support of the West is not only consistent with his grandfather's policy designed to protect his country's independence, but is also designed to provide economic and technical assistance without which he cannot possibly achieve the progress and development of the country.[41]

But Husayn has another reason for his commitment to the West. He believes that Islam and Arab traditions are opposed to Communism. "The concepts of morality and behavior of Islam," he says, "are the principles for which we in the free world stand." "Communism," he goes on to say, "denies all faiths and thus the very principles on which Arab nationalism is based."[42] Moreover, he maintains that Communism divides Arabs and he has refused to accept Soviet assistance and support on the grounds that Communist teachings are inconsistent with his country's principles and traditions. Though he follows a neutralist policy on the regional level, he does not subscribe to a neutralist

[41]Owing to the dwindling British economic aid to his country in the late fifties, Husayn turned to the United States and to some European countries, especially West Germany, for economic and technical assistance. Since 1970, he has also sought more often their political and military support.

[42]See *Life International*, pp. 80 and 84.

policy on the international level, even though the
Soviet Union and the United States have turned
away from the Cold War and entered a period of
detente.[43] He rejects the theory that local Communism and international Communism differ. The ultimate aim of all Communists, he asserts, is to deny
faith and undermine the very basis of Arab nationalism. These ideas, although some are vague and
abstract, can perhaps be more clearly understood
by noticing how they affect the conduct of his
policy both in domestic and foreign affairs.

VII

Husayn's foreign policy, contributing in no small
measure to the improvement of the country's
economy and the stability of the regime, has enhanced his own prestige and created the feeling
among his countrymen that his throne has become
essential to keep the country together and to speed
up its development along the path of progress and
prosperity. Husayn's success in domestic and foreign affairs may be attributed partly to a number
of able leaders who readily gave him support and
partly to the personal qualities and qualifications
which he has put into the service of the country.

What are these attributes and how did he secure
the cooperation of his country's leaders?

Although Husayn was young when he rose to
the throne and had a relatively short time to receive a solid education, his personal experiences
and exposure to events and situations, which he

---

[43]In an attempt to reduce Soviet influence in the Arab World, King
Husayn made use of his outspoken remarks about Communism to
strengthen his country's position in her relations with the United
States.

seems to have observed with a keen eye, provided him with an insight and deep understanding of men and public affairs. No ruler who has had the opportunity to witness or experience the problems and difficulties to which Husayn had been exposed would fail to acquire maturity and wisdom, unless he was utterly lacking in wit and sensibility. Husayn has been noted to possess a native intelligence and an agile mind; he also possesses will and moral courage which have often prompted him to act with conviction, even if his action ran contrary to the advice of counsellors.

Some of Husayn's admirers and critics maintain that most of his decisions and actions were based on intuition rather than calculation and that exigencies and auspicious circumstances turned out to be in favor of his actions. Whether by intuition or calculation he certainly proved to be a better judge of circumstances and the direction of public opinion than his counsellors. He seems to have been able to calculate how far he can go in his actions without a risk to his throne or a danger to the security of the country. His dismissal of General Glubb in 1956, his foiling of the military plot of 1957, the war against the PLO in 1970, and some of his marriages against the advice of many counsellors, are cases in point. His decision to go to war with Israel in 1967 has been faulted by some, because it resulted in the annexation of the West Bank by Israel and in heavy human and material losses,[44] and defended by others on the grounds that neither he nor his regime would have survived under the pressure of Arab public opinion

---

[44]Interview with Zayd al-Rifa'i, a former Jordanian Prime Minister and one of the King's close advisors ('Amman, June 12, 1977).

demanding Jordan's participation in the war.[45]
Though realizing the risk of going to war with Israel when the Arabs were not fully prepared for it,
his action was dictated partly by a sense of Arab
pride that he could not possibly remain idle when
all his neighbors were at war with the enemy but
mainly by his falling under Nasir's influence when
he went to see him in Cairo shortly before the war
broke out and gave his word that if Egypt were attacked, Jordan would be on his side. The risk of
defeat in the war and the overthrow of his regime
by an angry public opinion must have weighed
heavily on his conscience, but he also felt that Israel's attack on his Arab neighbors had been equally
an attack on his country for which he felt bound
in honor to defend. In the war of 1973, Husayn,
moved partly by public opinion and partly by his
recent rapprochement with Syria, sent a division
to fight with the Syrian forces but did not attack
Israel directly across the River Jordan because he
feared an Israeli counter-attack.

Some of Husayn's public pronouncements and
actions—disapproval of Nasir's policies at one time
and taking sides with him at another, criticizing the
Iraqi Ba'th leaders and cooperating with them and
others—gave the impression that he was inconsistent in his policies and strategy, but in reality he so
acted either because the interests of his country to
cooperate with an Arab neighbor prompted him to
do so or because he felt that cooperation in one
field—cultural or economic—can be maintained
apart from differences in the political field. He has
also shown a remarkable flexibility in his relations
with groups and leaders within his country. He has

---

[45]Interview with Sa'd Jum'a, Jordan's Prime Minister during the Six-
Day War of 1967 ('Amman, June 15, 1977).

never taken a stand against a leader of a group which was irrevocable. Moved by compassion, he has forgiven many an opponent, including Abu Nuwar, who had conspired against him and allowed him to return to service. He proved able to rise above personal vengeance and his generosity and tolerance turned a number of opponents into friends and supporters.[46]

A keen observer, Husayn came to know all the men around him and he chose the man to whom he could entrust the seals of his office in accordance with the demands of the occasion. True, his choice of First Ministers during the early years of his reign was largely determined by deference to constitutional procedure and the advice of privy counsellors; but very soon, especially after the dissolution of political parties, he made his own choice of Heads of Government and Chiefs of the Royal Cabinet. Before a prospective Premier is appointed, first he is tested for his fitness to become the Head of a Government by serving as Chief of the Royal Cabinet. After he forms the Government, the Premier receives from Husayn the full support to which he is entitled, not only to carry on the ordinary business of government efficiently, but, perhaps more importantly, to achieve the objectives for which he was called to power. No matter how able the Premier proved to be, however, he was not expected to remain too long in office, as another prospective Premier had already been wait-

---

[46]Shortly before his death in 1976, Sulayman al-Nabulsi, a former Premier, told me that he had respected King Husayn although he had serious disagreements with him, and the King often inquired about his health and visited him in his house when he was ill. Munif al-Razzazz, leader of the Ba'th Party in Jordan, spoke in the same vein to me in 1977, although his differences with the King were both personal and ideological.

ing for his turn, either to inspire confidence in the regime or to fulfill new functions laid down by the King. Only at times of national emergency did Husayn call upon his privy counsellors to nominate one of their number who could enlist the support of his peers to deal with the crisis. Husayn's desire to call on all men, each in his field, to serve the country has been with public approval and has left no doubt that no one in his realm would be deliberately excluded from service.

Because he had no male child from his first marriage, the question of succession weighed heavily on Husayn's conscience. The appointment of his brother Muhammad, eight years younger than he, as heir apparent was not considered satisfactory, because he lacked adequate education and sound judgment. After thorough scrutiny of other members of his house, his choice finally fell on Prince al-Hasan, who received a solid education at Harrow and Oxford. Well known for his integrity, sharp intelligence and attractive personality, his choice met universal approval. Returning in the spring for a short visit to 'Amman, al-Hasan called on his brother without having the slightest idea about the subject of his appointment as heir apparent. "Were you surprised?" I asked Prince Hasan. "It was quite a surprise and His Majesty's choice gave me confidence in the service of the country," he replied. His education at Christ Church completed in 1967, he returned to take an active part in the development projects of his country and to represent the King in various domestic and foreign functions whenever he was asked to do so on his behalf. In all his acts, Crown Prince Hasan proved equal to the task.

VIII

Although King Husayn has been able to hold the country together and establish a relatively stable regime, he has yet to take positive steps—indeed, an over-all plan of reforms—for the regime that has been evolving since the founding of the state to develop into a truly democratic system. As noted earlier, he is in favor of democracy in principle and wishes his people to enjoy democratic freedoms. True, the relative freedom of the press and the existence of trade unions and professional associations may well place Jordan in the forefront of Arab lands that are struggling today to establish stable regimes that would command the greatest public appeal. But Jordan's exposure to Arab revolutionary movements originating in neighboring countries—Syria, Iraq and others—and her incorporation of Palestinians who identify their political outlook with Pan-Arab and not with Jordanian aspirations rendered more difficult the task of developing Jordanian democratic institutions.[47]

After the Six-Day War, the question of Jordan's Parliament, representing equally Jordanians and Palestinians of the East and West Banks, became exceedingly difficult, as more than half the population—all Palestinians—had passed under Israeli occupation. Defying reality, King Husayn refused to

---

[47]For a statement voicing the demand of Jordanian intellectuals to have full freedom for the free expression of political opinion, see 'Abd-Allah al-Rimawi, "al-Umma al-'Arabiya Amam Masiraha" [The Arab Nation Facing Its Destiny] al-Akhbar ('Amman, October 26-28, 1978). For a more critical account of the regime, see al-Nizam al-Hashimi Wa al-Huquq al-Wataniya Li al-Sha'b al-Filastini [The Hashimi Regime and the National Rights of the Palestinian People] (Bayrut, 1974).

consider West Bankers outside his realm and continued to consult their leaders and pay the salaries of civil servants. However, when the Arab Heads of State, meeting at a Summit in Rabat in 1974, passed a resolution by virtue of which leadership of the West Bank and the Ghazza Strip became the responsibility of the PLO, the fate of Jordan's Parliament, claiming to represent Palestinians, was sealed. Acting under the advice of counsellors, including Palestinians, Husayn made no constitutional changes that would limit parliamentary representation to the East Bank on the grounds that such changes might be construed by Israel as a tacit recognition of its occupation of the West Bank. Though Parliamentary session was extended three years, Parliament was finally dissolved in 1974.

This action, the product of foreign and not of domestic conditions, affected adversely the process of democratic institutions in Jordan by the suspension of parliamentary elections for an indefinite period. Husayn could have governed by decree and dispensed with parliamentary control, nominal as this might have been, had he wanted to establish personal rule. But his commitment to democratic institutions in principle and his desire to achieve political participation prompted him to establish a National Consultative Council four years later which would function temporarily as a legislative body in the absence of Parliament. Composed of some 60 members representing various sections of the population, it was established by a decree on April 4, 1978.[48] The Council's functions are purely advisory. The draft laws that are pre-

---

[48]The 60 members, representing the various functional groups, are as follows: 20 former Ministers, including one former Premier to

pared by the Cabinet are submitted to the Consultative Council and issued as having the force of
laws, with the proviso that they will be submitted
to a future elective Assembly for final approval.
The President of the Council serves as a link between the Council and the Cabinet. The Council,
though appointed for only a three-year term capable of renewal, is not expected to last too long before a Parliament is elected to resume legislative
functions.[49]

To prepare the way for a democratic system,
King Husayn may well consider the existence of
institutionalized political groups, especially political
parties, as necessary instruments to allow existence
of opposition and prepare the new generation to
participate in politics. Because the political parties
that existed in the 1950s failed to operate within
Jordan's constitutional framework and represented
either Pan-Arab or international movements whose
goals ran contrary to Jordan's existence as a separate entity, they were abolished early in the fifties
and no new political parties have yet emerged.
Shortly before his assassination in 1971, Wasfi al-
Tal, then Prime Minister, began to organize a National Union representing various shades of opinion, designed to develop eventually into a political
party.[50] Even before he departed, however, al-Tal

serve as President of the Council, 13 former members of Parliament,
(excluding Senators), 13 West Bankers who live in Jordan, 12 lawyers, 7 doctors, 3 engineers, 3 ladies, 2 pharmacologists, 1 president
of the federation of farmer's unions.

[49]For the text of the law governing the establishment and operation
of the National Consultative Council, see *Qanun al-Majlis al-Watani
al-Istishari* ('Amman, 1978); and *al-Majlis al-Watani al-Istishari: al-Nizam al-Dakhili* ('Amman, 1978).

[50]For Wasfi al-Tal's plan to organize the National Union, see his
speech before Parliament on January 2, 1971, (see Hani Khayr, ed.,
Majmu'at al-Bayanat Al-Wazariya al-Urduniya) [A Collection of Cabinet Pronouncements of Jordan] ('Amman, n.d.), p. 196.

found it exceedingly difficult to reconcile the conflicting views of men who had agreed to cooperate
within the framework of the party. After his death,
there seems to be no great enthusiasm to revive the
plan and most leaders, discouraged by Arab frus-
tration with the party system, prefer to deal directly with the King rather than with political parties. Asked why he did not encourage the drive
toward the establishment of political parties, King
Husayn replied that the time has not yet come to
allow political parties to be recognized. Ever since
he came to the throne, he said, political parties had
been engaged in an intense struggle for power and
tended to confuse and divide public opinion rather
than to mobilize it to influence and guide the nation to do constructive work.

In a society which lacks cohesion and social solidarity a multiple party system seems to reflect the
fragmentation of society rather than to unify its divided forces into principal channels and therefore
tends to disrupt rather than encourage constructive work. Arab leaders who are in favor of democracy have, therefore, maintained that social
and economic development should first be
achieved before democracy is expected to work.
However, a beginning to organize institutionalized
political groupings might, indeed, be deemed necessary in order to educate the public and prepare it
for a truly democratic system.

Because Jordanian society lacks homogeneity,
composed of tribal, semi-tribal, native Jordanian
and Palestinian people, not to mention other non-
Arab groups, King Husayn has often sought to
keep his hold over the country by maintaining a
balance among the various sections of the country.
He has cultivated in particular friendly relations

with the tribes, who supported him against the rising influence of radical political parties, and solic-
ited native Jordanian support when he came into
conflict with Palestinians. Non-Arab groups, especially the Circassians, an active group in urban
centers, have been loyal to him and have always
supported his policies. More recently, he has often
made statements on behalf of the poor and working classes against the vested interests, as younger
leaders seem to have voiced criticism of wealthy
families and corrupt practices. Apart from occasionally resorting to playing off one group against
the other, he realizes the need to create out of the
fragmented Jordanian society a relatively homogeneous political community to which he could appeal in the name of Arab nationalism and the
Islamic heritage to play its role in the larger community of the Arab world and to have its deserved
position in the community of nations. Compared
with his neighboring countries, King Husayn can
indeed claim more than a modest success not only
in steering his country well in troubled waters, but
also in looking to the future with confidence concerning her stability, steady progress and prosperity.[51]

---

[51]Perhaps no better tribute has been paid to King Husayn than that
which Bahjat al-Talhuni, a former Prime Minister of Jordan, once
told me: "If some Arab countries owe their prosperity to the gift of
oil, Jordan is fortunate to have Husayn instead of oil."

Part Two

MILITARY LEADERSHIP

In the weakness of one kind of authority, and in the fluctuation of all, the officers of an army will remain for some time mutinous and full of faction, until some popular general, who understands the art of conciliating the soldiery, and who possesses the true spirit of command, shall draw the eyes of all men upon himself. Armies will obey him on his personal account. There is no other way of securing military obedience in this state of things. But the moment in which that event shall happen, the person who really commands the army is your master; the master (that is little) of your king, the master of your assembly, the master of your whole republic.

Edmund Burke, *Reflections on the Revolution in France* (1789)

CHAPTER IV

ANWAR AL-SADAT OF EGYPT

'Tis the height of merit in a man that
his faults can be numbered.
al-Mutannabi (d. 965 A.D.)

"Egypt," remarked Herodotus after a brief visit
to the country, "is the gift of the Nile"; without fresh water, the Nile Valley would have been
part of the Great Sahara that extends eastward
from the Atlantic Ocean. Because of the social
forces set in motion by "the gift of the Nile," Egypt
developed one of the most ancient systems of government, devised to maintain order and cope with
such complex problems as flood control, irrigation
and land tenure. The character of this system, described by most writers as authoritarian and highly
centralized, still predominates in contemporary
Egyptian society.

But Egypt's polity, though essentially the product
of internal forces, may be said to have also been
influenced by the central location of the country at
the cross-roads of three continents and two
oceans, which exposed her to foreign conquerors
and empire-builders who manipulated the political
processes to serve their own interests which were

not always compatible with the country's national interests. However, due either to internal weakness or to unfavorable international circumstances, the country had to submit to foreign domination—indeed, such domination often lasted for a very long time—but the people never tolerated foreign control nor did they ever give up the struggle to regain freedom regardless of how long that struggle might take.

Not infrequently Egypt's rulers, in their endeavors to repulse foreign invasions, found, in hot pursuit of the enemy, themselves becoming empire-builders by extending their control beyond Egypt's frontiers. In their pursuit of domination of foreign lands, however, they were often compelled to subordinate essential domestic needs to the requirements of hegemony and rivalry with other rulers. Once they were committed to foreign ventures, it was not easy to extricate themselves from those commitments, even when they appeared to have adversely affected the country's national interests.

Viewed in retrospect, Egyptian rulers fall into two main categories. First, those whose main concern was to attend to internal affairs and who paid little or no attention to foreign ventures, even if the circumstances for playing the game of empire-building were favorable. This category, which may be called the Egyptian school, maintained that Egypt's national interests could best be served by pursuing a policy of peace and cooperation with neighbors which encouraged the people to promote trade and improve internal conditions. Second, the category of rulers who were drawn into foreign conquests either in self defense or in pursuit of hegemony may be called the imperial or, in Arab parlance, the Pan-Arab school. In the modern age, beginning from Napoleon's conquest of Egypt in 1798—which brought the country into the sphere of international rivalry and competition—almost all of Egypt's rulers have been drawn willingly or unwillingly into foreign ventures, even though some may have preferred to follow a policy of peace and cooperation with foreign nations. Very few, however, went so far as to achieve their ambition by war and violent methods, as did Muhammad 'Ali, founder of the late ruling dynasty, and Nasir, the principal author of the Egyptian Revolution of 1952. Some, unable to avoid foreign entanglements, tried to use diplomacy and other peaceful methods in order to avoid the adverse effects of war and violence on the country's security and national interests.

To which of the two schools does Sadat belong?

In his autobiography, Sadat tries to draw a picture of himself as entirely different from Nasir, not only in style and temperament, but perhaps also in objectives.[1] In theory, Sadat and Nasir believed in the same principles which prompted them to participate in the Egyptian Revolution—the principles of national freedom, democracy, social justice and others—but Nasir, after he became entrenched in power, turned into an empire-builder and subordinated the principles of the Revolution to personal ambition. After he became President, Sadat began to reverse Nasir's policies on the grounds that Nasir had departed from the principles of the Egyptian Revolution. He also differed from Nasir

---

[1]See Anwar el-Sadat, *In Search of Identity: An Autobiography* (New York: Harper & Row, 1978). Hereafter cited as Sadat's *Autobiography*. In a slightly different version, though sometimes with further details, Sadat's story is set forth in a series of *Papers* published in the weekly *October* in Arabic, beginning from October 31, 1976 (Hereafter cited as Sadat's *Papers*).

in style and political methods, presumably because
the two had different upbringings and tempera-
ments. Since this essay is essentially a study of Sadat's leadership, only an indirect comparison with
Nasir's objectives and political methods will be attempted, as an essay on Nasir has already been
provided in another work.[2]

II

Sadat's fundamental ideas, goals and methods
may be traced back partly to a number of significant events and circumstances connected with the
social milieu in which he was raised and partly to
the events and activities he had experienced under
the Nasir regime.

The first important fact is that Anwar al-Sadat
was born to a relatively poor family—neither very
poor nor prosperous, although it owned a house
and a small farm—and that he was deeply affected
by the deplorable conditions in which the people
of his neighborhood lived. He was born in Mit Abu
al-Kum, a small village some twenty miles to the
southwest of Tanta, one of the central cities of the
Nile Delta, in the province of al-Manufiya, on December 25, 1918. The house in which he was born,
made of rough stone and sun-dried bricks—typical
in the area—consisted mainly of one large room
(the *qa'a*), which provided a meeting place for the
family where they gathered to chat, eat and sleep,
and some smaller rooms for the cattle and storage.
In an interview with Sadat, he said that he was
born in the *qa'a* and recalled that in the winter he

---

[2]See my *Arab Contemporaries* (Baltimore: The Johns Hopkins University Press, 1973), chapter 4.

used to sleep with other children on a straw mat, close to an oven, used daily for baking bread, to keep warm. The *qa'a*, though relatively spacious, was a closed room having only a small door and no windows. Only one small opening above the oven allowed the smoke to escape. This primitive system of heating and ventilation in the countryside must have survived from Pharaonic times.

Young Anwar seems to have been happy in that environment. He used to leave at dawn to work on the farm and help both his family and neighbors, as cooperation among farmers was customary and made all feel as if they belonged to one big family. This was the way of life in all other villages—the perennial way of life in the countryside—and the people of the Delta, especially in the Manufiya province, have been renown for their good nature, lightheartedness and industry.[3] Manufiya is a small and densely populated province; its farmers have won the reputation of being cooperative and hard-working and seem to have a greater attachment to their land than other farmers. For this reason, Sadat still visits his birth-place every year, despite official preoccupations, and often spends his holidays there.[4]

Second only to his environment was the influence of his grandmother—his father's mother. His father, a small functionary, married a Sudanese woman while with the Anglo-Egyptian Army in the

---

[3]In contrast with the people of the Delta, the people of Upper Egypt (al-Sa'id), though also hard working like other peasants, are austere and suspicious, especially to outsiders. For a description of life in the countryside, see al-Sharbini, *Hazz al-Quhuf Fi Sharh Qasid Abi Shaduf* (Cairo, 1963).

[4]See Sadat's *Autobiography*, pp. 2-3; Sabri Abu al-Majd, *Ma' al-Sadat: al-Masira al-Tawila 'Ala Tariq al-Nidal* [With Sadat: The Long Procession on the Path of Struggle] (Cairo, 1976), pp. 36-37.

Sudan. When Anwar was born, his mother was at Mit Abu al-Kum, and both he and his mother stayed with the grandmother. His mother and grandmother took very good care of him and gave him attention and encouragement. "Who had the greater influence on your life," I asked Sadat. "My grandmother," he replied. She was a remarkable woman—wise, experienced, and possessing a strong personality. In the absence of the father, she looked after the family and supervised work on the family's farm.[5]

Before he went to bed, the grandmother used to recite the *mawawil* (folksongs) which seem to have inspired him with courage, enthusiasm and a high sense of patriotism. One of the *mawawil*, which she recited with pride, touched upon the exploits of an uncle—it was indeed not only the epic of a courageous horseman who fought gallantly in a lost battle, but also a legend of the nationalist war fought by the Egyptian Army against the British occupation of the country in 1882. After defeat at Tal al-Kabir, the hero of Mit Abu al-Kum refused to surrender to the British and made his way back to his native village. Upon arrival, he was surrounded by fellow villagers who were anxious to be given an account of the nationalist war by one of its heroes. Before reaching his house, the horse fell dead from exhaustion and the horseman, though still alive, was stained with blood. He was taken to his aunt's house and, half suffocating, told the tragic story of the Egyptian Army led by Arabi Pasha—it was, he said, a "betrayal." Arabi's name had become a household word for his courage and defiance of the British, and the tragedy of his

[5]The writer's interview with President Sadat (Cairo, December 17, 1977).

Army's demise was commemorated in the *mawa-wil* which young Anwar had learned from his grandmother. From early childhood, these folk-songs inspired him, as they inspired other young men of his generation, with patriotism and hatred of the foreign domination of the country.[6]

Not only was the care of the family the responsi-bility of the grandmother, but also the schooling of the children. The course of study at the Azhar, a thorough grounding in the traditional disciplines of literature, theology and law, was given to all who aspired to have an education. But Anwar's father, like his grandfather, was given a secular education which enabled him to get a job in the Egyptian Army; the grandmother decided that Anwar should pursue the same course of study as his father. At first she made him join the *kuttab*, the Quranic school in the village, where he learned the Qur'an by heart; then she made him join a Coptic school at Tukh Dalka, near an ancient monastery, not very far from Mit Abu al-Kum. Since no means of transportation existed, Anwar had to commute on foot. The school, attended by Christian and Muslim boys, gave Sadat not only an education in modern disciplines, but also taught the spirit of toleration and cooperation with members of the Coptic com-munity.

In 1924 his father suddenly returned home fol-lowing the expulsion of the Egyptian Army from the Sudan in retaliation for the assassination of Sir Lee Stack, Sirdar (Commander) of the Egyptian

---

[6]For the story of Sadat's grandmother and the *mawawil*, see Sadat, *Ya Waladi: Hadha 'Amuk Jamal* [My Son: This is Your Uncle Jamal] (Cairo, 1957), pp. 93ff. In his *Autobiography*, Sadat gives an account of other legendary figures such as al-Sharqawi and Zahran who dis-tinguished themselves in anti-British activities and other heroic acts (Sadat's *Autobiography*, pp. 5-6).

Army, by an Egyptian patriot. Anwar joined his father in Cairo, where he resumed his work as a government functionary, and the youth pursued his studies first in a private school and then in a government public school.

In Cairo, young Sadat was exposed to a new social environment which had a profound impact on his future career. At home, he heard his father complaining about the loss of his job in the Sudan as a result of British action against the rising tide of Egyptian nationalism. In school he found his fellow students excited by the events in Cairo and participated himself in street demonstrations. He also learned about events in the Sudan and student political activities, expressed mainly in street demonstrations. Young Sadat, half-Egyptian and half-Sudanese, felt highly indignant about the occupation of the Nile Valley—his parents' homeland—by the British.

No less significant was the inspiration Sadat derived from the accounts of the activities of prominent nationalist leaders, whether Egyptian, like Mustafa Kamil and Sa'd Zaghlul, or foreign, like Mustafa Kamal (later Atatürk) of Turkey and others.[7] To his father's generation Kamal was the hero who saved Turkey—the country for which Egyptians had the greatest admiration before World War I—from foreign domination. As a token of admiration for Turkish leaders, the father named his sons—Anwar, 'Atif and Tal'at—after them. Following World War I, when Kamal fought for his country's independence, the Egyptians expressed great enthusiasm for him and Ahmad Shawqi, the poet laureate, sang his praise in verse, calling him the

---

[7]In his *Autobiography*, pp. 12-13, Sadat cites other names whom he admired. See also Sadat's *Papers, op. cit.*, p. 11.

Khalid of the Turks, after the name of Arab hero Khalid Ibn al-Walid, who commanded the Arab conquests of Syria and Iraq in the seventh century A.D. Sadat and other officers, who took part in the July Revolution of 1952, derived inspiration from the Kamalist movement, though the Egyptian Revolution followed a different course under Nasir's leadership.[8]

Most of Sadat's heroes—Napoleon, Atatürk and others—had a military background. It was therefore natural that Sadat, after he completed high school, should seek a career in military service. A post in the Army was highly prized in the public eye; to young Sadat it was considered an opportunity to achieve national goals. But it was almost impossible for a young man like Sadat to enter the Military Academy as admission was restricted to only a few known for their loyalty and devotion to the regime.[9] Nonetheless, the course of events helped him to enroll in the Military Academy. In 1936, following the signing of a treaty of alliance with England, Egypt was allowed to enlarge her Army and participate not only in the defense of her territory but also in the joint control of the Sudan under the Agreement of 1898.[10] For this reason the War College was reorganized as a new Military

---

[8]In an interview with the writer, Sadat stated that he and other Free Officers were inspired by Kamal, but his successors failed to live up to the ideals of their leader. See also Sadat's *Ya Waladi*, p. 53; and Sabri Abu al-Majd, *op. cit.*, pp. 45-48.

[9]For details about admission to the Military Academy, see Abu al-Majd, *op. cit.*, pp. 59-64.

[10]England came to a quick understanding with Egypt mainly because of the rivalry with Italy over control of the Mediterranean Sea. By enlisting participation of Egypt in the defense of the Nile Valley, she sought to grant satisfaction to Egyptian nationalist aspirations on the one hand and to oppose Italian designs in the Eastern Mediterranean on the other.

Academy and its doors were thrown open to a larger number of young men and not just to a select few. Nevertheless, it was not easy to get admitted unless the applicant was sponsored by a person of influence. Since his father, a functionary in the Army, had known a person of influence in it, Sadat was finally admitted. Some of his future friends, on the other hand, including Nasir, were at first turned down.

Sadat was in his true element in the Academy. He took his work very seriously and proved to be a model cadet both in class and in military exercises. He also had a strong thirst for learning and applied himself to his homework thoroughly and kept up with national and international affairs. Since there was then a need for more officers for the newly reorganized Egyptian Army, he was graduated in February 1938, after only a two-year period of training, though a three-year course was normally required.

Graduating as a second lieutenant, Sadat first was officially posted to an infantry regiment (though in practice he was commissioned as a signal corps officer) near Alexandria; very soon he was transferred in July to Mankabad, where he met and fell under the influence of Nasir. But before he joined the Free Officers Movement under Nasir's leadership, he seems to have headed an independent revolutionary group which carried out its own clandestine activities against the regime. Only after he was arrested and thrown into prison in 1942 did he suspend the independent activities of his group and turn over its leadership to Nasir. He rejoined the Nasirite organization only after his release from prison in 1944.[11]

---

[11]Some of my informants seem to be dubious about Sadat's claim

III

Sadat's interest in politics was aroused long before he entered the Military Academy, but he was drawn into revolutionary activities only after he had left the Academy. He passed through radical changes in his life and his activities changed from one type to another—he began as a terrorist, then he became a revolutionary leader, and finally rose to the highest position in the state as President. His career falls into three periods: in each he played an entirely different role from the other, though in all he sought to achieve essentially the same cherished goals and national objectives. These periods are as follows:

First, the period in which he became engaged in underground activities and sought by terrorist methods to undermine the Old Regime and prepare the way for a revolutionary change. Second, the period in which he participated in the establishment of a revolutionary regime in 1952 and served under Nasir's leadership till 1970. Third, the current one in which he succeeded Nasir as President and promised to inaugurate a new era of peace and liberal reforms. During the third period, Sadat's personal qualities and qualifications have been put to the test; it is, indeed, in this period that his performance as a leader and his methods can be taken as the fulfillment of his goals and ultimate objectives. In retrospect, it appears that almost all his life has been in preparation for this highest position where at last he can make final decisions in

that he had an independent revolutionary group of his own before joining the Nasir group, though he certainly had influenced a group of young nationalists during and after the 'Uthman Amin affair (see p. 136-37 below).

accordance with his goals, tempered only by personal experience.

In the first two periods, Sadat revealed two distinct sets of qualities. In the first he reflected the character of a radical activist who was determined to undermine and ultimately destroy the Old Regime; in the second, following the July Revolution of 1952, he completely changed from an activist into an almost subservient instrument in the hands of Nasir, a posture which superseded the image of the fearless officer who spent years in prison in pursuit of nationalist goals.

Before the July Revolution, Sadat joined a few officers engaged in political activities against Britain, presumably on the grounds of her interference in domestic affairs after independence. Under the influence of 'Aziz 'Ali al-Misri, well-known for his pro-German sympathies before World War I, Sadat became engaged in pro-Axis activities for which he was arrested and thrown into prison for most of the war years.[12] No sooner had he escaped from prison (1944) than he resumed his clandestine activities and joined the Free Officers Movement under Nasir's leadership. In 1946, Sadat was implicated in the assassination of 'Uthman Amin 'Uthman, a former Minister of Finance, because he made statements considered highly unpatriotic and called for close Anglo-Egyptian cooperation.[13] Sadat's trial, which lasted almost three years, fo-

---

[12]For Sadat's own story of this period, see *Revolt on the Nile* (London, 1957), pp. 36-38; 45-55; and *Autobiography*, pp. 24-40. See also my " 'Aziz 'Ali al-Misri and the Arab Nationalist Movement," *St. Antony's Papers*, ed. Hourani (London, 1968), Vol. IV, pp. 140-63.

[13]'Uthman, in his call for an Anglo-Egyptian alliance, was reported to have described Egypt's relations with England as inseparable as Catholic marriage. Such a statement, tantamount to treason in the eyes of Egyptian nationalists, was the reason for the assassination

cussed public attention on his nationalist activities long before he participated in the July Revolution.[14] Young and imbued with a sense of patriotism, he won the reputation of the fearless and defiant leader reminiscent of the heroes commemorated in the *mawawil* that he had heard from his grandmother.

After the July Revolution of 1952, in the preparation of which he seems to have taken an active part, Sadat's role completely changed from that of an agitator and clandestine terrorist to a defender and staunch supporter of the new regime presided over by Nasir, even when he disagreed with some of Nasir's actions. His submission to Nasir earned him the nickname of "Colonel Yes, Yes," because whenever his opinion was sounded by Nasir, he invariably agreed with him, simply saying "yes, yes, *rayyis* (chief)." In so doing, he gave the false impression that he lacked the ability of independent judgment and acted as the soldier who followed blindly military orders even when they appeared to him to be wrong. For this reason, few predicted that he would survive very long after he succeeded Nasir as President.

However, Sadat's support for Nasir was not simply blind submission and this calls for an explanation. There are two schools of thought concerning Sadat's relationship with Nasir. One holds that

on the grounds that the man who made such a statement had no right to live in Egypt.

[14] For an account of the trial and imprisonment of Sadat, see his *Autobiography*, pp. 59ff; and Sabri Abu al-Majd, *op. cit.*, p. 181ff. Sadat did not directly participate in the plot of assassination of 'Uthman, but he was in contact with the young man who carried it out (the writer's interview with 'Abd al-'Aziz Khamis, one of the 26 young men who had been imprisoned for the crime [Cairo, December 11, 1977]).

Nasir, especially after his successful nationalization
of the Suez Canal, had dominated all his followers
and nobody could oppose him—those who did
were relieved from office and fell from grace. Witnessing the fate of such leaders as General Najib,
the Salim brothers, Khalid Muhyi al-Din and others, Sadat prudently kept quiet in order to save his
own skin. This dissimulation, as one informant
friendly to Sadat told me, was not a sign of weakness but a manifestation of prudence, as it protected Sadat from Nasir's whims and saved Egypt
from falling in the hands of Nasir's self-seeking entourage. The other school argues that Sadat shared
Nasir's views on almost all national issues because
he deeply felt that after the downfall of the Monarchy, Nasir was the only leader that could hold
the country together and achieve the goals in
which he believed. True, Nasir may have become
too authoritarian and dealt harshly with opponents
with whom probably Sadat would have dealt dif-
ferently, but these were after all differences in
style and political methods and not in principles.
According to this school, Sadat's support for Nasir
was not sheer dissimulation but a personal conviction that Nasir was achieving goals in which he believed. It follows that he and other supporters of
the Nasir regime were just as responsible as Nasir
for the actions, as well as the blunders, committed
under the regime. Accordingly, Sadat's differences
with Nasir, as reported in his *Autobiography*, are
either afterthoughts to justify the changes of policy
which he had to make under his regime or matters
of detail writ large.

Needless to say, there are some elements of truth
in each school. Sadat asserts that he was, and still
is, an admirer of Nasir. He has said time and again

that Nasir, despite certain personal failings, was a great patriot whose integrity, dedication and national commitments were beyond reproach. Moreover, Sadat felt that Nasir and his fellow officers worked so assiduously to carry out the July Revolution of 1952 that he felt it was his duty to support him regardless of personal considerations. He also felt that the new regime was indeed in need of a strong man who could inspire confidence and possess the requisite leadership qualities—personal integrity, moral courage, popular appeal and others—that would enable him to achieve national goals and hold the country together. He maintained that in countries undergoing rapid social changes there was need for a strong leader who could take full responsibility and achieve national goals. He saw in Nasir the man who possessed the requisite leadership qualities and who could achieve the objectives of the July Revolution. For this reason, when Nasir replaced General Najib as Head of State, Sadat urged his fellow officers to give him full responsibility. He also supported him against rival leaders and groups who challenged his authority.[15] Thus nobody would have expected Sadat to criticize Nasir openly, though he might have disagreed with some of his actions, as public criticism was taken to undermine the regime. Whether Sadat often told Nasir his personal views, as he claimed in his *Autobiography*, is an open question.[16] I have it on the authority of some informants that, not infrequently, Sadat would retire to his native town whenever the relations between

---

[15]See Sadat, *Qissat al-Thawra Kamilatan* [The Full Story of the Egyptian Revolution] (Cairo, 1955), pp. 204-211; and 'Abd al-Latif al-Baghdadi, *Mudhakkirat* [Memoirs] (Cairo, 1977), Vol. I, p. 240.

[16]Cf. Sadat's *Autobiography*, pp. 143, 169-170, 189-190.

master and disciple were strained, but the disciple always returned whenever the master inquired about his health and welfare.

Sadat's behavior patterns may have also helped to avoid conflicts with Nasir. Impatient by nature with bureaucratic routine, he claimed that he was a politician and not an executive—he served only once as Minister without portfolio in 1954. Whether as writer or Speaker of the National Assembly, he tried by his ability to charm people to sway public opinion in favor of the regime rather than against it. He kept in constant touch with the press and published a number of books and pamphlets in which he expounded the goals of the July Revolution and consequently won Nasir's goodwill rather than his wrath.[17]

Although a struggle for power among top leaders began soon after Nasir assumed full responsibility, it became more vocal after nationalization of the Suez Canal, especially between Nasir and Marshal 'Abd al-Hakim 'Amir, Minister of War and Commander of the National Forces, as the former began to concentrate power in his hands and dominate the country. Nasir, by nature jealous of his power and suspicious of other leaders, began to rely on younger officers, to whom he entrusted important posts to counter the power of top leaders. Since Sadat revealed no desire to compete with peers for higher stakes, he kept out of the power struggle. For this reason, Nasir had greater appreciation of Sadat's personality and character and eventually chose him as his successor.

The question of succession weighed heavily on Nasir's conscience, especially after he became ill

[17]See Musa Sabri, *Watha'iq (Documents) of May 15* (Cairo, 1977), pp. 272-273.

and his health began to deteriorate. There were three officers whom he seriously considered as suitable candidates—Husayn al-Shafi'i, Zakariya Muhyi al-Din and Anwar al-Sadat. As to the first, though he enjoyed his confidence and served as Vice-President earlier, Nasir doubted his ability to bear the burden of office. The second, whose experience was acknowledged by all, prompted Nasir to nominate him as a successor when he resigned after the Six-Day War on June 9, 1967, hoping that Muhyi al-Din's liberal and pro-Western leanings might save Egypt by coming to an understanding with the West.[18] The third, appointed Vice-President by Nasir on December 20, 1969, only shortly before the latter's death, was not highly rated by his peers as he had neither held a high executive post nor was considered to possess the strength of character to carry the country behind him.

Nasir, ill and disenchanted with his entourage, seems to have come at last to the conclusion that Sadat and Shafi'i were the only two top leaders whom he could trust and who would follow the policies he had laid down for the country. Since he considered Sadat to possess greater ability than Shafi'i, he appointed him First Vice-President and Shafi'i Second Vice-President. Upon his nomination as Vice-President, Sadat prudently deferred to other senior officers, and told Nasir that he was prepared to serve as Presidential Adviser, but Nasir, on the day of his departure to an Arab Sum-

---

[18]Nasir entrusted Muhyi al-Din with the Premiership after he had withdrawn his resignation under public pressure to remain in office. But Muhyi al-Din, disagreeing with Nasir on the measures to be taken to improve the country's conditions after the Six-Day War, very soon resigned. Nasir never again called on him for a high position, though Muhyi al-Din was considered in certain political circles as a possible successor to Nasir.

mit Conference in Morocco, called Sadat to be sworn in as Vice President and act as deputy in his absence. Sadat accepted the appointment as a matter of duty and proved, after he succeeded Nasir, equal beyond expectation to the task he was called to fulfill.

IV

Sadat's tenure of the Vice-Presidency lasted not quite a year (December 1969 to September 1970); it was too short for anyone to consolidate his position before rising to the Presidency. Nasir had so towered over all other leaders that anyone who stepped into his position would appear too small in the public eye. Nor was Nasir's entourage—'Ali Sabri, Sha'rawi Jum'a, Sami Sharaf and others—in favor of Sadat's accession to the Presidency, since they considered themselves the men closest to Nasir and, therefore, the custodians of the regime bequeathed by him over which only one of their number, rather than an outsider, should preside. Since Sadat was not a member of the inner circle and it was suspected that he might depart from Nasir's policies and come to an understanding with the West, he seemed to the Nasirites unsuitable to deal with the Soviet Union, an ally of Egypt. A struggle for power was therefore inevitable, and the Nasirites, encouraged by the Soviet authorities, were waiting for an opportunity to overthrow him, even if he were prepared to accommodate to them.

Nasir's war of attrition with Israel led to no conclusive results. Egypt suffered a state of no war and no peace and her economic conditions were deteriorating. The Treasury was virtually empty and the country had to rely on her own resources, as no foreign aid was extended. "All that we received from the outside world," Sadat remarked, "was abuse."[19] For these, if for no other reasons, both foreign and native observers did not think Sadat could survive very long.

Once in the saddle, however, Sadat proved to possess certain qualities of survival—prudence, resourcefulness and readiness to act quickly—which enabled him to respond with greater moral courage to the challenge of the office than his opponents had anticipated. True, before he became President his executive experience was relatively limited, but he stood close to the centers of power and, observing with a keen eye how the men around Nasir conducted themselves, he was able to appreciate the points of strength and weakness of his opponents and knew how to expose them. So long as Nasir was alive, he kept out of the struggle for power among men he did not respect. Whether he did so on the grounds of loyalty to Nasir or lack of interest is an open question. But after he achieved power, he did not hesitate to act resolutely against his opponents whenever he was challenged by them.

The struggle for power ensued immediately after Nasir's death. Shafi'i, Second Vice-President, was no real threat; he remained in office until he retired four years later. Zakariya Muhyi al-Din, nominated by Nasir as his successor in 1967, seems to have expected the Presidency to be offered to him merely on the grounds of personal ability and long experience, but he would not fight for it. The group that presented the real threat consisted of

---

[19]Sadat's *Autobiography*, p. 214.

'Ali Sabri, former Premier and President of the
Arab Socialist Union; Sami Sharaf, head of the
Presidential Office; Sha'rawi Jum'a, Minister of Interior; General Mahmud Fawzi, Minister of War;
General al-Laythi Nasif, Commander of the Presidential Guard; and Muhammad Hasanayn Haykal,
former Editor of *al-Ahram* (the leading newspaper
in the country) and Minister of Information. Preferring to return to *al-Ahram* and at that time on
good terms with Sadat, Haykal refused to align
himself with Sadat's opponents and warned of the
dangers of plotting against the new regime.[20] But
the others, especially the triumvirate—'Ali Sabri,
Sami Sharaf, and Sha'rawi Jum'a—were determined to take a firm stand against the incumbent.

As Vice-President, Sadat stepped into Nasir's position in an acting capacity; he had yet to be confirmed by a plebiscite. At the outset, he contended
that he should continue to govern as Vice-President until the "consequences of Israeli aggression"
were removed, in accordance with Nasir's instructions on June 10, 1967.[21] But since Sadat felt that
his opponents might justify their challenge to his
authority on the grounds that he was President
only in an acting capacity, he decided to strengthen
his position by an appeal to the public. A plebiscite,
held on October 15, 1970, confirmed him as President. It was the first setback for the opposition, often called the central power bloc, and the plan of
plotting was changed. Whether individually or collectively, the bloc began to raise obstacles intended
to weaken Sadat's position in the public eye, preparing for a plot to overthrow him that would be

[20]See M.H. Heikal, *The Road to Ramadan* (New York, 1975), pp. 108-
110.
[21]Sadat's *Autobiography*, p. 204.

carried out on the grounds that he had departed from Nasir's policy and was unable to act in accordance with the national interest.

Because of the state of no war and no peace, Sadat had to act on certain pressing problems relating to the Arab-Israeli conflict. For instance, he had to decide on whether to renew the ceasefire (beginning on August 8, 1970) which was to expire very soon and the war of attrition would be resumed. Some of Sadat's advisors, either sympathetic to or in league with the power bloc, urged resumption of the war as a matter of national pride. Since he realized that the country was in no position to resume the war, Sadat twice extended the ceasefire (September 1970 and February 1971), as there was a growing public opinion in favor of suspension of hostilities. This public attitude developed partly as a result of economic difficulties and partly from a feeling that even at the height of the Egypto-Soviet friendship under the Nasir regime, the Soviet Union had not given Egypt full support to force Israel to withdraw from the occupied territory.

Moreover, Sadat made a number of decisions which his opponents considered to effect a change in the Socialist regime established by Nasir. In December 1970, he issued a decree lifting all state custodianship of private property. As a result, private enterprise received an impetus which led to the growing enlargement of the private sector to the satisfaction of the business community and shopkeepers. His action was construed by the Soviet Union as evidence that he was encouraging free enterprise as a means to come to an understanding with the West. For this reason suspicion between Sadat and the Soviet leaders became

deeper and the Soviet protégés—Sadat's opponents—were encouraged to intensify their opposition to him.

Matters came to a head on the question of unity
with Syria and Libya. Unlike Nasir, Sadat was not
very enthusiastic about regional coordination—
much less about Arab unity—but he was anxious
to secure economic assistance from Libya, if she
were to join Egypt in an Arab Union. Since a unity
plan with Syria and Libya had already been laid
down by Nasir shortly before his death, Sadat
thought that the implementation of the plan might
improve Egypt's economic conditions. In April
1971, Sadat, accompanied by 'Ali Sabri, President
of the Arab Socialist Union, and Sha'rawi Jum'a,
Minister of Interior, went to Libya to negotiate the
plan of unity. In private talks, 'Ali Sabri and
Sha'rawi Jum'a seem to have discouraged Qadhdhafi from commitment to unity, but a federal
plan, which Qadhdhafi—an outspoken protagonist
of Arab unity—could not possibly turn down was
proposed by Sadat. It was accepted by both Qadhdhafi and Asad as the basis for a broad Arab
unity plan.[22]

Back in Cairo, Sadat called a meeting of the Supreme Executive Committee and submitted the
unity plan for approval. Unexpectedly, it was rejected by five members and approved by three
only—Sadat, Vice President Shafi'i and Premier
Fawzi. This was the first open confrontation between Sadat and his opponents; it was the first
trial of strength which the power bloc put forth

---

[22]Cf. Sadat's *Autobiography*, pp. 217-218. For text of the plan, see Muhammad Hafiz Ghanim, *Ittihad al-Jumburiyat al-Arabiya* (Union of
Arab Republics) (Cairo, publications of the Egyptian Society of International Law, 1972).

against Sadat. Realizing that if he failed in this trial he would be powerless, Sadat proposed to submit the plan to the Central Committee of the Arab Socialist Union, a higher authority than the Supreme Executive Committee. When the Central Committee met on May 1, the power bloc tried to force rejection of the plan but failed. The plan was ratified and Sadat won the first round against his opponents.

Earlier, when Sadat had proceeded to take a decision on the Rogers Plan, the power bloc won a majority at a meeting of the Supreme Executive Committee (January 1, 1971) which voted to resume the war of attrition on the grounds that Egypt was capable, with Soviet arms, of winning the war. Sadat, realizing that the action of his opponents might put him in an embarrassing situation, suggested that he was prepared to resume the war provided Egypt would receive the SAM batteries promised by the Soviet Union for defense of the country against Israeli raids. But he also proposed that he had to allow an extension of the ceasefire for one month in accordance with the Rogers Plan.

On February 4, 1971, Sadat announced his readiness to open the Suez Canal, if Israel were to withdraw her forces in Sinai to the Passes and to allow an extension of the ceasefire for six months rather than three. More significant, indeed, was his declaration that he was prepared to sign a peace agreement with Israel and restore diplomatic relations with the United States. Public opinion, contrary to the contention of Sadat's opponents, welcomed his peace initiative—it was the first bold declaration ever made by an Arab leader to sign a peace agreement with Israel.

Failure of the central power bloc to oppose Sadat through official channels, prompted the leading members of the bloc—'Ali Sabri, Sami Sharaf and Sha'rawi Jum'a—to initiate plots to conspire against him with the assistance of Soviet agents in Cairo. Sadat issued orders to watch their activities carefully and began slowly but confidently to make preparations to dismiss them from official positions. Though aware of the Army's support for his policy, he thought it was his duty as Commander-in-Chief to consult the Army on his move to get rid of his opponents. The Presidential Guard, set up by Nasir to protect him against a sudden assault, was under the command of General al-Laythi Nasif whose loyalty to the power bloc was taken for granted simply because he was a former protégé of Nasir. Sadat had no difficulty winning Laythi's allegiance to him. He won even greater success when he induced General Sadiq, Commander of the National Forces, to side with him against his Chief, General Fawzi, Minister of War, who was in sympathy with Sadat's opponents. Both generals Sadiq and Laythi, disenchanted with the condescending Soviet attitude toward Egyptian officers and Soviet failure to provide Egypt with adequate defensive weapons, were prompted to turn against the central power bloc, because their victory over Sadat would result in an increase of Soviet influence in Egypt. Without even the need to put the Army on the alert, Sadat was now ready to topple his opponents by a stroke of the pen as the Army's loyalty was undivided.[23]

---

[23]In his *Autobiography*, Sadat stresses the support of public opinion but made no reference to his effort to ensure the support of the Army in the dismissal of his opponents.

Before he took any formal action, Sadat called the Soviet Ambassador to inform him of his decision to strip first 'Ali Sabri, considered the leading Soviet protégé, from all official powers save his membership in the Arab Socialist Union, as this was an elected body and dismissal from it would be dependent on a vote of its members. "I am prepared to tolerate differences of opinion," Sadat pointed out as his reason for action to the Soviet Ambassador, "but I cannot tolerate a struggle for power."[24] He went on to explain that his action should not be construed as unfriendly toward the Soviet Union, even if 'Ali Sabri were considered a friend of the Soviet Union—at least he was so depicted in the press—nor to affect the friendly relationship between the two countries. On May 1, on the occasion of Labor Day, Sadat made a speech in the People's Assembly in which he denounced 'Ali Sabri and his group, who claimed to have inherited legitimate power from Nasir, even though Nasir bequeathed no such power to them, as self-seeking. On May 2, the day following his speech in the People's Assembly, Sadat issued a decree, which was published in the press, dismissing 'Ali Sabri from all posts, except his membership in the Socialist Union, because it was an elective position. A fortnight later Sadat proclaimed that Sabri's followers, Sha'rawi Jum'a, Sami Sharaf and others, were dismissed and put under arrest pending trial on the grounds that they were planning a plot to overthrow the regime because he had dismissed 'Ali Sabri.[25] Meanwhile, Sadat issued a decree dissolving leadership of the Arab Socialist Union, in

[24]Sadat's *Papers* (December 19, 1976), p. 19.
[25]Tape-recordings of conversations between 'Ali Sabri and his followers were discovered and considered as evidence of conspiracy

which 'Ali Sabri was a member; when the new elections were held Sabri failed to be reelected. Sabri and his followers, sentenced by a special tribunal for life, were thrown into prison and the central power bloc ceased to exist. Relieved of domestic pressures, Sadat turned to foreign affairs.

V

From the time of Napoleon's descent upon the Nile Valley at the turn of the nineteenth century, which brought Egypt into the sphere of international rivalry, Egypt's rulers often became involved in foreign adventures which led to foreign interventions. The July Revolution of 1952, claiming to mark a departure in traditional policies, declared as its aim putting an end to foreign domination and achieving domestic reforms. In their endeavors to achieve national freedom, however, Egypt's new rulers became increasingly involved in foreign affairs which prompted them to subordinate consideration to domestic defense and security plans. True, Nasir's initial foreign involvements—Israel's invasion of Ghazza in February 1955, the Czech (Soviet) arms deal, and the tripartite attack on Egypt in 1956—were essentially defensive in character. But very soon he found himself tempted into empire-building. In the wake of the tripartite attack on Egypt, which was occasioned by the upsurge of Arab nationalism, he was offered in effect, and accepted, leadership of the Pan-Arab movement on the grounds that in an Arab Union, of which his country formed a part—indeed, a central part—all Arabs, with whom his country-

---

against the regime (See Sadat's *Papers, op. cit.,* [December 19, 1976], p. 20).

men shared the bonds of language, culture and history, would live in security and prosperity and occupy their rightful place in the community of nations. But after the United Arab Republic was established, his appetite for empire-building was whetted and he did not shrink from using violence to achieve his goal; indeed he went so far as to call on all the Arab people, over the heads of their rulers, to overthrow their regimes if they were to oppose the achievement of Arab unity, claiming that he was responding to the call of destiny—a call to play the role of a Pan-Arab leader determined by the historical process in which he was involved.[26] But the union that he erected lasted scarcely three years, partly because it was forged with inadequate preparation, but mainly because Syria was governed not as an equal but as a subordinate partner in the union.

Sadat belongs to a different school. He is not an empire-builder who aspires to preside over a Pan-Arab Union; he is essentially an Egyptian patriot who wishes to attend primarily to his country's national interests. However, he was caught by the legacy of his predecessor's deep involvement in foreign adventures from which he has not yet been able to extricate his country. In practice, Sadat followed Nasir's foreign policy in the early seventies for two important reasons. First, he continued to pursue the path of Arab unity as a means to secure Arab support for Egypt in foreign affairs. Second, Egypt was still in need of economic and political backing which only Arab countries advocating Arab cooperation would provide. For these and other reasons, he could not possibly have de-

---

[26]See my *Arab Contemporaries*, p. 57.

parted completely from Nasir's foreign commitments.

After he consolidated his position, Sadat began to reconsider his country's relations with its neighbors and with the Great Powers. Very soon he began to realize that Arab unity did not provide the political and economic assistance which his country needed to improve its conditions and obtain support in foreign affairs. Meanwhile, finding the Soviet leaders unwilling to take him into their confidence, he began to have second thoughts about Soviet ability to give Egypt political and military assistance. Before his death, Sadat maintained, Nasir himself realized that the Arab-Israeli conflict could not be resolved by dependence on Soviet support alone, and came to the conclusion that American participation was necessary, if Israel were to withdraw from the territory occupied in 1967.[27] Invoking Nasir's authority to justify a change in his policy may have been an afterthought, but it is also true that Soviet leaders, finding Sadat unwilling to accommodate to their pattern of cooperation, were not prepared to support him. It was rumored that Premier Kosygin, after he attended Nasir's funeral in September 1970, left Cairo with the impression that Sadat was not his country's man.

Even before Nasir's departure, there was already a growing opinion in Egypt in favor of an understanding with the United States and of disenchantment with the Soviet Union, stemming mainly from a feeling that the Soviet Union was not prepared to assist Egypt to regain its lost territory. According to Sadat, Nasir himself had often com-

---

[27]Sadat's *Papers* (December 12, 1976), p. 17; and Heikal, *op. cit.*, p. 87.

plained about Soviet inability or unwillingness to understand Egypt's attitude toward Israel and Soviet lack of enthusiasm about lending him support. Since Sadat did not expect greater Soviet support for him than for Nasir, he was prepared to trade American for Soviet friendship. Needless to say, Sadat was mentally prepared to bring Egypt's dependence on the Soviet Union to an end and sought by an understanding with the United States to improve his country's economy and enhance its position in world affairs.[28]

In view of Egypt's strained relations with the United States under the Nasir regime, Sadat began indirectly to approach the American Government. In May 1970, when diplomatic relations were still ruptured, Nasir himself addressed President Nixon and asked whether the United States was unwilling or unable to solve the Arab-Israeli conflict. This initiative resulted in the steps taken under the Rogers' Plan, which Sadat, after Nasir's death, pushed a step further when he proposed on February 4, 1971, to offer peace and open the Suez Canal, if Israel were to withdraw her forces from Sinai to the Passes.

Sadat's readiness to resist Soviet pressures and come to an understanding with the United States aroused Saudi interest and prompted King Faysal to offer Egypt economic assistance and repair her relations with the United States. The Saudi leaders, alarmed by increasing Soviet influence in the Red Sea and the Indian Ocean, saw in Sadat a possible ally to check Soviet penetration and persuade the United States to exert her influence over Israel to

---

[28]Sadat's *Papers* (December 5, 1976), p. 16. For a study of Egypt's relations with the Soviet Union, see Karen Dawisha, *Soviet Foreign Policy Towards Egypt* (London, 1979).

withdraw from occupied Arab territory in accordance with UN Resolutions 242 and 338, which the United States itself had accepted in principle. The initial rapprochement between the Saudi leaders and Sadat began in the fall of 1970, immediately after Nasir's death, bringing increasing economic and political support which not only bolstered the Sadat regime against mounting economic difficulties, but also prepared the way for him to deal directly with the United States. As an honest broker, King Faysal was able to persuade Sadat to give up his dealings with Qadhdhafi, with whom Faysal had been disenchanted, and offered to mend his relations with other Arab countries. Since Egypt had already been on good terms with Syria, Faysal offered his good offices to bring about reconciliation between Egypt and Jordan. Saudi support for Sadat, despite occasional differences, continued after Faysal's death (though considerably reduced after the Camp David agreement), as the Saudi leaders could not possibly allow Egypt to fall under Soviet influence.[29]

The Soviet Union was not unaware of the fact that Egypt was slipping from its hands under Sadat's leadership, but it could do nothing to stop it despite several attempts to repair the situation. In his *Autobiography*, Sadat puts the blame on Soviet leaders. They always promised, he said, to provide Egypt with much needed defensive weapons, but they failed to live up to their promises, and when they did deliver some weapons, the delivery was

---

[29]The writer's interviews with the late Muhammad Hafiz Ghanim, former Deputy Premier and President of the Egyptian Society of International Law; and Mustafa Mar'i, former Minister and member of the Egyptian Academy (Cairo, December 14, 1977). See also Heikal, *op. cit.*, pp. 119-120.

very slow. Nor were the promises given without reservations; the Soviet leaders demanded a veto on the use of weapons, ostensibly on technical grounds, but in reality to restrain Egypt from going to war with Israel. Since a veto would compromise Egypt's freedom of action, especially in the case of a sudden attack, Sadat felt compelled to reject it.[30] It seems that the Soviet leaders gave the impression they were more interested in extending their influence to the eastern Mediterranean and the Red Sea, presumably to counter-balance American influence, than in the defense of Egypt or the recovery of occupied Arab territory from Israel.[31]

Sadat deeply felt a let down by his Soviet ally when his drive to recover occupied Arab lands was frustrated while Israel was receiving full American support politically and militarily. He was hurt in particular by Soviet failure to support him in 1971, a year which he called "decisive," by withholding delivery of weapons and by the joint Soviet-American communiqué (May 1972) in which relaxation of the Middle East crisis and reduction of the supply of weapons were stressed. He held that the Soviet leaders consciously tried to bring him to his knees in order to accept their conditions.

Sadat speaks of the Soviet leaders as being by nature very suspicious, though lack of confidence on both sides seems to have been the underlying factor. Even before he became President, Sadat

---

[30]See Sadat's *Autobiography*, pp. 220-21; and Heikal, *op. cit.*, pp. 170-72.

[31]Hermann F. Eilts, American Ambassador to Egypt (1973-79), made the following comment: "The Soviet Ambassador in Cairo always insisted to me that there was never any condition on Egypt's right to use arms to defend itself in the event of an attack. There was a Soviet requirement to approve the use of some arms in the event Egypt contemplated an attack of its own."

was not fully confident that Soviet leadership was prepared to support Egypt against her enemy. After he became President, lack of Soviet confidence must have been aggravated when he dismissed, in a struggle for power with his opponents, the pro-Soviet leaders and began to improve his relations with the West. Sadat's decision to seek Western support may have met the approval of moderate Arab leaders, but it could hardly endear him in pro-Soviet circles. The expulsion of Soviet military technicians (about 15,000) in 1972, though resented by the Soviet leaders, did not really turn them against Egypt, as they sided with her and Syria in the October War of 1973, both militarily and diplomatically.[32] However, finding Sadat increasingly leaning toward the West, the Soviet leaders refused to replace the weapons Egypt lost during the war or provide spares for aircrafts that had already been delivered. Overreacting to the Soviet attitude, Sadat denounced with sharp words the Soviet leaders and finally unilaterally terminated the Egypto-Soviet treaty of friendship and cooperation in 1976, including the ending of Soviet facilities in Egypt, and almost irreversibly turned to the United States for support. If Egypt is ever disappointed by the United States and sees the need to seek Soviet support again, she will probably have to do so under other leadership.

However, Sadat's break with the Soviet Union and the assertion of his country's independence did not bring about that immediate American support he may have expected. Before Sadat became President, William Rogers came very near to offering a plan acceptable to moderate Arab leaders as

---

[32]Cf. Sadat's *Autobiography*, p. 264.

a basis of settlement, but it was unacceptable to Israel.[33] After his expulsion of the Soviet experts, Sadat was expecting American support for Egypt's legitimate claims, but Nixon did not take immediate action. However, initial contacts were established between Hafiz Isma'il, Sadat's National Security expert, and Henry Kissinger, Nixon's National Security Advisor, and the conversations were later continued without interruptions between Kissinger, who became Secretary of State, and Isma'il Fahmi, the Egyptian Foreign Minister. Sadat did not expect reversal of American support for Israel but he sought American assistance in recovering the territory occupied by Israel in 1967, since the United States had accepted the UN Resolutions 242 and 338 in which the principles of peace and withdrawal were embodied. Very soon he began to realize that the United States was reluctant to put pressure on Israel and that substantial concessions, both political and territorial, were expected to be granted if Israel were to accept the principle of withdrawal.[34] The lesson that Sadat learned from his contacts with the Great Powers was that Egypt had to help herself before those Powers—indeed, any other power—could assist her. In one of his conversations with Kissinger, Isma'il carried back to Sadat a message which implied this lesson—he was told that "the United States regrettably could do nothing to help so long as Egypt was the defeated party and Israel maintained her superiority."[35] Sadat concluded that Egypt herself had to

---

[33]For an account of the abortive Rogers peace initiative, see W.B. Quandt, *Decade of Decisions* (Berkeley, 1977).

[34]See Heikal, *op. cit.*, p. 203.

[35]Sadat's *Autobiography*, p. 238.

exercise the pressure on Israel—a pressure that would break the deadlock and bring Israel to the negotiating table on parity with Egypt. This message did not necessarily mean that Kissinger advised Egypt to go to war with Israel, but it confirmed the view held by many an Arab leader that the Arab lands Israel had taken by force could not possibly be recovered without force.

True, the original purpose of the October War of 1973 was to break the deadlock between Israel and the Arabs but in reality it was the product of several other forces. There was first the contention of Arab thinkers who held that a peaceful settlement with Israel might lead eventually to the acceptance of Israel as a member state in the regional system which was unacceptable to them. There was also the argument of extremists who asserted that Israel would never give up occupied Arab lands (i.e. in 1967)—much less the lands taken in earlier wars—save by war and their views were shared by an increasing number after Sadat failed to achieve a settlement despite his leanings toward the United States in 1972 and early 1973. Still others called for war not only as a means to recover lost Arab territory but also, perhaps more importantly, to overcome the feeling of indignity and injured pride that Israel had inflicted on the Arabs in three earlier wars. Had Israel, after the Six-Day War, tried to conciliate Arab feelings and alleviate their fears and suspicion by an offer of withdrawal from the lands she occupied in 1967, an atmosphere of goodwill might have been created for peaceful settlement. But the threats, massive retaliations and arrogant statements by Jewish leaders about Israel's might and military superiority accentuated Arab resentment and induced them never to give up fighting and come to terms with Israel. Indeed, Jewish claims to an invincible Israel and Arab inability to use modern weapons strengthened Arab determination to fight Israel at the earliest possible moment to disprove Israeli claims.

However, the immediate aims of the October War, at least as agreed upon between top Egyptian and Syrian leaders, were more modest and limited in scope, as both Syria and Egypt did not yet feel sufficiently equipped to wage an all out war that would enable the Arabs to drive Israeli forces from all territory occupied in 1967. And yet the initial stages of the war went beyond expectations of both victors and vanquished—it is reported that General Dayan wept and said in despair that the "fourth temple" was collapsing and Golda Meir, the Prime Minister, sent a message of "save Israel" to the United States which prompted Nixon and Kissinger to start an airlift which delivered tanks and weapons direct to the battlefield and enabled the Israeli Army to take the offensive during the last five of the fifteen-day war. Arab *amour-propre* may have been rehabilitated, and doubts about Arab ability to stand up to Israel's military discipline were removed, but the immediate objectives of the war were not achieved. As one Arab writer remarked, "no praise can be too high for the men of all ranks who made (the war) possible," but, "the initial successes were not exploited with sufficient energy or imagination." [36] Since Israel and the Arabs were not fighting a war in a vacuum, the war could not have ended by the victory of one contender against another without the consent of the two Great Powers.

The Nixon-Kissinger diplomacy, with Soviet tacit

---

[36]Heikal, *op. cit.*, p. 207. See also Ahmad Baha' al-Din *Wa Tahattamat al-Ustura 'Ind al-Zuhr* (The Myth Collapsed by Noontime) (Cairo, 1974).

agreement, was based on the assumption that a settlement of the Arab-Israeli conflict would become possible only if the fourth Arab-Israeli war were to end with no-victory and no-defeat for either side. Realizing that neither one could win over the other without the support of the two Great Powers, Egypt and Israel seem to have been ready for compromises; but Nixon's domestic troubles at home frustrated his partner in the field from receiving sufficient support to play a more constructive role in the ensuing negotiations between Arabs and Israelis. The October War, rendered inconclusive by massive American military support for Israel, was the Arab's lost opportunity to recover their territory by force.

Apart from the political consequences, the October War destroyed Israel's "myth of security," to use Sadat's words, as the Arabs proved they could not be kept permanently at arms length from Israel. Peace with the Arabs, the American policy makers began to argue, had become necessary if Israel were to live in security. Since the parties concerned were not yet prepared to sign a comprehensive peace treaty satisfactory to all, as the initial meeting of the Geneva conference demonstrated, a short-term bilateral agreement between Israel and her Arab neighbors became the alternative— perhaps as a face-saving device—if the peace process were not to turn to another war. But Kissinger's shuttle diplomacy, for which he was credited with bringing Arabs and Israelis to the negotiating table, failed to provide the atmosphere necessary to pursue a peaceful settlement.[37]

One of the consequences of Kissinger's diplo-

---

[37]Ambassador Hermann F. Eilts, maintaining that Kissinger's diplomacy did not intend to create an atmosphere leading to an overall settlement, made the following remark: "It was intended to unlock

macy, in fact if not in intent, was Arab relapse into disunity. Syria, though it had accepted the first interim agreement, was not prepared to accept a second agreement which only Egypt had accepted against Syria's objection.[38] Nonetheless, Sadat was determined to leave no stone unturned in his search for peace, hoping that a settlement satisfactory to Jews and Arabs might eventually be in the best interests of the Arabs, despite increasing criticism of his peace initiative in the Arab world.

Early in 1977, when the new American administration began to pay attention to Middle Eastern problems, Sadat was ready to participate in the peace process that had slowed down under the former administration. Encouraged by public and private pronouncements favorable to the Arabs made by President Carter, Arab diplomats became very active in Washington and New York. However, initial negotiations revealed that Israel continued to demand territorial concessions for security requirements, since the Arabs refused to accept her as a full partner in the Arab World—an argument which many Americans, in public and private quarters, have accepted at face value. Believing that Israeli leaders might be more flexible if met by Arab leaders directly at the negotiating tables a number of American and European statesmen hinted on more than one occasion that if the Arabs and Israelis were to talk directly to one another without an intermediary, negotiations might prove more satisfying.[39]

---

the immediate doors to specific problem areas to move in the direction of an overall settlement." For a more favorable account of Kissinger's shuttle diplomacy, see Edward R.E. Sheehan, *The Arabs, Israelis, and Kissinger* (New York, 1976).

[38]See p. 221, below.

[39]Several Israeli leaders have time and again complained about Arab

Renewed calls for direct talks whether from an American source or elsewhere, seem to have had an effect on Sadat, who had already begun to realize the futility of indirect talks.[40] He seems to have sounded some men close to him, who advised against direct talks, but hoping that a meeting with top Israeli leaders might speed up the peace process, he decided to proceed himself to Israel and negotiate directly with them. In a speech at the People's Assembly (November 9, 1977), he reiterated his intent to settle the Arab Israeli conflict by peaceful methods, and went on to declare that he was prepared to go to the end of the world—even to the Knesset—to negotiate for peace.[41] His offer, responded to by an invitation from Prime Minister Begin to address the Israeli Parliament, set in motion his historic journey to Jerusalem (November 26, 1977) in which he offered, on behalf of the Arabs, his proposals for a peace settlement to the Israeli leaders. In brief, he demanded complete

refusal to talk with them directly, and Golda Meir, a former Israeli Premier, is reported to have once said that if Arab leaders would only talk directly with them, there would be no difficulty in coming to an agreement.

[40]I have it on the authority of some of my informants in Cairo (December 1977) that the idea of direct talks came either from an American source or from the President of Rumania, during Sadat's visit to Bucharest. Sadat himself said, in a public statement, that the idea of direct talks came to his mind on his way back from Bucharest to Cairo in 1977. It is also said that during a meeting of Arab delegates in New York early in 1977, Secretary of State Vance suggested negotiations on the Arab-Israeli conflict, presumably through an American intermediary, but Moshe Dayan demanded direct talks. Isma'il Fahmi, Egypt's Foreign Minister, declined. Informed about the suggestion, Sadat seems to have thought that the time for direct talks had come, and decided to take the initiative himself and negotiate directly with Israeli leaders. Sadat's trip to Jerusalem was his own innovation.

[41]See Ministry of Information, *Speeches and Interviews by President Sadat on the Occasion of His Visit to Jerusalem* (Cairo, 1977), p. 51.

withdrawal from all Arab territory occupied by Israel in 1967 and a homeland for the Palestinian people on the West Bank and in Ghazza, the form and future of which were to be decided by self-determination as *quid pro quo* for recognition and acceptance of Israel in the Arab World and agreement on all relevant security requirements.

The world, taken by surprise, hoped that the psychological barrier that Sadat had removed by his journey might at last lead to a final settlement of the Arab-Israeli Thirty-Year War by peaceful methods. But Begin, in reply, made no gesture to reciprocate Sadat's peace offer save that he was prepared to negotiate Sadat's peace proposals. Whether at their meeting in Isma'iliya on Christmas Day or in subsequent negotiations between their representatives, the two leaders never really came to a meeting of the minds, not even on how to keep the peace process going. Sadat, in an effort to reach an overall settlement, insisted that an agreement on general principles should first be reached leaving to Arab and Israeli negotiators all matters of detail to be worked out later. Begin, to whom all matters of detail were as important as principles, refused to commit himself on general principles and offered Sadat Sinai but refused to recognize a homeland for the Palestinians or their right to self-determination. Only self-rule within Israeli occupation for a five-year period, presumably based on Begin's conception that the West Bank (Judea and Sumaria) belonged to Israel as a matter of historical right, at the end of which the status of Palestinians would be reviewed without a promise of sovereignty or the right to decide on their future status was offered. The question of a settlement with Syria was not even on the agenda for discus-

sion on the grounds that Asad was not prepared to
make concessions on the Jawlan Heights. Begin's
plan remained the guidelines for subsequent Israeli
negotiations.

Since no change in Begin's stand seemed feasible, despite attempts to resume negotiations in
Egypt, England and elsewhere for possible alternative plans, Sadat turned again to the United States.
By his journey to Jerusalem, Sadat perhaps sought
by direct negotiations to achieve peace without an
intermediary. Now he began to have second
thoughts about his short-cut diplomacy.

President Carter, realizing that without American
participation peace in the Middle East could not be
achieved, invited both Sadat and Begin to a Summit at Camp David which in effect changed the direction of the peace process from a comprehensive
into a bilateral settlement. When Sadat visited Jerusalem, he had in mind to draw Israel into negotiations leading to a settlement of the Arab-Israeli
conflict in all its aspects. But when he went to
Camp David, he was drawn into negotiations
which resulted in meeting not the minimum demands of the Arabs as a whole but essentially
Egypt's own needs.

Sadat continued to assert that his purpose was to
pursue the peace process until a comprehensive
settlement was achieved. By enlisting American
participation in the peace process as "a partner"
(to use his own words), he hoped that American
pressure might be brought to bear on Begin to
agree on a general declaration of principles embodying Arab demands of withdrawal and self-determination for the Palestinians. Since these demands were consistent with the essential elements
of American policy, he took it for granted that Car-

ter would support him in his dealings with Begin and a warm friendship developed between the two leaders.

To Begin, however, the situation appeared entirely different. Counting on the pressure his American constituency could bring to bear on the American President, he was able to take advantage of Sadat's dependence on Carter. Already alienated from his Arab supporters, Sadat tried in vain to overcome his isolation by obtaining favorable terms at Camp David. Though Begin offered the tempting prize of Sinai, which Sadat could not easily turn down, he insisted on a limited autonomy for the West Bank and Ghazza which made it exceedingly difficult for Sadat to accept without risking complete isolation from the Arab World. Still believing in the advantages of peace, he put aside the advice of counselors to reject Begin's limited autonomy plan, though in a moment of despair he almost contemplated a return to Cairo to declare the failure of his peace initiative. President Carter, for personal prestige as well as domestic reasons, urged Sadat to accept an agreement that fell short of expectations, notwithstanding Arab rejection of a settlement that appeared both bilateral and one-sided, contrary to Sadat's pledge to resolve the Palestinian question in all its aspects. Instead of becoming a stepping stone for Palestinian self-determination, Camp David proved a victory for Begin's plan. Not only did Begin secure acceptance of his limited autonomy for the West Bank with no promise of sovereignty or self-determination after a five-year period, he also succeeded in asserting his own interpretation of the agreement, including continuation of the policy of land settlements which ran contrary to the spirit of the agreement. Moreover, he rejected the possible establishment of a Palestinian State on the West Bank and participation of the PLO in any future negotiations with Palestinians. Small wonder that almost all Arab countries, moderates and extremists, rejected the agreements and went so far as to impose political and economic sanctions against Egypt.

Still counting on American support, Sadat has not lost faith with his peace initiative and he is still hopeful that a settlement favorable to the Palestinians is feasible. In an interview with the present writer, he maintained that the establishment of autonomy in the West Bank and Ghazza necessarily will enable the Palestinians to exercise their inherent rights of self-determination despite Israeli efforts to establish settlements in the occupied territory.[42]

However, neither the negotiations for the establishment of autonomy nor an agreement to revise or supplement the Camp David peace plan have yet shown signs of hope. Unless a radical change in Israel itself takes place in favor of a Palestinian homeland and self-determination, whether produced by internal or foreign pressures, no prospect for an overall settlement is expected in the near future.

VI

Sadat's involvement in foreign affairs, especially the Arab-Israeli conflict, left him virtually little or no time to attend to internal affairs. Since the public, the politically conscious literate in particular,

[42]The writer's interview with President Sadat (Cairo, March 14, 1981).

had become increasingly impatient with the repressive measures enforced under the Nasir regime, one of Sadat's early decisions after he became President was to repeal those measures and inspire confidence in his regime that it would take no indiscriminate actions. He promised that he was prepared to transform the regime ultimately into a democratic system under which all individuals would enjoy freedom and equal opportunities. Selecting competent Premiers to whom he could delegate responsibility, he gave evidence that he was not planning to rule as a dictator. These changes, which he collectively called the Corrective Revolution (*al-Thawra al-Tashihiya*), were in his eyes the continuation of the Revolution of 1952.[43]

Apart from the promises of reform and constitutional changes, relaxation of repression and censorship of the press were perhaps the first noticeable signs of change from the former regime. These initial measures and free expression of political opinion enjoyed by writers encouraged some of them to indulge in a trenchant attack on the Nasir regime and expose its abuses and repressive measures. Indeed, there was a lively debate in the People's Assembly voicing criticism which no government under Nasir would have tolerated. Though the economic system continued to be socialist, relaxation of its application and encouragement of free enterprise, made in response to the demands of the business community, met almost universal approval as the need to attract foreign investment and increase

---

[43]Coincidentally, Sadat and Asad came to power in the same year and both called the actions they had undertaken as a "Corrective Revolution," on the grounds that they did not depart completely from the previous regimes but were only to modify and "correct" them.

production were considered necessary steps to improve economic conditions. A new Constitution, striking a balance between collectivism and free enterprise and stressing individual freedoms, was issued in 1971. No custodianship or confiscation of private property, not even nationalization of a single economic enterprise, was to be allowed unless absolutely needed.[44]

A greater excitement was aroused when Sadat promised to allow political parties to be organized. Under the Nasir regime, no political parties were permitted; only the Arab Socialist Union (ASU), representing various corporate bodies, was in existence, though the need for a multiple party system was acknowledged in principle.[45] Sadat tried to liberalize the regime by recognizing the need for new political parties in principle, but he moved slowly and cautiously to allow the formation of political parties in order to avoid a return to the pre-Revolutionary regime when political parties, indulging in a vain struggle for power, undermined the very system under which they were permitted to operate.

In his opening speech to the People's Assembly, convened following the general elections of 1971, Sadat promised that three "tribunes" (*manabir*) would be allowed to be formed within the ASU, presumably as a first step toward the ultimate establishment of a multiple-party system.[46] In a speech to the People's Assembly, Sadat announced

---

[44]See Articles 34-35, *Dustur Jamhuriyat Misr al-Arabiya* (Constitution of the Arab Republic of Egypt).

[45]For Nasir's views about political parties, see my *Arab Contemporaries*, pp. 55-56.

[46]The tribunes within the ASU did not actually begin to take form until five years later.

that three political parties, representing three shades of opinion within the Assembly, would be allowed to be organized in accordance with a new law which the Assembly had already passed on July 7, 1977.[47]

The three parties that came subsequently into existence were as follows: (1) the Egyptian Party, composed of some 318 members, led by Mamduh Salim, then Prime Minister, who won a majority in the elections of 1977 and formed a government; (2) the Liberal Socialist Party, composed of some 20 members, led by Mustafa Murad; it differs from the Egyptian Party only in placing a greater emphasis on moral and religious values; (3) the Marxist Group, led by Khalid Muhyi al-Din, composed of only 4 or 5 members and which stressed collectivist doctrines to a greater degree than other parties.[48]

Sadat's move to allow the formation of parties was hailed by the politically conscious public as a step in the right direction, but there was a demand for the granting of democratic freedoms without restrictions. On August 23, 1977, on the occasion of the anniversary of the two founding leaders of the Wafd Party—Sa'd Zaghlul and Mustafa al-Nahhas—Fu'ad Siraj al-Din, former Secretary of the Wafd Party, made a speech in which he called for the formation of a new nationalist party which would stress liberal and democratic freedoms within the framework of a socialist society. Trying

---

[47]For text of the law and the introductory memorandum for the enactment of the law, see People's Assembly, *Report of the Legislative Committee Concerning the Draft Law for the Organization of Political Parties* (Arabic) (Cairo, 1977).

[48]Some twenty members in The People's Assembly, preferring not to belong to any political party, were collectively called Independent Members.

to strike a balance between the public and private sectors, he declared that the socialism of the new party, consistent with the platform of the ASU, would be shorn of foreign (Marxist) doctrines.[49] Although the proposed new party was welcomed by a surprisingly large section of the literate, especially younger men, it was attacked by protagonists of the regime and leaders of the Egyptian Party on the grounds that Siraj al-Din, as Minister of the Interior, was largely responsible for the abuses and corruption of Wafdist governments in the pre-Revolutionary period. Despite opposition, however, a petition, signed by more than 600 men, including 22 members of the People's Assembly, was submitted to Sayyid Mar'i, President of the Assembly (Speaker of the House), in January 1978, demanding formal recognition of the party. Sayyid Mar'i, finding the petition consistent with the law governing the formation of political parties (which requires a minimum of 20 members of the People's Assembly), passed it on to President Sadat for approval. The Neo-Wafd Party, under a new label, became the fourth political party.

Demands for pushing the democratic process a step further in a country that has become appreciative of democratic freedoms were both right and a healthy sign for progress and development, though certain errors in exercising these rights were not unexpected. At first a few members of the People's Assembly and liberal writers in the press voiced criticism of various governmental actions, but their criticism was quite moderate and con-

---

[49]For text of the speech, see Fu'ad Siraj al-Din, *Limadha al-Hizb al-Jadid?* [Why a New Party?] (Cairo, 1977). It is said that almost a quarter of a million copies of the speech were purchased within a few weeks.

structure.[50] Sadat, as Head of the State, was not necessarily the direct target for criticism, only the Government was censured; but when criticism touched on foreign policy—the peace initiative with Israel and dealings with the United States and the Soviet Union—he obviously was directly involved and seems to have felt that the critics exceeded the limits and their criticism was inconsistent with the national interest.

As a process, democracy can always be improved upon, and it certainly has not yet reached a high stage of development in Egypt; but Sadat, denouncing his critics as having been irresponsible by subordinating national to private interests, holds that the democratic process cannot proceed too quickly and certain restrictions should be imposed on those who wish to go too far too soon. His critics maintain that the democratic process should continue to develop without interruptions, if it is to mature and become meaningful. For this reason, when he moved to restrict criticism—including the expulsion by the People's Assembly (May 1978) of two of its members—his action was considered a setback to the democratic process. In protest against this action, Siraj al-Din declared the self-dissolution of his party. Criticism by liberal writers in the press prompted Sadat to order the arrest of some 60 writers and leaders, including Haykal, former Editor of *al-Ahram*, who were detained or kept under house arrest, pending investigation, on the grounds that they undermined the regime. Haykal, writing in the foreign press, said that he

---

[50]Criticism varied from such chronic matters as corruption, food shortages, housing and black-marketing problems to faults in the Aswan Dam, and deterioration in the levels of education and morality.

was in favor of non-alignment; he criticized Sadat for his leaning toward the United States and abandonment of the Soviet Union, just as he had criticized Nasir for total dependence on Soviet support and antagonizing Western countries. He also criticized Sadat's peace initiative on the grounds that it failed to settle the Arab-Israeli conflict and undermined the Arab negotiating position. He gave Sadat, however, full credit for starting the democratic process but regretted his move to restrict it, a move which might lead to total suppression.[51]

In order to demonstrate his firm belief in the advantages of parliamentary democracy and give it a practical expression, Sadat allowed the formation of two parties in 1978. First, the National Democratic Party, which he took the lead in organizing, differed only in name from the Egyptian Party, led by Mamduh Salim. Very soon most members of the Egyptian Party resigned to join the National Democratic Party. To enlist the support of the Coptic Christian community, which seems to have voiced certain grievances against the regime, Sadat chose Fikri Makram 'Ubayd, brother of the former Secretary of the Wafd Party, to become the Secretary-General of the new party.[52] Second, he encouraged formation of the Socialist Labor Party,

---

[51]For Haykal's criticism of Sadat's foreign policy, see M.H. Haykal, *Hadith al-Mubadara* (Discussion of the Initiative) (Bayrut, 1978); and for an account of the interrogations before the Socialist Prosecutor, see M.H. Haykal, *Waqai' Tahqiq Siyasi Amam al-Mudda'i al-Ishtiraki* [Proceedings of the Political Interrogations Before the Socialist Prosecutor] (Bayrut, 1979).

[52]In entrusting his party's second highest ranking position to a Copt, Sadat has followed in the footsteps of Sa'd Zaghlul, hero of the Egyptian Revolution of 1919 and leader of the Wafd, who sought by his choice of a promising young Coptic nationalist as Secretary of the Wafd to supersede religious by national identity.

headed by Ibrahim Shukri, a former Secretary-
General of the Misr al-Fatat (Young Egypt) Party,
founded by Ahmad Husayn in the early thirties to
organize the new party as a counterpart to his National Democratic Party. In order to play the role
of a loyal opposition, Shukri took a more critical
attitude toward the regime, especially on foreign
policy issues, than Sadat had perhaps expected.

It is true that Sadat has always advocated political democracy in principle, as evidenced in his
writings and public statements before and after he
became President in 1970; but his conception of democracy seems to stress procedural rather than
substantial matters. Criticism of governmental acts
relating to procedure and technical matters are allowed, but not on matters of high policy. Sadat is
in particular opposed to criticism leveled by persons considered self-seeking. Only persons concerned about the country's reputation and national
interest are considered the true advocates of democracy. Criticism, he said, should be exercized
with self-restraints. The standard of restraints, according to Sadat, are religion and traditions, and
the critics should be men well-known for their
honesty, straight-forwardness and fairness.[53]

When Sadat was challenged by advocates of the
democratic freedoms, he sought public backing by
a nation-wide plebiscite (May 16, 1978) in order to
curb the activities of radical (Communist) and reactionary (liberal) leaders whom he denounced as
obstructing his efforts to establish a working
democratic system. He called the contest with his
opponents "a moral crisis," because he felt democ-

---

[53]See Sadat, *Qissat al-Thawra Kamilatan* (Cairo, The Hilal Books,
nd.), pp. 19-20.

racy cannot possibly work in the absence of moral principles.[54]

In 1979-80, Sadat took two formidable steps to insure that the democratic process conformed to religious and moral principles which he considered necessary for the development of democratic institutions in Egypt. The first was to establish the press as a "Fourth Power"; the second, a "Law of Shame," to hold critics liable to penalties, if they made statements contrary to morality and the national interests. On the occasion of signing a peace treaty with Israel, a plebiscite was held on April 19, 1979, first to secure public approval of the establishment of peace with Israel, and second, to reorganize the country's democratic system. The People's Assembly was disolved and the election returns showed that the country was overwhelmingly in favor of Sadat's actions.

In 1980, two laws were enacted for the reorganization of the democratic system. The first, issued on June 28, 1980, provided for the establishment of a Consultative Assembly, composed of some 210 members (two-thirds elected and one-third appointed by the President), to operate as a prototype of a Senate, in an advisory capacity. The second law, issued on July 14, 1980, provided for the establishment of the press as a Fourth Power. The idea that the press is a "Fourth Power" is a sym-

---

[54]See his Speech on the Anniversary of the July Revolution (July 22, 1978), in al-Ahram, Cairo, July 23, 1978. Some thinkers, especially those who advocate positive philosophy, have criticized Sadat for the re-introduction of religious and moral values into State institutions and consider Sadat's reforms as a set-back in the development of secular thought in Egypt. See Ghali Choukri, Egypte Contre Revolution (Paris, 1979); and al-Nahda wa al-Suqut fi al-Fikr al-Misri al-Hadith (Revival and Decline in Modern Egyptian Thought) (Bayrut, 1978), and Fauzi M. Najjar, "How Genuine Is Egypt's Democracy," The New York Times, June 1980.

bolic acknowledgement of its significance in the democratic system, but its formal establishment as a "Power" within the State might lead, as Mustafa Mar'i stated, to its domination by the Executive.[56]

Sadat's action may seem as an attempt to grant the press independence, since it had already been nationalized and brought under state control under the Nasir regime. By establishing the press as a Fourth Power, Sadat seemingly moved toward eventual termination of State control. According to the present arrangement the press has been given a semi-autonomous status under the control of a Higher Press Council, composed of the editors of newspapers and periodicals, the Dean of the Lawyers Association and some other prominent men of the media, presided over by the Speaker of the Consultative Assembly. However, since most members of the Higher Press Council are editors of nationalized newspapers (though not the editors of party organs), indirect government control may eventually disappear.

Sadat, however, has not been vindictive or harsh with critics; he has, indeed, shown tolerance on the whole with political opponents, compared with his predecessors. Instead of the harsh methods of the Nasir regime, he has warned those who fail to observe self-restraints by the enactment of a Law of Shame, which holds critics liable to penalties only if their criticism were to undermine the regime or the country's reputation abroad. Asked by the present writer if this law would not discourage constructive criticism, Sadat replied that nobody

---

[56]For a defense of the freedom of the press and criticism of its establishment as a Fourth Power, see Mustafa Mar'i, *al-Sahafa Bayn al-Sulta wa al-Sultan* [The Press: Between Power and Authority] (Cairo, 1980).

has yet been brought to trial in accordance with
this law, nor will it be applied except to those
"who have lost the veil of shame." Well-wishers of
the regime, however, hope that the law will eventually be revised or replaced by another in conformity with the democratic system which Sadat has
always promised to establish.

VII

From childhood, Sadat has been noted for his
courage, dash and adventurism. After more than a
quarter of a century of experience in public offices, he has not mellowed—on the contrary, he
has shown an ability to assume full responsibility
and take actions involving great risks since he became President which demonstrates that he possesses even greater moral courage than he had displayed before. The liquidation of his opponents in
May 1971, the expulsion of Soviet military technicians in 1972, the October War of 1973, and the
historic journey to Jerusalem in November 1977,
despite mounting Arab opposition, are cases in
point. True, Sadat's initial actions have been taken
in auspicious circumstances, and his gambles are
likely to involve risks which might affect adversely
the national interests in the long run. But Sadat,
with great courage, seems to be prepared to take
them.

Corollary to Sadat's propensity to take risks, he
is capable of taking extreme positions, if they appear to him to be right or in the national interest—
he will go, in his words, to "the end of the world"
in search of an answer, or a clue, to a problem.
For instance, when he came into a conflict with
Soviet leaders and decided to lean toward the
United States, he terminated his dealings with the

Soviet Union almost to the point of no return.

In like manner, when he realized that the use of violence was the only method of forcing Israel to withdraw from occupied Arab territory, he was all for war and for carrying it out against the suspension of fighting by a ceasefire, as suggested by the Great Powers—USSR, USA and Britain. At that stage, such an action was unthinkable to him, though a ceasefire in the first week of the October War might have been in Arab favor.[56] In 1977, when Sadat came to the conclusion that peace and direct negotiations with Israel were the only possible means of achieving a settlement with Israel, he did not shrink from reversing his former position in favor of war, when he realized that peace was the key to the dilemma. In both situations, when he was for war or for peace, he was quite earnest and in accordance with his system of thought each position was right in its time.

Sadat's swinging, like the pendulum, from one extreme to the other may give the impression that he is an erratic—or, as referred to in the press, the zigzag—leader. His swinging may give the impression that he relies on tactics and lacks the ability to work out a strategy. But in reality his sudden change of direction only appears abrupt and is not without transition. In all important matters Sadat is calculating and takes quite a bit of time in making up his mind; once he makes a decision, he will announce it to the public as if it had been made almost on the spur of the moment, and will proceed to carry it out with determination and vigor. In the implementation of a decision, he is a master of tactics.

Sadat has been praised not only for his courage

[56]Cf. Sadat's *Autobiography*, pp. 252-54, 256-59.

and patriotism, but also for his loyalty and personal integrity. As noted earlier, his almost blind subservience to Nasir was partly due to a sense of patriotism because he believed that Nasir's leadership was necessary for the country and partly due to his personal loyalty to a comrade revolutionary leader to whom he was attached from almost the beginning of the Free Officers Movement. After he became President, he has continued his personal attachment to friends who had supported him in the past and tried to help them in reduced conditions and in events that have turned against them. When the former Shah of Iran found it difficult after his fall from power to receive adequate medical care in Western countries, Sadat at once offered moral support, as a gesture to acknowledge Iran's assistance to Egypt during the October War of 1973. Despite the tense relations between Iraq and Egypt following the Camp David agreements, Sadat has not failed to extend indirect support to Iraq in its wars with Iran. These and other instances have demonstrated Sadat's loyalty to friends and allics.

Sadat often betrays impatience, however, partly because he is short of temper, but perhaps mainly because of the pressure of work and lack of interest in matters of detail, despite his readiness to delegate responsibilities to ministers.[57] In his negotiations with Israeli leaders, especially with Begin, who always paid particular attention to details—in-

---

[57]In an interview with Mamduh Salim, former Prime Minister, I was told that Sadat tends to distribute responsibility among his Ministers and that he (Mamduh Salim) had been given some 90 specific assignments, presumably falling within Presidential power, to relieve him of the pressure of work, in addition to his functions as Premier (the writer's interview with Mamduh Salim, Cairo, December 13, 1977).

deed, he often gave the impression that details were almost as important as basic issues—Sadat often became very impatient, because he held that basic issues should be overriding, though not infrequently he proved capable of suppressing impatience with understanding and tolerance.

"Are your decisions and actions based mainly on empirical or intuitive reason?", I asked Sadat. "Mainly on intuition," he replied. But he went on to explain that apart from taking a comprehensive view of a situation he always tried, according to his system of thought, to deepen his understanding with relevant facts and conditions. "I always try to weigh a particular decision on the scale of its chances of success and failure—I do my calculations *(hisabat)*—before I act," he pointed out. Though he is well-read and keeps himself informed on all important matters, he seems to grasp thoroughly only the fundamental elements of a question by an overview rather than by the analytical process of details. He is fond of discussing spiritual and ethical problems, and has been influenced in particular by writers, like Lloyd Douglas, who are concerned with spiritual and humanistic matters. He has read, I am told, all of Douglas' works. Moreover, Sadat is a writer in his own right; his style, though repetitious, is clear and lucid.[58]

Stepping into the position of Nasir, who possessed an impressive charisma and stood in the popular imagination as a national hero, Sadat is still struggling to create an image for himself as a

[58]Unlike Winston Churchill, who was honored as a great statesman by the Nobel Prize for literature (though he was not certain he deserved the prize as a writer), Sadat was honored with the prize for an unfinished peace, shared with Begin.

patriot who has been able to have his country rehabilitated from injured pride. Unlike Nasir, he
sought to win the masses not by the appeal to an
ideology, but by improvement of social conditions.
From childhood he has been concerned about conditions of the people and hopes that by talking can-
didly about the complexity of domestic conditions
he may go down in history not as the politician
who sought applause by rhetorical speeches, but
the patriot whose record of achievements shall
speak for him. And his career may well prove
eventually that his promise was fulfilled.[59]

---

[59]For an expression of some of Sadat's ideas about social reform, see
his "Where Egypt Stands," *Foreign Affairs*, Vol. 51 (October 1972),
pp. 114-123.

CHAPTER V

HAFIZ AL-ASAD OF SYRIA

> Two powers are unconquerable—the
> power of God and the power of the
> people. We, leaders of the Ba'th Party,
> hope to achieve our national goals by
> dependence on these two powers.
>
> Hafiz al-Asad

Syria, in the broad historical-geographical sense of the term, is the home of the founding fathers of Arab nationalism and became in the subsequent development of the nationalist movement the fountain of that movement. Whether in Damascus, Bayrut or Istanbul—where the concept of the Arab awakening (*al-nahda al-'Arabiya*) had first been initiated—Syrians proved to be the most vocal and articulate about the goals and character of Arab nationalism and sought after separation from the Ottoman Empire and emancipation from foreign control, to bring together all Arab lands into a form of unity in which Syria would play the central or pivotal position in a grand Arab Union. For various reasons—geographical, historical and otherwise—the Syrian leaders may have a just claim for their aspiration to play such a role, not only because they were the forerunners of the Arab nationalist movement but also because in an overall Arab union their country would be the bridge

which connects the Arab Crescent, the Arabian Peninsula and the Nile Valley. Above all, the Syrians have displayed a deeper sense of commitment to Arab unity notwithstanding that local feeling in some parts of Syria is by no means less strong than in other Arab lands.

But the course of events following World War I ran contrary to their expectations. The whole area from the Nile to the Euphrates valleys had first fallen under foreign control, which undermined Arab independence, and then divided into two zones of British and French interests. Because of the superiority of British power in Egypt and Iraq over the relatively insecure French position in Syria and Lebanon, Syria's aspirations to play the pivotal role in the Arab World had necessarily become subordinate to the rival Egyptian and Iraqi claims to Arab leadership. Owing to the dynastic rivalry between the Saudi and Hashimi Houses—the first predominating in Arabia and the latter confined to Iraq and Transjordan—Saudi Arabia sided with Egypt in her historic rivalry with Iraq which tipped the balance of power in favor of Egypt. Had Saudi Arabia supported Syrian leadership, a balance between the two historic rivals might have been maintained and Syria would have been able to play a more constructive role in such unity schemes as Greater Syria or the Fertile Crescent, notwithstanding Egyptian opposition. As a result, Syria's vision of Arab unity remained unfulfilled.

Looked upon from this perspective, Syria's regional and foreign policy objectives become more meaningful than if viewed in terms of its internal or communal structure. From the time when the first constitutional experiment was undertaken under the Faysal regime (1918-20), Syria tried to form a federal union comprising not only Lebanon but also Palestine and Transjordan, which were under British control. She also tried unsuccessfully to link Iraq with its regime first under some form of a dual monarchy and later under a republican regime. Though the goal of Arab unity seemed like a mirage, almost all regimes remained committed to it. No leader or group who aspired to achieve power could solicit public support if they failed to pay at least lip service to Arab unity. Even the Communist Party, though loyalty to internationalism is overriding, has embodied in its platform the principle of Arab unity.[1]

The rise of Israel to statehood and the conseᶋquent inability of Arab states to prevent its expansion provided another compelling reason for unity, not only among the dismembered parts of geographical Syria but also among other Arab countries, if they were to stand up to the challenge of Israel. How was it possible, it is often asked, that a small, new country like Israel could defeat seven larger and already established Arab states? The older leaders, in defending their position, maintained that they were utterly unprepared because they needed weapons which the Western Powers who sympathized with Zionist claims denied them. But others, who said that weapons could have been obtained from other sources, argued that the seven Arab countries were defeated precisely because they were seven and not one united Arab

---

[1]It was perhaps for this reason that Antun Sa'ada, leader of the Syrian Nationalist Party, advocating only Syrian rather than Arab unity, had very limited support in Syria (though not in Lebanon), because he did not include in his platform other Arab lands—an essential element in the principle of Arab unity—though Iraq was later included as part of Syria in his unity scheme.

State, which could have prevented the rise of Israel by having one Arab Army under one command and prosecuting the war to achieve one common purpose and not the diverse purposes of rival Arab leaders. Bickering and lack of common purpose exposed the bankruptcy of older leaders, who put their own narrow interests above Arab national interests and thus allowed the Jewish community to impose its will against the general Arab will. Nor were the older leaders aware that what their countries needed after independence was reconstruction and development, if the independence that they had just won from the European Powers were to be protected.

For a long time the young generation had been lecturing the older about the need for progress and Arab unity and had warned that unless Arab lands pursued the path of progress and development, they would face disaster. But only one group, the Ba'th Party, was capable of giving their call to reform and Arab unity an articulate expression and they presented it to the public with greater vigor and deeper sense of conviction than others.[2] What helped the Ba'th emerge as the most active party was its appeal to the new generation that was then challenging the leadership of the old generation and its stress on Arab unity at a time when the old leaders were charged with Arab defeat in the Palestine wars. In its platform of the "One Arab Destiny," combining a social reform program implied in the general slogans of Arab unity, freedom and

[2]There were other young leaders and groups with like programs— Socialists, National Democrats and others in Iraq, Egypt and elsewhere—who contributed to the generational upsurge against older leaders. As an organized group, the Ba'th had greater appeal to younger men in civil and military ranks.

socialism, the Ba'th seemingly offered the Arab
World a remedy for all its ills.

Though the Ba'th Party formulated a platform
for all Arab lands and appealed to all the Arabs to
unite and form "One Arab Nation," its founding
leaders were Syrians and their ideology for Arab
unity was seen from a Syrian perspective. In line
with earlier compatriots, the Ba'th leaders had
their base of operation in Syria and hoped that
their country would eventually lead in the achievement of Arab unity. Whenever leadership of Arab
unity passed to other hands—Egypt, Iraq or other
countries—Syria very soon felt the need to re-assert her role as the champion of Arab unity under
a new leadership.

The gospel of Arab unity, an overriding principle
of the Ba'th Party, prompted the Ba'th leaders to
propose unity schemes to Egypt and Iraq—their
two rivals for Arab leadership—on two different
occasions, but the Ba'th was not the first Syrian
political party that sought unity with other Arab
countries.[3] In their first experience with unity in
1958, the Ba'th leaders failed not because they
sought unity with Egypt, but because the Syrian
aspiration to play a meaningful role in the unity arrangement under Nasir's leadership remained unfulfilled. After Egypt, the Ba'th leaders made still
another attempt at unity with Libya, the Sudan
and Iraq. These attempts, stressing form rather
than substance of unity, remained viable only on
paper and practical plans failed to materialize. But
Syria has not given up her Pan-Arab aspirations

[3]For earlier attempts at achieving unity with neighboring Arab countries see M. Khadduri, "The Scheme of Fertile Crescent Unity," in
Richard N. Frye, ed., *The Near East and the Great Powers* (Cambridge, Mass., 1951), pp. 137-77.

and the Ba'th Party today, under the leadership of
Hafiz al-Asad, may still try to fulfill them. President Asad, with a new style and diplomatic skills,
is exerting his utmost efforts to lay the ground for
the fulfillment of his party's promises.

For an understanding of Asad, a little background about his life and social environment is
necessary. Asad's fundamental ideas and policies,
as well as the major issues and problems facing
him, will be the object of this study. Although he is
the central figure, the role of the Ba'th Party and
other organizations will also be discussed.

II

Some of Asad's goals and actions can be traced
to certain facts and events connected with the social milieu in which he was raised. The first important fact is that Asad was born into a family belonging to the 'Alawi community, and he was
deeply affected by the isolation and deplorable
conditions in which the people of that community
lived, notwithstanding that his own family was neither poor nor prosperous. He was born on October
6, 1930, at Qirdaha—a small town near the Mediterranean port of al-Ladhaqiya (Latakia)—where
most of the villagers were engaged in agriculture
and were small landholders. Almost all the inhabitants of that town and the hillside villages of the region near Ladhaqiya belong to the so-called
Nusayri or 'Alawi sect—a sub-division of the Shi'i
community, one of the two major divisions of Islam. Almost all of this closely-knit community used
to live in the secluded mountainous area between
Ladhaqiya and Antioch, where they had some natural defense against oppression under Ottoman
rule.

After World War I, when Syria was separated from Turkey, the 'Alawi community began to find greater freedom under new rulers and its young men enrolled in government schools and entered the military service. Like other young men who adopted Arab nationalism as a symbol of identification, the 'Alawi youth were able to mix with their Sunni compatriots and participate in public life and occupy high positions in the state. It was in this new social environment when sectarianism had just begun to be superseded by Arab nationalism that Hafiz al-Asad was born. From his high school days, young Asad became an ardent nationalist, as it was considered a duty for young men to adopt an Arab nationalist identity. For Asad, to identify as an Arab nationalist also meant a reaction against his community's exclusiveness as well as a desire to participate in the Arab nationalist movement which promised greater opportunities for progress and development.

The second important fact about Asad's life is that his father, who had an appreciation for culture, was keen to give him the best available education despite his meager resources, in order to enable him to enter public life and improve the family's social status.[4] Under Ottoman rule, children of the Sunni community were allowed to study at government schools, though in practice only children of relatively well-established families could take advantage of such an opportunity.[5]

---

[4]In an interview with Asad (Damascus, January 19, 1980), the writer learned that Asad's father was well-read in Arab history and literature and recited poetry. He took a keen interest in the Arab nationalist movement and inspired his son with nationalist feelings before the son went to school and became involved in political activities.

[5]In the other Arab provinces, educational facilities were made available to loyal Sunni families, but rarely to children of minority groups.

While children of minority groups, especially non-Muslims, attended private communal or missionary schools, the children of the 'Alawi and Durzi communities had very limited opportunities to study beyond the *kuttab* or Quranic schools. As a result, illiteracy and ignorance were more widespread in these communities than others, not to speak of the discrimination and oppression to which these communities had been subjected. But after Syria was separated from Turkey and educational facilities became available to all, the minority communities began to take advantage of this opportunity and improve their conditions.

After five years at the Qirdaha School, where students receive primary education, Hafiz al-Asad went to the Ladhaqiya Preparatory School (al-Tajhiz) and spent some six or seven years completing his primary and high school studies. Although it was not far from home, his mother, who was concerned about his upbringing, went to live with him and provide the necessary requirements for his comfort. It was in this school that young Asad revealed his talents first as a diligent student and later in political activities, in which he became deeply involved in the final year of high school. It was fashionable in those days that students often took to the street in support of popular demands, as students in Syria—indeed, in many other Arab countries—had become highly politicized and participation in public affairs was considered a national duty. On more than one occasion, Asad led student demonstrations and made fiery speeches which received the acclaim not only of the fellow students of his school but others as well. True, these activities often kept the students away from homework, but Asad was able to make up for his deficiencies. After high school, students often entered higher institutions of learning as a means to seek a career in politics. Asad had no hesitation in continuing his studies beyond the high-school level and chose to enter the Military Academy.[6]

Before study in higher institutions of learning became free in recent years, only children of relatively well-to-do families could afford to pursue their studies in colleges such as law and medicine; high school graduates from families of modest income would ordinarily enter either the Military Academy—if they were fortunate enough to be among the relatively few selected for admission, as the need for cadets was then very limited—or the Teachers' College. Asad was indeed fortunate that his physical fitness—he was tall and personable—and his scholastic record qualified him for admission without difficulty in 1952.[7] After two or three years at the Military Academy, he graduated as Air Lieutenant in 1955. He continued further military training in Syria and Egypt and distinguished himself in practical aviation, for which he received prizes for his performances, and graduated as squadron leader in 1957. In 1957-58, he received further training in aviation in the Soviet Union and passed with distinction.

---

[6]The writer's interview with George Saddiqni, a fellow student at the Ladhaqiya High School, and one of Asad's associates in political activities. Now he is a member of the Syrian National Command of the Ba'th Party (Damascus, June 23, 1979). For some sidelights on Asad's high school days, see Muhammad Shakir Adima (ed.), *al-Yubil al-Dhahabi li-Thanawiyat Jul Jamal Bi al-Ladhaqiya* [The Golden Jubilee of the Jul Jamal Secondary School] (Damascus, 1977).

[7]Before he was admitted in the Military Academy, Asad told me that he was persuaded to study science though his personal inclination lay in literary studies. Because of his keen interest in nationalist activities, he chose to enroll in military training.

It is significant to note that while Asad was engaged in military service, both as cadet and Air Officer, he never lost sight of politics. Indeed he regarded military training as part of his preparation
for the nationalist activities in which he had been
involved since his high school days. While he was
still in high school at Ladhaqiya, he joined the
Ba'th Party when it was formally organized in
1947 and was entrusted with the leadership of a
unit for students. But it was after he graduated
from the Military College that he became fully involved in the activities of the Ba'th Party.

Syria's marriage with Egypt to achieve Arab
unity, in which the Ba'th Party took an active part,
was a turning point in Asad's career. Like many
other leaders, he envisioned the union as the fulfillment of a fundamental national goal and hoped
that it would open a new horizon for Ba'thist
members. Although a number of Ba'th leaders—
Akram al-Hawrani, Salah al-Din al-Baytar and others—were given high posts in the new regime, they
were shorn of real power. It was soon realized that
Nasir had no great interest in Ba'th teachings and
demanded the dissolution of the Ba'th Party—indeed, he demanded the dissolution of all Syrian political parties—and tried to administer Syria directly through his own appointees.[8]

Disenchantment with the Nasir regime began to
spread into the Syrian Army soon after Nasir demanded that all Syrian officers refrain from political activities. He dismissed some from service and

---

[8]As Salah al-Din al-Baytar once told me, Nasir tried to administer
Syria as one of Egypt's northern provinces and not as a full partner.
See Ahmad 'Abd al-Karim, *Adwa' 'Ala Tajribat al-Wihda* [Light on
the Unity Experience] (Damascus, 1962), pp. 139-43.

transferred others to Egypt, replacing them with Egyptian officers.[9] Among those transferred to Egypt were Asad and some of the officers who ruled Syria after secession from Egypt—Salah Jadid, Amin al-Hafiz and others. Virtually relieved from official work, they began to meet secretly and discuss Syria's difficulties under Egyptian rule. Asad said that he wasted his time by shuttling every day between home and office doing virtually nothing constructive. It became clear that the services of Syrian officers were neither needed nor appreciated by their Egyptian superiors. Secret contacts with fellow officers at home indicated that their condition was not much better, and led them to believe that unity with Egypt could not last too long.

Informal meetings among the Syrian officers led gradually to serious talks about the need for action. They decided to form a secret military organization which later came to be known as the Military Committee of the Ba'th Party. By 1960 the Committee began to meet regularly, composed first of five members. Later the number rose to more than a dozen.[10] The founders, whether by accident or design, belonged to the 'Alawi (Shi'i) community, because they came originally from the same locality and shared the same views about Syria's subordination to Egyptian rule. Upon the enlargement of

[9]Nasir dismissed no less formidable an officer than General 'Afif al-Badhri (al-Bizri), Chief of Staff, on the ground that he had communist leanings, though al-Badhri had cooperated with the Ba'th Party and supported union with Egypt (See Ahmad 'Abd al-Karim, op. cit., pp. 131-33.

[10]The five founders of the Military Committee were Muhammad 'Umran, Salah Jadid, Hafiz al-Asad, 'Abd al-Karim al-Jundi and Ahmad al-Mir. For the origins and composition of the Committee, see Colonel Muhammad 'Umran, Tajribati Fi al-Thawra [My Experience in the Revolution] (Bayrut, 1970), pp. 18-19.

the Committee, members of other groups joined
and, by gradual process, the full implication of
which they themselves did not always perceive,
they tried to take over leadership of the Ba'th
Party from older members.[11] They maintained that
the older leaders—'Aflaq, Baytar and Hawrani—
had betrayed the party by acquiescing in Nasir's
demand to dissolve the party. As a result, the unity
achieved under Nasir had become entirely different from that enshrined in the Ba'th program. Nor
did Nasir pay attention to other Ba'thist teachings,
least of all the principles of liberty and democracy
which the Ba'th Party had stressed. The Committee, accordingly, sought cooperation with members
who had little or no sympathy with older leaders
and called for the revival of the Ba'th Party under
new leadership. It is true that Syria's secession
from union with Egypt was carried out by an alliance of diverse military groupings, including Ba'th
officers, but the most instrumental officers were
opposed to unity in principle and the Ba'th officers
played a marginal role in the break-up of the
union. They began to come to the fore in Syrian
politics only after secession had been achieved.[12]

In 1961, when Syria declared her secession from
Egypt, Asad and the other members of the Military

---

[11]Though conscious of their minority origin, they all spoke in the
name of nationalism and stressed Ba'thist principles. There is a tendency among Western writers to overemphasize the communal or
religious background. See Nickolas Van Dam, "The Struggle for
Power in Syria and the Ba'th Party, 1958-1966," *Orient* (Hamburg)
No. 1 (March 1973).

[12]For an account of the forces and events that led up to the break-up
of the Syro-Egyptian union and its subsequent development, see
Robert Mertz, *United Arab Republic, 1958-1961: Arab Unity on Trial*
(Ph.D. unpublished dissertation at SAIS Library, Johns Hopkins University, 1975).

Committee were stationed at the Suez Canal Zone. Though opposed to secession, they were arrested by the Egyptian authorities on the grounds that all Syrian officers had been engaged in secret activities against unity with Egypt. Asad told me that before they were released and sent back to Syria, they served 52 days under arrest. Back in Damascus, they were relieved from service by Syria's new rulers and were entrusted with civilian posts. Asad was given a modest job in the department of overseas transportation. Some 63 officers—some were either Ba'th members or Ba'thist sympathizers—were dismissed from the Army. It did not take long before these officers, disenchanted with what they called the "Separatist Regime," began to establish secret contacts with fellow officers in the Army and moved to overthrow the regime by a military coup (March 8, 1963) on the grounds that it betrayed the principle of Arab unity and therefore was unworthy of survival. The faction that carried out the coup was a mixture of Ba'thist and Nasirite officers who, supported by Iraq and Egypt, denounced the Separatist Regime as anti-nationalist and gave as excuse for deposing it Syria's isolation from its neighbors. A month earlier (February 8, 1963), the Ba'th Party in Iraq, in cooperation with a group of Army officers friendly to Egypt, was able to overthrow the Qasim regime in Baghdad and extend support to the Syrian Ba'th Party to seize power.

The number of the officers who took part in the military coup was very limited—perhaps the most active was Salim Hatum—because Salah Jadid, 'Umran and Asad were then outside the Army. No sooner had the coup begun than they returned to important military posts and the position of the

Ba'th members in the Army began to improve.
Very soon, these officers became very active, and
sought by cooperation with Iraq to strengthen their
position in the Ba'th Party. Negotiations with Nasir,
in which Iraq participated, did not materialize to
restore unity, and Syria reverted to an isolationist
policy in which factionalism and a struggle for
power among rival officers ensued. Three officers—Amin al-Hafiz, Salah Jadid and 'Umran—distinguished themselves as a power bloc which ruled
Syria from 1963 to 1966. At the outset, Amin al-Hafiz, cooperating with Jadid, eliminated 'Umran; and
then Jadid, cooperating with Hafiz al-Asad, eliminated Amin al-Hafiz. In 1966, Jadid, Chief of Staff,
became the strong man who had the Army under
his control. Entrusting the nominal posts of the
Presidency and Premiership to civilians—Nur al-
Din al-Atasi and Zu'ayyin—he ruled Syria with an
iron hand from 1966 to 1970. Meanwhile, Hafiz al-
Asad, at first cooperating with Jadid and satisfied
with the portfolio of Defense, eventually came into
conflict with the Jadid regime because of disagreement on fundamental national issues. Since he was
in control of the Army and Air Force, he moved to
depose Jadid and his faction from their position of
power and establish his own regime without much
difficulty.

III

Hafiz al-Asad's star had begun to rise when he
sided with Salah Jadid in his struggle for power
with Amin al-Hafiz. It was a protracted and tenu-
ous struggle which lasted almost three years, from
1963 to 1966, in which a number of factions were
involved. Outwardly there was no question that

both the Jadid and Hafiz factions were loyal to the
Ba'th Party's principles of Arab unity, freedom and
socialism. But in practice, the Hafiz faction, seeking cooperation with Nasir, accepted his perception
of Arab unity; while the Jadid faction, opposed to
Nasir, held that Arab unity under Nasir's leadership meant Syria's subordination to Egypt and acceptance of the Nasirite pattern of authoritarian
rule. The Hafizites retorted by labeling the
Jadidites as *"qatriyyin"* (regionalists or advocates
of local Syrian feeling considered to be opposed to
Pan-Arab goals) and accused them of promoting
communal interests, because Jadid and his followers belonged to the 'Alawi sect and came originally
from the same locality, while Amin al-Hafiz and
his followers belonged to the Sunni majority and
advocated Pan-Arabism which prescribed Arab
unity as an overriding principle. Moreover, the
Sunni community, comprising the merchant class
of the big towns and cities, was opposed to nationalization of industry and prevailed over the
Hafizites to relax socialist measures, while the
Jadidites, reflecting the feelings of the poorer minority communities, attacked the Hafizites for their
disregard of Ba'thist socialist principles. Polarization between the two factions reached the high-
water mark when both factions, unable to reach
an agreement, resorted to force to settle their differences. Victory of one military faction and its assumption of control of party and state would mean
that the other faction would be thrown out of its
military posts and perhaps liquidated. For this reason the struggle for power had become, in the final
analysis, a struggle for survival.

On February 23, 1966, Jadid seized power by a
military uprising. Hafiz resisted, but the Army

units in the principal cities of Halab (Aleppo), Hums, Hama and Dayr al-Zur supported Jadid. Hafiz al-Asad, in command of the Air Force, tipped the balance by his support of Jadid. Amin al-Hafiz and his faction were arrested and thrown into prison. The civilian leaders of the Ba'th Party fled the country.

Jadid, who held the position of Assistant Secretary General of the Ba'th Party and headed the Military Committee (composed of Ba'thist officers in control of the Army), saw no reason under the new regime to assume nominal titles as Heads of State or Government. He did not even demand to become the Secretary General of the Ba'th Party. There was no question that he emerged as the regime's strong man and the highest positions in the State were entrusted to three civilian protégés— known as the triumvirate of three doctors (as they were physicians by profession)—Nur al-Din al-Atasi, President of the Republic, Yusuf al-Zu'ayyin, Prime Minister, and Ibrahim Makhus, Minister for Foreign Affairs. The three principal military posts—the portfolio of Defense, Chief of Staff and Military Intelligence—were given to three officers—Hafiz al-Asad, Ahmad Suwaydani and 'Abd al-Karim al-Jundi—who had supported him in his struggle for power with Amin al-Hafiz. In addition to the portfolio of Defense, Hafiz al-Asad continued as acting Commander of the Air Force. He was therefore potentially capable of becoming more powerful than Jadid, because the Army and Air Force remained under his control. So long as Asad was on good terms with Jadid there was no question that final decisions were made by Jadid. Very soon, however, the relations between Jadid and Asad began to change.

As the experiences of Syria and other Arab countries have demonstrated, once the military are in the saddle, factionalism leads to a struggle for power and each faction seeks to eliminate the other until a strong military leader eventually emerges who will hold power in his hands and keep the Army firmly under his control. These experiences with military factionalism have been shared by other nations, especially in countries undergoing rapid social change.

Dissension and conflict in the military have arisen either for personal reasons or for lack of agreement among military leaders on essential political questions. Even if the military leaders are guided by well-known doctrines of an established political party, disagreement on the interpretation or the application of those doctrines often gives rise to rivalry and dissension among quarrelsome leaders and groups. As a consequence, no sooner had the Jadid regime begun to operate than differences ensued between Jadid and Asad and their followers. Polarization between the two factions led to a struggle for power rationalized on differing interpretations of doctrines which the two factions had accepted in principle.

How did the conflict among the military begin?

From the time the Ba'th Party achieved power in 1963 there had already been in existence two major groups within the party: one, a left-wing, asserting radical socialist doctrines and the other, a right-wing, stressing moderate socialist views. There were also differences on priorities. The nationalist-minded members stressed the principle of Arab unity as overriding while those who advocated freedom and collectivist principles did not wish to see these principles abandoned or neglected simply because Arab unity had to take precedence when Syria and Egypt agreed to unite under Nasir's leadership. These and other differing views were reflected in the Army, accentuated by factional and personal reasons. In order to resolve the issue, civilian leaders often appealed to the military for support which in effect meant that the military members of the Ba'th Party were invited to become the arbiters whenever there were political or ideological differences among civilian leaders. Since a well-organized Military Committee had already been in existence, the military members of the Ba'th Party became the strongest power bloc after secession from Egypt. The military, opposed to the leaders who had agreed to dissolve the Ba'th Party under Nasir's leadership, supported the left-wing group who sought to get rid of the right-wing group—'Aflaq, Baytar and others. Though moderate leaders tried in two party congresses—the sixth (1964) and seventh (1965)—to reconcile the military with civilian leaders by focusing attention on principles rather than on personalities, the issue remained unresolved and the trend was unmistakably toward the domination of the party by military leaders. The assumption of power by Jadid in 1966 was a victory for the faction that stressed socialist doctrines and the older leaders were pushed to the background.[13]

Very soon, the Jadid faction, supported by radical elements, moved further to the left by offering new interpretations of Ba'thist principles. For in-

---

[13]Though opposed to the old leadership, it was the younger civilians rather than the military members who pressed for the expulsion of the old leaders—'Aflaq, Baytar and Akram al-Hawrani—from the Ba'th Party (the writer's interview with President Asad, Damascus, January 19, 1980).

stance, they talked about "Scientific Socialism,"
which was understood to mean Marxist Socialism,
and began to apply it by nationalization of land in
the countryside and industry. True, this was not
the first time nationalization was enforced—indeed, it was first introduced by the Nasir regime
and stopped after secession—but the Jadidites carried it a step further by applying it to private ownership in urban areas. Most members reacted negatively and urged moderation. But the conflict
between left- and right-wing groups continued unabated, which undermined the position of the
whole party in the country. Hafiz al-Asad, urged
by moderates to save the country from falling into
radical hands, warned against departure from established Ba'thist teachings. He began to criticize
nationalization of small industries which unnecessarily aroused public concern and pointed out that
while Arab Socialism prescribed public ownership
of industry it also encouraged free enterprise in
the private sector and recognized the principle of
private property.

The Jadidites, gradually losing ground in the
party and throughout the country, began to depend solely on loyal members who supported the
regime while civil servants suspected of disloyalty
were ignored and looked upon with disfavor. As a
result, the Jadidites gradually lost the confidence
of the people as a whole. In an effort to strengthen
their position, they resorted to high-handed methods which aggravated the situation and increased
tension in the country.

Nor was the isolation of the regime confined to
domestic affairs. It was also reflected in the conduct of foreign affairs. Ideological in outlook, the
Jadidites often looked upon their Arab neighbors

with a critical eye and branded the moderate regimes of Jordan and the Arabian Peninsula as the
allies of imperialism and backwardness. Only the
regimes that advocated radical and revolutionary
doctrines were considered progressive and nationalist, as in Egypt, Iraq and Algeria. This attitude
was reflected in the press and broadcasts and in
official statements made in regional and international councils. The Syrian people began to feel the
impact of isolation, as it affected their own personal as well as the country's trade relations with
their neighbors. Even travel to Lebanon, a country
closely connected with Syria, was prohibited without official permission from the Ministry of Interior, although the crossing of frontiers between the
two countries had required no such permits in the
past.

  This situation was accentuated when the clouds
of war with Israel appeared on the horizon and
fighting became imminent in the spring of 1967.
The Jadidites seem to have been bent on entering
into a confrontation with Israel—indeed, some of
their statements about Israeli retaliation were pro-
vocative and highly inflammatory—and consciously sought to involve Nasir, hoping that war
with Israel might enhance their prestige in the
Arab World, as Israel would be compelled to fight
on two fronts. Even after Egypt had lost the war,
the Jadidites urged that the fighting be continued
on the Vietnam model, and appealed to the people
to engage the enemy and prolong the war. Hafiz
al-Asad, Minister of Defense, rejected this strategy
and called their attention to the fallacy of compar-
ing the Arab-Israeli War with the Vietnam War. He
conceded that popular support was necessary, but
pointed out that the reorganization and strengthen-

ing of the Syrian Army was the only guarantee against renewal of fighting with the highly mechanized Army of Israel. Asad's strategy, supported by most of the officers, enhanced his position in the Army.

Asad tried to persuade the Jadidites to change their policies at several meetings of the Ba'th Party but failed. At the Fourth Regional and the Tenth National Command Congresses (1968-69), he appealed to them to respond to public appeals to relax Marxist measures, but, by rhetorical statements and the pressure of activists, they dominated the meetings. As a last resort, Asad proposed to establish a National Front in order to solicit the support of other parties. He also called for the promulgation of a new Constitution and the holding of elections for a National Assembly. But all his efforts were in vain.

Matters came to a head on the question of supporting the PLO in its struggle for power in Jordan in September 1970. Considering King Husayn as an obstacle to a hard-line policy against Israel, the Jadidites decided to intervene in favor of the PLO. Asad objected on the grounds that the Army had not yet been sufficiently strengthened and its intervention might lead to war with Israel, but the Jadidites rejected his warning. They dispatched a force that was intercepted by the Jordanian Army and the intervention, despite heavy initial Jordanian losses, failed to rescue the PLO from defeat.[14]

The fiasco in Jordan heightened the tension within the Ba'th Party and the Jadidites decided to

---

[14]In 1980 Asad resorted to the same method of trying to put pressure on King Husayn to postpone an Arab Summit meeting in 'Amman, though it is doubtful that he intended to go to war with Jordan if King Husayn failed to accommodate to the Syrian demand.

get rid of Asad and his followers. Asad was not unaware of Jadidite intentions; therefore, he and his
close supporters began to make preparations to remove the Jadidites from power. During October
and early November the two contending factions
were closely watching each other before they
clashed; by the middle of November Jadid finally
issued orders to dismiss Asad and his followers
from the Army. In full control of the Army, Asad
replied by alerting the chiefs of divisions to be
ready. Moreover, the Air Force Command was on
his side.

Asad proved equal to the occasion. On the eve of
his move to depose Jadid, he met with his principal supporters to review the situation. They were
aware that the Jadidites had become very unpopular and the country was ready for a change of regime. Since the key military posts were in the
hands of officers sympathizing with Asad's position, it was decided that Asad should proclaim
publicly his assumption of supreme command and
present himself directly to the nation as temporary
Chief of State until new elections for the Presidency and the People's Assembly would be held.
Jadid and his faction, including the President of
the Republic and the Cabinet, were denounced as
traitors who betrayed the Party and the country
and were therefore unworthy to remain in power.

It was a bloodless *coup d'état*. At midnight (November 16, 1970) the Chief of Military Police dispatched a detachment with instructions to inform
the Heads of State and Government, Cabinet Ministers and a few others in high positions, that they
were from that moment under house arrest.[15]

---

[15]They were told that if they were to remain quiet and confined to
their houses, their lives would be secure and receive their regular

Some, like Jadid and Zu'ayyin, were detained and later thrown into prison. Ibrahim Makhus, the Foreign Minister, fled the country and found asylum in Algeria. Still others, considered dangerous to the regime, were arrested and imprisoned.[16]

The move to bring the Jadid regime to an end was not called by Asad's supporters a "revolution" but a "corrective movement" *(Al-haraka al-tashihiyya)* designed merely to get rid of a handful of extremists who had departed from Ba'thist teachings as set forth in Party Congresses and had imposed Marxist doctrines and unpopular measures considered alien to the Party. Nor was Asad's seizure of power considered a military uprising, as no military action was in fact necessary. The top military leaders, aware of tacit public support, felt confident of their ability to remove the Heads of State and Government and others in high offices who had become puppets in the hands of Jadid, without firing a shot.

The purpose of the "corrective movement," Asad declared, was to confirm the goals of the Ba'th and its platform, made public in 1963 (when it first achieved power) and reiterated in 1966. The fundamental points embodied in the proclamation issued by the Temporary Regional Command (set up on November 16, 1970) were as follows:

1. A Progressive National Front, composed of all political parties and groups, would be established under the leadership of the Ba'th Party.
2. A People's Assembly, representing various na-

---

pension, but if they were to engage in surreptitious activities they would be thrown into prison.

[16]Most of those under arrest were later released, but the principal figures—Jadid, Zu'ayyin and Atasi—as well as a few others are still in prison today.

tional organizations and groups, would be called to prepare a draft permanent Constitution and to function as a legislative body.

3. Social and economic programs would be laid down, designed to reconstruct an equitable society in which the individual's dignity and freedom are respected.

4. The Armed Forces, designed to achieve national objectives, would be organized and strengthened.

5. A law for the reorganization of local administration would be enacted.

6. In foreign affairs, the new regime promised to promote Arab cooperation and the achievement of Arab unity with Egypt and other progressive countries such as Libya and Sudan. It also promised support of the Palestine Liberation Organization (PLO), the strengthening of relations with the Soviet Union and other progressive countries, and support of National Liberation Movements throughout the world.[17]

From the moment he seized power, Asad consciously tried to rule not only in the name of the Ba'th Party, but as leader of the country as a whole who would put all national organizations, including his own party, in the service of the nation. The regime over which he presided may be said to be based partly on Ba'thist teachings, but mainly on Syria's past experiences and on Asad's own interpretations of his Party's guidelines. He

---

[17]For text of the Proclamation, see *Al-Ba'th*, Damascus, November 17, 1970. These points were reiterated by Asad in a speech to the public (December 5, 1970) on the occasion of a rally organized in support of the new regime. For text of the speech, see Ministry of Defense (Public Affairs Division), *Majum'at Khutab Hafiz al-Asad* [Compilation of Asad's *Speeches*] (Damascus, 1971), Vol. I, pp. 21-29. (Hereafter referred to as Asad's *Speeches*).

said time and time again that he was in favor of democracy. Popular participation, he insisted, was the best safeguard against recurring military uprisings. Nor could reform and development be carried out unless the regime is spared instability and civil strife among rival political and religious groups. But he is not unaware that a stable and viable regime cannot be constructed overnight. It has to evolve from existing institutions and improvised in the light of past experiences.

Ever since he seized power, Asad has proceeded with full vigor and determination to reconstruct a regime that would achieve the objectives set forth in his proclamation on November 16, 1970. Before he took any positive step, he had first to remove some of the harsh measures adopted by the former regime such as martial law and other security regulations which had existed since the Six-Day War. Moreover, restrictions on travel were abolished and Syrians living abroad were encouraged to return. Amnesty to all who left the country for political reasons since the first military coup took place in 1949 was granted. Regulations governing foreign trade were liberalized and private enterprises encouraged. Wages and family allowances were increased and the prices of essentials— flour, tea, coffee, sugar—were reduced to assist the poor and low-income earners. These and other measures were needed before conditions that had deteriorated under previous regimes began to improve.

In order to achieve popular participation, Asad began to take preparatory steps for the establishment of a popularly elected People's Assembly. On February 16, 1971, a decree was issued to establish a temporarily appointed People's Assembly composed of 173 members, representing various national organizations and corporate bodies, whose functions were to prepare a draft Constitution (to be submitted to the public for approval by a plebiscite) and approve all the laws and decrees that had been issued since the regime was set up on November 16, 1970. The Assembly, convened on February 22, 1971, and presided over by Ahmad al-Khatib (Temporary President of the Republic), began to prepare a draft Constitution.

On March 12, 1971, Asad was elected President of the Republic by a national plebiscite upon his nomination by the People's Assembly and the recommendation of the Regional Command. He appeared before the Assembly for the oath on March 14, 1971, and promised to achieve Syria's national aspirations.[18] The Assembly set to work and passed a number of laws and regulations, including a law for the reorganization and the distribution of powers among local administrative councils and a law for the abolition of illiteracy. It took more than a year before the draft Constitution was ready for debate by the Assembly on February 20, 1973. It was finally submitted for approval by a national plebiscite on March 12, 1973, and was promulgated on the following day.[19]

The Constitution provided that Syria is an Arab country and its people part of the Arab nation which aspires to form a federation of Arab Republics. Its system of government, based on Ba'thist teachings, is democratic and socialist, designed to achieve freedom and justice for all. Islam is de-

---

[18]For text of the speech, see Asad's *Speeches*, Vol. I, pp. 149-55.

[19]For text of the Constitution, see People's Assembly, *Dustur al-Jumhuriya al-'Arabiya al-Suriya* [Constitution of the Syrian Arab Republic] (Damascus, 1973).

clared to be the religion of the President of the Republic and a source for legislation. The Ba'th Party is a "leader party"; but will cooperate with other parties in a National Progressive Front. Though the form of government is Presidential, a Cabinet headed by a Prime Minister is appointed by the President and made responsible to him. The President, elected directly by the people, is not responsible to the People's Assembly. He is leader of the Ba'th Party in the capacity of a Secretary General. Since its establishment in 1973, he has also become the head of the National Front and chaired its meetings. Thus Asad has virtually brought under his control all national organizations. But as member of the Ba'th Party, he has to abide by the decisions of its Regional and National Commands.

Even before he achieved power, Asad often urged the Ba'th Party to cooperate with other "progressive" parties and national organizations which have similar goals. He realized that before the Ba'th Party could claim popular support, cooperation with other groups was necessary before the principles of Arab unity, freedom and socialism were fully accepted. In 1969, the Communist Party proposed to collaborate with the Ba'th Party on the basis of a National Front, but the Jadid regime, bent on the monopoly of power, was not in favor of collaboration. Afer he seized power, Asad abandoned that policy and began to negotiate with other parties to form a National Progressive Front. In 1971, a committee representing various political groups met to discuss the charter of the Front, composed of the following parties:

1. The Ba'th Party, called the "leader party," represented by nine members.
2. The Arab Socialist Union Party, often called

the Nasirites and led by Fawzi al-Kayyali, represented by two members.

3. The Syrian Communist Party, led by Khalid Bakdash, represented by two members.
4. The Arab Socialists, led by 'Abd al-Ghani Qannut, represented by two members.
5. The Union Socialists, led by Fa'iz Isma'il, represented by two members.

The aims of the Front, as stated in its Charter, were as follows:

1. Liberation of the Arab territory occupied by Israel in 1967 (this is regarded as an overriding objective and precedes all others).
2. Decisions on all matters relating to war and peace.
3. Approval of a Five-Year Plan laid down by the government to achieve social and economic development.
4. Approval of plans for national education which would create public opinion in support of the battle of liberation and the establishment of an Arab socialist society.
5. Implementation of democratic institutions which would enable the public to exercise its rights to achieve national aims.
6. The development and strengthening of the Army as the shield of the country and the means for its liberation. All forms of conflict and strife within the armed forces are prohibited. Therefore all parties except the Ba'th Party should abstain from establishing contacts with the armed forces or from fostering dissension or conflict within the Army. Similarly, parties other than the Ba'th should abstain from contacting students or involving them in political activities.

7. Before the goals of the organization are achieved, the Front will lay down a transitional program of social change to prepare the country for ultimate changes.

8. In foreign affairs, the charter stressed the need for cooperation with other Arab countries to liberate Arab lands occupied by Israel and to use all possible means to achieve national goals. Arab unity is deemed essential to resist Zionist encroachments and achieve national goals. Support for the rights of Palestinians is considered one of the Front's primary objectives. Not only Zionism is declared the principal enemy of the Arabs but also the powers that give it support. The socialist countries, especially the Soviet Union, are considered friendly powers and the Front aims at cultivating and strengthening relations with them. It also seeks cooperation with Islamic and other countries of the Third World. Indeed, all countries, including Europe and the West, that might give positive support to the Arabs are considered friendly countries. Finally, the Front will give support to all world progressive and national liberation movements which seek emancipation from foreign domination and pursue social and economic development.[20]

Second only to the Ba'th, the Communist Party is the most highly organized and active political party in the country. Yet it was assigned only two seats in the Front—an equal number of representatives with the other small parties—presumably on the grounds that the Front is not a coalition Govern-

[20]For text of the Charter, see Ba'th Party, *Charter of the National Progressive Front* (Damascus, 1972).

ment but a forum in which differing views are presented. The Ba'th Party, as the "leader party," is alone responsible for all the decisions carried out by the regime. This arrangement allowed the Communist Party to feel free to hold its own views on public affairs and in the party's congresses sharp criticism was often leveled against the regime for the deterioration in economic conditions.[21] In its Seventh Regional Congress (December 1979), the Ba'th Party felt the need to pay attention to differing views of other members of the National Progressive Front and sought their cooperation in an effort to improve social and economic conditions.[22]

As the "leader party," the Ba'th depended more heavily on its own organizations and tried to bring them into full operation within the State. Under the former regime, the Jadidites paid little or no attention to the Party's apparatus and depended only on a few loyal members to control the Party and run the country. To restore confidence, Asad urged all members to participate and assume responsibility for the work assigned to them. Party Congresses—National and Regional—met regularly every four years to scrutinize the work of the regime and make recommendations on all matters concerning domestic and foreign policy. The Party's apparatus was set to carry out the recommenda-

[21]See the opening speech of Khalid Bakdash, Secretary General of the Communist Party, before the Fourth Communist Party Congress, September 26-28, 1974 (Damascus, 1974); and the Communist Party Central Committee, *Taqrir al-Maktab al-Siyasi* [Report of The Political Bureau] (Damascus, 1977).

[22]In his statement at the opening meeting of the Ba'th Regional Congress (December 22, 1979), Khalid Bakdash urged further cooperation between his party and the Ba'th both in domestic and foreign policy, especially stressing the need for cooperation with the Soviet Union and other socialist countries (see *Kalimat Khalid Bakdash* [The Bakdash Statement], Damascus, 1979).

tions proposed by the Party's Congresses. The Regional Command, composed of twenty-one members, addressed itself to internal affairs. The National Command, composed of a dozen members, dealt with foreign affairs. Both are ordinarily headed by Asad as Secretary-General of the Ba'th Party, but in practice his functions are exercised by two deputy Secretaries-General and Asad chaired the meetings only when the two Commands met to discuss fundamental questions of policy.[23] In his capacity as Secretary-General of the National Front, composed of seventeen members representing the various parties and groups that form the Front, the decisions taken are submitted to the Cabinet for execution. Moreover, Asad often discusses major issues with leading members of the Party and seeks the advice of counsellors from various organizations before he makes public statements about policies. Often his statements were taken to represent the official position of the Ba'th Party, because he had already consulted leading members of the Party. So central has his position become in the country that he has officially been called Leader of the Procession *(Qa'id al-Masira)*, a symbolic identification of his leadership with the "Arab revival" which the Ba'th Party claims to

---

[23]At its last meeting (December 5, 1979), the Regional Command Congress established a Central Committee, composed of 75 members, as a new organ whose functions were to elect from its own members the new members of the Regional Command and to act on behalf of the Regional Congress on all matters relating to regional affairs until its next meeting four years later. Another committee, called the Control and Supervisory Committee, composed of five members was set up to deal with possible irregularities in the conduct of party members (for composition of these new organs, see *al-Thawra*, Damascus, December 8, 1979).

represent in its efforts to construct an Arab socialist society.[24]

Asad is the last to claim that Syria has become a
socialist society; he concedes that it has just begun
to develop along the lines laid down by the Ba'th
Party. In order to achieve its goals, the Ba'th Party,
in cooperation with other groups, is engaged in
laying down ambitious programs designed to transform society step-by-step from a traditional to a
modern nation-state. But Asad and his followers
are not unaware of the difficulties that they have
to overcome before the country is placed along the
path of progress and development.[25]

Whether it is the legacy of the Jadid or earlier
regimes, the Army has not yet been brought under
full control and the officers are still in the habit of
using their influence for personal advantages. Asad
has spoken frankly on the subject with the military
to restrict their influence, but personal influence
has not yet been completely eliminated. Even more
widespread are the corrupt practices of bribery
and nepotism which are compounded by inflation
and higher prices, despite disciplinary measures
and an appeal to the bureaucracy and national or-

---

[24]When the Seventh Regional Congress was in session in December
1979, the writer was on a visit to Damascus and had the opportunity
of learning at first hand the composition and working of the principal organs of the Ba'th Party.

[25]The projects of social and economic development are embodied in
five-year plans, two of which have already been carried out by the
Ba'th Party since Asad had come to power in 1970. It is deemed outside the scope of this work to discuss developmental plans and problems (a summary of the plans may be found in *Tishrin*, Damascus,
December 5, 1979). For a critical evaluation of economic development, see the report of the Central Committee of the Syrian Communist Party, entitled *Taqrir 'An al-Wad' al-Iqtisadi Fi al-Bilad* [Report
on the Country's Economic Conditions] (Damascus, 1978).

ganizations to improve the conditions of civil servants and employees and inspire high morale and
efficiency.

Above all, Asad has to deal with the lingering
sectarian problem *(al-ta'ifiyya)* which has become
a serious threat to the very existence of the regime.
The Sunni-Shi'i tension in Syria—indeed, in some
other Arab lands too—seemed to have subsided
after World War I, when Arab nationalism began
to supersede religious identity, but in recent years,
when the 'Alawi community became active in politics, the sectarian tension has been heightened, especially under the Jadid regime, as an increasing
number of Army officers belonging to this community began to occupy the highest positions in the
State. Asad, though himself an 'Alawi, has shown
no sign of sectarian bias and has done his utmost
to stress nationalism as a symbol of unity; but
Sunni extremists, especially the Muslim Brothers,
have become too active and have consciously
aroused sectarian feeling against the 'Alawi community as a means to undermine the regime. The
Muslim Brothers, opposed in principle to secular
nationalism, have criticized Arab nationalists even
in countries governed by Sunni rulers. But in Syria
their opposition to 'Alawi rulers has found an appeal in circles opposed to the Ba'th Party for political reasons that have nothing to do with sectarianism. Leaders of the Muslim Brotherhood who have
been caught in sabotage activities, like the recent
attack on the Aleppo Military Academy and elsewhere, have been arrested and tried for subversive
activities; but the sectarian question as a whole is
in need of a constructive approach as its roots go
deeper in society than a struggle for power among
rival political leaders. So long as the Sunni-Shi'i di-

vision of society continues to exist, as the classic
example of confessional division in Lebanon demonstrated, it is bound to be associated with political
activities. Though Asad has proved to be immune
to sectarian influences, he has yet to inspire the
men around him to follow his example and to deal
with the situation not as a political but as a social
problem which should be handled with care and a
high degree of toleration and patience.

IV

In foreign affairs, where communal dissension
had little or no direct influence, Asad proved more
successful in pursuing national objectives than in
domestic affairs, and his reputation as a skillful
diplomat enhanced his prestige and strengthened
his hold over the country. Isolated from the outside world under the Jadid regime, Syrians welcomed Asad's policy of repairing Syria's relations
with Arab neighbors and opening her frontiers for
travel without restrictions. Asad's frequent visits to
Arab countries and his negotiations for Arab economic cooperation improved Syria's trade relations
and secured new sources for economic development. His cooperation with Sadat in the planning
and execution of the October War of 1973, resulting in the recovery of some Arab lands occupied
by Israel in 1967, and in the rehabilitation of Arab
pride by victory in the initial stage of the war,
placed him in Arab opinion as an able strategist
and, in his subsequent negotiations with Kissinger,
as the diplomat who could stand firm in asserting
Arab national interests. Considering himself a
spokesman for the Arabs, he asserted Arab national—not only Syrian—objectives, such as Arab

unity, defense against foreign encroachments and others, because the regime over which he presided is the instrument of a party that claims to achieve Arab national and not only local interests.

Asad's foreign policy objectives, however, stem partly from Ba'thist teachings but mainly from Syria's historical role in inter-regional affairs. Asad realized that Syria cannot long isolate itself from Arab interdependence. Since his high school days, he had been lectured by nationalist teachers on Arab unity and almost all the country's leaders had either paid lip service to it as an ideological goal or called for it to divert attention from internal dissension and rivalry among competing groups. By his adoption of Arab unity and other nationalist symbols, Asad's horizon has been widened from that narrow and exclusive communal environment of his locality to the higher national and inter-regional levels which provided a greater opportunity for his generation to improve conditions by cooperation with other communities. When he left school, Arab unity had already become to him a meaningful objective and not a fanciful ideal, and when he entered politics he began to cooperate with other young men to achieve it. Despite disappointments with unity under Nasir's rule, he supported the principle of Arab unity after Syria's secession from Egypt and sought to achieve it by other means.

In agreement with other Arab leaders, Asad maintains that Israel is an obstacle to Arab unity, because its creation was from the beginning facilitated by Arab dissension and lack of agreement on how to deal with the powers that were concerned with the Palestine problem. Had the Arab countries been one state, or had their forces and resources been entrusted to one leadership, it would have been exceedingly difficult for Zionists to establish a Jewish state, and if it were established in the territory assigned to it under the partition plan of 1947, it would not have been able to become so powerful as to threaten its neighbors. Asad therefore has good reason to believe that Arab unity is the best guarantee against Israeli attacks, as the combined Arab human and material resources would enable the Arab countries first to contain and ultimately to reduce Israel from its present preponderant position. It is therefore not surprising to find Asad's mind so preoccupied with the problems of Arab unity and Israel's threats to the Arab world.

However, Asad has found that despite the dangers posed by Israel and its periodic attacks in massive retaliations the Arabs have not been induced to unite. He is not unaware that there are other factors, internal and external, working against Arab unity, but he is confident that the Arab people as a whole aspire to unite and that their leaders will ultimately be able to achieve unity. Nor can Arab unity be achieved overnight. The experience of unity under Nasir has taught many a Pan-Arab leader that a colossal amount of preparation and spade work are needed before the steps to achieve it could be undertaken.[26]

In these circumstances, Asad has come to the

---

[26]In his speech before the final session of the Twelfth Congress of The National Command (July 24, 1975), Asad expounded his views about Arab unity and other political goals which the Congress adopted as representing the official views of the Ba'th Party. For text of the speech, see the National Command (the Ba'th Party), *Nidal Hizb al-Ba'th al-'Arabi al-Ishtiraki*, 1943-1975 [Struggle of the Arab Socialist Party, 1943-1975] (Damascus, 1978), pp. 200-219; and Cultural Committee (the Ba'th Party), *al-Tadamun al-'Arabi wa al-Wihda al-'Arabiyya* [Arab Solidarity and Arab Unity] (Damascus, n.d.) pp. 4-40.

conclusion that what the Arab countries need today is not immediate unity, but Arab solidarity *(al-
tadamun al-'Arabi)* as a step—indeed, an almost
prerequisite step—for ultimate unity. Because the
Arab countries today vary in their political regimes
and in the stages of development, cooperation and
coordination in social and economic development
are obviously essential before steps for unity can
be undertaken, though all share the same historical
and cultural heritage and have a community of interests. Asad is not particularly concerned about
the variety of existing political regimes in the Arab
world, as was Nasir, who prescribed that no country could join Egypt in unity before it had adopted
a socialist model. To Asad, solidarity and cooperation among Arab countries, despite their differing
systems, are more important today than unity, and
should take precedence over it and perhaps over
other national goals. Above all, the threat of Israel,
let alone the injury caused by its arrogance and
display of military power, ought to be a force
strong enough to bring about cooperation and
unity despite disparity in their political regimes.[27]

But if one or two of the Arab countries wish to
unite with Syria, short of an over-all Arab union,
Asad would welcome such a move and would be
prepared to support it. The triparite unity agreement with Egypt and Libya, to which the Sudan
adhered, is a case in point. But Asad is not in favor
of setting forth conditions for unity that would be
impossible to accept, and when Libya and the Su-

---

[27]Asad's views about Arab unity and Arab solidarity, which the Ba'th
Party has officially adopted, have been fully elaborated and com-
mented on by the Cultural Committee (headed by George Saddiqni)
in a number of studies. See Cultural Committee (Ba'th Party), *Silsilat
al-Fikr al-Qawmi al-Ishtiraki* [Serial on Arab Socialist Thought] (Damascus, n.d.) nos. 1 ff.

dan failed to give substance to the unity scheme, he continued to deal with them without reference to unity.

In accordance with Arab solidarity, Asad offered Syria's friendship and cooperation to all other Arab countries irrespective of differences in their internal systems, as he considered cooperation among the Arab countries against Israel more important today than a debate about the form of regimes; least of all did he choose to weigh them on the scale of ideology. He was the first to recognize Sultan Qabus as the new ruler of 'Uman after Sultan Sa'id Bin Taymur was overthrown in 1970. His relations with Jordan is a striking example of his determination to coordinate the foreign policy of the two countries on the basis of mutual interests. Before he seized power in 1970—when he was still Minister of Defense under the Jadid regime—he saw the futility of the conflict between the PLO and King Husayn, as both were equally exposed to danger from Israel, and criticized Jadid for his encouragement of the PLO to engage in a futile struggle for power in Jordan, though Asad was and still is a great supporter of the PLO movement. After he seized power, Asad began to normalize Syria's relations with Jordan and though he has taken steps to bring about coordination between the two countries, relations are far from having been repaired.[28] Above all, he has established good working relationships with Saudi Arabia, which had been disrupted under the former regime, and he found in the late King Faysal readiness to cooper-

---

[28]See note 14 above. Jordan's strained relations with Syria today, caused partly by its support for Iraq, is not expected to last too long, since Jordan's traditional policy is to maintain neutrality with neighbors rather than to take sides in a conflict among them.

ate not only for the mutual interests of their countries but for Arab interests as a whole. This cooperation has continued between Asad and the present Saudi leaders.

Asad's relations with Iraq were governed by a somewhat different set of principles. Since both Iraq and Syria have been ruled by two branches of the same party—both of which consider the principle of Arab unity as overriding—they were expected to unite at the earliest possible moment when the Ba'th Party achieved power in both countries in 1963 and then when the Iraqi Ba'th Party seized power again in 1968. Instead of solidarity and cooperation, an ideological warfare, compounded by personal and local differences, not only prevented unity but fostered dissension and hostilities among the top leaders of the two countries who claimed to be governed by the same set of principles.[29]

Syria's relations with Egypt were weighed by an altogether different scale of criteria. After Nasir's departure, Sadat abandoned Nasir's Pan-Arab drive which brought in its train Arab dissension following the Six-Day War of 1967. Divorced of ideological outlook, Egypt's relation with her Arab neighbors are now being governed by strategic considerations and Egypt's own domestic needs. At first, Asad was quite sympathetic with Sadat's position and was prepared to deal with him on his own terms. The primary factor that prompted Asad to cooperate with Sadat was Egypt's strategic position vis-á-vis Israel; for in the event of a joint

---

[29]For the Syrian Ba'th criticism of the Iraqi rulers, see National Command (Syrian Ba'th Party), *Tahlil Dawr Hukm al-Yamin al-Mashbuh Fi al-Iraq wa Mawqifuna Minhu* [Analysis of the Role of the Right-Wing Rule in Iraq and our Attitude Toward It] (Damascus, n.d.).

action to force Israel to withdraw from occupied
Arab territory, Egypt's role would be indispens-
able, as the combined Syro-Egyptian operations in
the October War of 1973 demonstrated. Asad
agreed with Sadat on the need to bring the conflict
with Israel to an end provided the other Arab
countries concerned—the confrontation states—
would act in concert. But he was opposed to separate deals with Israel on the grounds that any bilateral agreement between Israel and a single Arab
country, especially between Israel and Egypt,
would undermine the position of all other countries. For this reason, Asad was prepared to negotiate the first round of agreements as a step toward
a comprehensive settlement which would establish
peace with Israel as *quid pro quo* for its withdrawal from all Arab lands occupied in 1967. But
when the second Sinai Agreement was signed
(1975), Asad reproached Sadat for entering, without prior consultation with other confrontation
states, into a bilateral agreement the beneficiary of
which—contrary to the larger Arab interests—was
Israel, with little or no important benefit for
Egypt.[30] The rift between Asad and Sadat was
patched up, thanks to Saudi good offices, and Sadat seems to have pledged not to enter into a separate peace agreement again. But when he decided
to embark on his peace initiative and visit Jerusalem in 1977, although he did inform Asad, he did
not heed the warning that such a step might lead
to another separate agreement unless he secured
an Israeli commitment to withdrawal from all ter-

---

[30]For Syrian objections to the Second Sinai Agreement, set forth in a
booklet by the Defense Minister, see Brigadier Mustafa Tallas,
Dirasa 'Askariya Fi Itifaq Sina' al-Siyasi [A Military Study of the Sinai
Political Agreement] (Damascus: Ministry of Defense, The Political
Bureau, 1976).

ritory occupied in 1967.[31] It is true that in his initial negotations with Begin, Sadat demanded withdrawal from all occupied Arab lands as a condition for comprehensive settlement, but he seems to have failed to persuade Begin to accept his terms. Consequently, his acceptance of the Camp David compromise alienated the other Arab parties concerned and prompted them to take diplomatic actions which isolated Egypt from almost all other Arab lands.

If Asad failed to dissuade Sadat from dealing with Israel, he did succeed in impressing on the Iraqi leaders the need to end the ideological conflict between Iraq and Syria and to bring the two countries closer to cooperation and perhaps to unity than at any time before. Camp David, it is true, brought almost all Arab countries to stand together against Sadat's action; but in his dealings with Iraq, Asad was able to go a step further by proposing unity between the two branches of the same party as a step before unity between the two countries could be achieved. Even before pending issues were resolved, however, a struggle for power among Iraqi leaders ensued which postponed action indefinitely. Relations between the two countries have been so strained that Syria condemned Iraq when it went to war with Iran in 1980.

The civil war in Lebanon, a country with which Syria is closely connected, is so vital an issue that

---

[31]Sadat went to Syria for consultation with Asad in a meeting at the Damascus International Airport (November 15, 1977). After Sadat's departure, Asad said at a press conference that he failed to persuade Sadat to stop his bilateral negotiations with Israel, contrary to previous promises not to negotiate a separate peace agreement.

Asad was not expected to react with indifference.[32] Before he came to power, the relations between Syria and Lebanon had deteriorated and the borders between them were closed. Asad put an end to isolation and a new chapter of cooperation was expected to open, especially since Sulayman Faranjiya (Franjieh), then President of Lebanon, was on good personal terms with him. Soon after he came to power, Asad was caught in the events of the civil war which prompted him to take actions not entirely agreeable to the competing parties in Lebanon.

The forces that brought about the civil war were in the making long before Asad seized power in 1970. But his support of the PLO, whose local military arm—The Sa'iqa (the storm)—was an appendage of the Syrian Army, triggered the clash between the competing Lebanese groups in a struggle for power. The inability of the PLO in Jordan to use that country as a base of operation for raids on Israel since 1970 prompted it to increase its activities in southern Lebanon. Since the Lebanese Government tried to restrict PLO military activities because they escalated Israeli retaliations, the PLO supported the left (essentially Muslim) bloc against the right (essentially Christian) bloc, hoping that the victory of the left would allow greater freedom of action for the Palestinians to deal with Israel from Lebanon's southern border.[33]

---

[32]The origins and events of the civil war are deemed outside the scope of this study (see note 35, below).

[33]In accordance with the Cairo Agreement (1969) between the Lebanese Government and the PLO, the Palestinian guerillas were allowed to establish military bases in southern Lebanon provided they carry out their operations inside Israel.

Very soon, however, Asad began to realize that Syrian support for the left would considerably undermine the right and create resentment which might prompt the Christians to seek Israeli support (signs of such possible support had already become known to him) and intensify the struggle and prolong the civil war. He offered his good offices to reconcile the two warring blocs, which he found Faranjiya quite prepared to accept, but leaders of the left, who had won an initial victory, hoped to end the struggle by a defeat of the right which would establish a new balance in the Lebanese confessional structure in favor of the Muslim community.

Since Asad saw grave dangers from allowing an intensification of communal antagonism, to which he was opposed in principle, he decided to intervene in 1976 by military action in order to bring the two parties to reason and end the civil strife. His intervention, which met the initial approval of almost all Lebanese quarters and was supported by other Arab states, saved Lebanon from being split into two separate entities but it did not bring that peace which was desired by all the parties concerned. The Lebanese central Government, undermined by continuation of the war, lacked the strength to impose order and Asad, criticized by both the right and the left, could not give the central Government adequate support save by keeping his military force in the country—an unenviable position in which he finds it more excruciating to continue than to get out. The intervention has become burdensome and costly, although inaction would have brought further disaster by eventually allowing Israel to become the arbiter between the two warring factions with the consequent increase of its threats to his country.

Asad deeply felt that his intervention in the Lebanese civil war was a national duty. Syria and Lebanon are so closely connected by geography and history that no major event has ever occurred in one country without having an impact on the other. If Syria were to play a stabilizing role in the region, the events of the civil war in Lebanon could not be taken with indifference by Syrian leaders.[34] More specifically, Asad felt that if he did not intervene, foreign intervention would be inevitable; consequently, his regime would be undermined and his image in the Arab world tarnished. Above all, if the civil war were prolonged, the country might split into two states, a Muslim and a Christian, the latter becoming a base of operation for Israel against Syria. It is tempting to agree with Asad that if Lebanon were to remain intact, he was bound to intervene and support the central Government rather than allow division and win one part but alienate the other.[35]

Asad's relations with the Great Powers seem to be governed by forces arising essentially from regional rather than global sources. As member of a party that shares with the West certain cultural and moral values, he perhaps would have preferred to be on the side of the Western democracies in the East-West conflict.[36] But the existence of

---

[34]Some Christians in Lebanon have construed Syrian interventions as a pretext to dominate the country and eventually to annex it as part of Greater Syria. For Christian fear of domination, see Rashid Aoun and Elias el-Hayek, *Syria's Design for Lebanon* (Washington: Lebanese Information and Research Center, 1979).

[35]For the background of intervention, see Asad's *Speeches*, Vol. VI (1976), pp. 101-154. See also Adeed I. Dawisha, "Syria in Lebanon: Assad's Vietnam," *Foreign Policy*, (Winter, 1978-79), pp. 135-150; and *Syria and the Lebanese Crisis* (London, 1980).

[36]See George Tu'ma (Tomeh), "Syria and Neutralism," *The Dynamics of Neutralism in the Arab World*, ed. F.A. Sayegh (San Francisco, 1964), p. 124.

Israel in the heart of the Arab World has aroused deep concern and prompted some of the Arab countries to seek the support of the Soviet bloc, because the Western Powers have taken an active part in Israel's creation and maintenance by providing her with weapons and economic assistance. Asad's concern is even deeper, as he warned the Arab World of Israel's seemingly expansionist policy not only because it occupied part of Syrian territory without any visible sign or willingness to return it but also, citing the views of Zionist extremists, because of Israel's alleged ultimate objective of establishing an empire extending from the River Nile to the Euphrates.[37]

Of the two Super Powers, Asad realizes that the United States is the Power that has greater influence in world affairs and can have a more decisive role in the peaceful settlement of the Arab-Israeli conflict. He would have preferred to cooperate and indeed to depend to a greater extent on the United States than on any other Great Power. But the United States, Asad held, is so deeply commited to the support of Israel that she has in fact if not in name become "the ally of our enemy." Small wonder that he cannot depend on American goodwill to achieve an equitable settlement of the Arab-Israeli conflict, as his experiences under the Nixon and Carter administrations have demonstrated, although he concedes that Carter seemed to admit the validity of Arab rights and recognized in particular the Palestinian right to have a homeland and participate in the choice of the form of government by self-determination.

Asad maintains that since Israel has been receiv-

---

[37]See Asad's *Speeches*, Vol. 1 (1970-71), p. 165; Vol. III (1972-73), p. 21.

ing major military and financial support from the United States, presumably for defense though in reality for asserting its preponderant position in the Arab World, he was and is still bound to depend on Soviet support, as the only means to stand up to the challenge and defend both his country and other Arab lands from Israeli encroachments. In offering its assistance, Asad goes on to say, the Soviet Union has not demanded special privileges from Syria nor was he prepared to compromise his country's independence in dealing with it or with any other power. For long Asad resisted the temptation of entering into formal alliance with the Soviet Union, but Syria's conflicts with Egypt and Iraq and Israel's recurring threats to Lebanon seem finally to have forced him to enter into a formal Soviet alliance to strengthen Syria's position vis-à-vis its neighbors, as Egypt and Iraq had done before him.[38] Syria, however, had already signed trade agreements with the Soviet Union and paid in cash for the weapons and services that have been extended to her. Asad had often reiterated the special friendship that has existed between his country and the Soviet Union, because the Soviet Union has actively supported the Arabs against Israeli attacks, and he seems to have maintained on the whole good personal relations with Soviet leaders. But Asad has not always acted in accordance with Soviet demands, as his intervention in Lebanon, which ran contrary to Soviet policy in supporting left-wing groups, has demonstrated. Nor has he been engaged elsewhere in revolutionary activities inspired or supported by Soviet orientation or resources. In his foreign policy, Asad has

---

[38]The Egypto-Soviet treaty, signed in 1972, was terminated in 1975 (see p. 156, above).

been primarily concerned with regional and not global conflicts.

More specifically, Asad is now preoccupied mainly with the Arab-Israeli conflict. He has accepted the principles enshrined in the United Nations resolutions 242 and 338 and agreed to make peace with Israel, which no Arab revolutionary leader except Sadat has yet accepted, provided Israel would withdraw from the territories she had occupied in 1967. He also supported the Palestinian demand to establish a homeland on the West Bank and in Ghazza and their claim to exercise the right of self-determination concerning their future, whether to establish an independent state or to associate with another country. In accordance with the Arab declaration at Rabat (1974), recognizing the PLO as the sole representative of the Palestinian people, he has continued to support that organization in its struggle to assert Palestinian rights. For this reason, when Sadat undertook his peace initiative and signed the Camp David and subsequent agreements without consultation with or participation of the other parties concerned, including the PLO, Asad denounced Sadat's actions because he failed to honor his promise to act in concert with other Arab countries and abandoned the principle of withdrawl from occupied Arab territories in accordance with UN resolutions 242 and 338.

V

Situated at the cross roads of the Levant, Syria has been exposed to the invasions of armies and ideas from all sides throughout its history. As a result, Syrians have always been fearful of foreign pressures and their concern about their newly won freedom from foreign control has rendered the country extremely vociferous and difficult to govern. Since independence, Pan-Arabism has inspired Syrians with the sense of a mission that all Arab lands, especially those surrounding them, should unite in one Arab State, in order to become strong enough to assert independence and resist foreign pressures. The Ba'th Party has given a practical expression to this sense of a mission, embodied in the three slogans of unity, freedom and socialism.

In an attempt to overcome internal difficulties, Syria has been grappling with the problem of establishing a stable regime capable of achieving national aspirations. Yet, ever since French control was terminated and independence achieved, Syria has witnessed no less than some twenty violent changes of government, not counting attempts to change that failed to materialize, which made it exceedingly difficult to do anything constructive. The manifestation of this internal turbulence has been seen by outside observers as constant shifting of power, anti-Western feeling (often depicted in the press as xenophobia) and isolationism. Instability may be inherent in a fragmented society, but in Syria the problem has been compounded by regional cross-currents, and foreign pressures.

To the outside world the present regime might not seem different from others which have preceded it, save that it has survived more than a decade. But to Syrians stability is very important; for, if any constructive work is ever done, public order and a viable regime to enforce it are necessary. From the day Asad seized power, his regime has been received with overwhelming relief because he put an end to an unpopular regime that ruled by terror and kept the country in complete fear of alienation contrary to Syrian aspirations to cooperate with Arab neighbors and achieve national goals.

Asad's greatest asset for survival is his sensitivity to the popular demand (to which former rulers had paid little or no attention) to overcome alienation and isolation from Arab neighbors by opening Syria's borders and promoting solidarity and cooperation with them. Solidarity and Arab unity—the first adopted by the Ba'th Patry as a means to achieve the other as an ultimate goal—are symbols of identification for Syrians who aspire to play a meaningful role in the Pan-Arab movement. From his early school days, Asad has firmly believed in Arab unity and after achieving power he found in it a worthy goal to rally the country in his drive to resist foreign encroachments and cooperate with countries prepared to support him. He has often said that he deeply felt that these goals should be realized as a national duty—a feeling shared by the Syrian people as a whole who consider their country the cradle of Pan-Arabism and therefore have an obligation to achieve it.

Asad has often reminded us that it was this obligation which prompted him to enter politics; the fact that circumstances gave him an opportunity to assume power does not in his eyes mean that he sought power for the sake of power. "If I ever felt that I have failed in my duty," he once said, "or that I lost the confidence of my people, I would never stay in power for a single moment." He never considered himself, in his own words, "an aspirant for power" (*min huwat al-sulta*); author-

ity to him is responsibility and its assumption is a
form of national duty.[39]

Idealistic as these claims may seem, Asad is appreciative of the power he wields and has indeed
tried to be moderate and realistic in his approach
to solving problems. True, he belongs to an ideological party and in some of his public statements
he is still in the habit of reiterating Ba'thist slogans,
but he no longer utters them as abstract words
without qualifications. He is well aware that Arab
unity, freedom and socialism are goals not for immediate applications but for the future. The
achievement of any one is not an easy undertaking;
it requires hard work and preparation before it is
translated into reality. He has learned this lesson
since the Ba'th Party achieved power in 1963. He
realized that most of the Ba'th leaders who preceded him had failed because they tried to put
Ba'thist teachings into practice by imposing them
on the country by force without its having been
prepared for them. He insisted that these teachings
should be applied in a manner that would improve
conditions and serve the national interests. No
party will ever succeed, he admonished his followers, if it alienates the people and imposes its doctrines by force, as the experiences of the Jadid regime have demonstrated. Thus, socialism to him is
not necessarily the abolition of private property or
nationalization of industry, but the use of the
country's resources for public welfare in an equitable manner and the encouragement of private
enterprise without necessarily compromising collectivist doctrines.

---

[39]See Asad's *Speeches*, Vol. VI, (1976), p. 106.

No less significant are Asad's attitudes in public pronouncements and in private conversations. While in public speeches he has revealed a certain emotionalism and used some harsh words, in private conversations however he has shown patience, calmness and willingness to listen to his visitors without revealing signs of discomfort or irritation even if their views run contrary to his convictions. But when his turn to state his own position comes, he always presents his views and arguments with clarity, candidness and self-assurance which often inspired sympathy with him. No matter how sharply disagreement may be with a visitor, he rarely raises his voice or reacts with anger. Cordiality and respect seem to have always prevailed in his dealings with others.

Though Asad is considered a moderate, he can be firm and even ruthless when the occasion calls for it. He does not hesitate to bring to trial and order execution of persons who disturb public tranquility or conspire against the regime, whether it takes the form of a military plot or communal instigations. The recent 'Alawi-Sunni antagonism in Aleppo and several other towns, stirred by opponents to the regime, are cases in point. Asad's reaction was prompt and exemplary—these incidents, he warned, should be stopped immediately because they disturbed public order, hurt the progress of the country and undermined his efforts to achieve national objectives.[40]

Both as national leader and Head of State, he

[40]The writer was on a visit to Syria in June 1979, when the conspiracy at Aleppo Training Academy occurred and the subsequent trial and executions were carried out. Though feeling among the rank and file rose high, the public as a whole condemned the outburst of sectarian strife and supported Asad in his stand against a Sunni-Shi'i rift.

has been able to impress his followers with his
dedication and straightforwardness in the service
of the country. His honesty and integrity have
never been in question. Some of his followers, his
brother Rif'at in particular, have been the subject
of public criticism for alleged personal gain and
corruption, for which Asad has been reproached.
But in reality he has never closed his eyes to corruption or irregularities (including vain attempts to
curb his brother's exploits) and has indeed reduced, if he has not completely eliminated, these
practices whether in civilian or military circles. In
a traditional society undergoing rapid change, corruption and nepotism are not expected to be completely eradicated overnight. Asad has counselled
patience and appealed in the name of national
pride to stop these practices; indeed, a herculean
cleansing of the Augean stables from these corrupt
practices is needed. He himself has led a fairly austere private life and set an example of public service deviod of personal gain or self-indulgence in
worldly affairs. He is married and has five children (four of them boys) and his private life is essentially simple. He neither drinks nor smokes and
he spends most of his time in attending to public
duties. For this reason, if anything went amiss, it
has become almost customary that someone else in
his regime would be blamed. But there is no doubt
that Asad bears ultimate responsibility, as all political decisions are made either directly by him or
under his general instructions and guidance.

"Asad is the first military man I have met," said
one of his admirers, "who governs with the mind
and manners of a civilian leader."[41] I have also

---

[41]The writer's interview with Fadil al-Ansari, member of the National Command (Damascus, June 16, 1979).

been told by another keen observer that whenever Asad is drawn into the company of military peers, he can equally be as popular and influential as with civilians. Experts may disagree on whether a good soldier can become a good politician; the latter must possess certain elements of flexibility which a good soldier might not tolerate and therefore be unable to become a good politician. Though Asad is not the first military man who succeeded in becoming a politician, he seems to be one of the few who could combine soldierly and civilian qualities. He has conducted himself as the man made of both velvet and steel and he is capable of meeting challenges in accordance with the need of circumstances.

Often branded by outside observers as stern and mysterious, Asad is quite candid and open not only to people who know him well, but also to others, including foreign visitors. He is known to admirers as a kind and congenial person—often called a humanist (insani)—because he sympathizes with the poor and the oppressed and has paid attention to persons who had rendered service to the country.[42] Not infrequently, he speaks about justice, both in relation to national and international questions, and is concerned about moral and religious values whenever they are disregarded by malefactors.[43] Though conspiracy against the state or the regime are taken very seriously and culprits severely pun-

---

[42]Asad's instructions for the care of children who lost their parents in military operations is often cited as an example of his sympathy with people who suffered deprivation. These children are now being taken care of by the State until they come of age and complete their education.

[43]A decree was issued in 1979 to punish persons who commit immoral acts, especially by assaults on women and children, by either a fine or short-term imprisonment.

ished, Asad harbors no ill-feeling against men who conspired against him personally.

But neither Asad nor his regime have yet attained sufficient security and stability to be immune from violent changes, because harmony and cohesion have not yet been achieved by a people still struggling to form a modern nation-state. Above all, confessional and communal divisions have often diverted attention from concerted action to larger national issues. Asad is not unaware of these internal handicaps in his long struggle to achieve national unity and progress. He is never discouraged, because he is a very patient man and an optimist by nature. He often tries to impart this optimism to his people and tells them to be patient and tolerant, as he is confident that they possess abundant potentialities.[44]

VI

Shortly after independence, Syria passed under military rule and experienced a chain of violent changes and instability in her regimes. Violent changes and instability have created a feeling of personal insecurity and no leader today who seeks power by violent methods can persuade the public to support him. For almost a decade, Asad has been able to maintain public order and achieve relative tranquility despite attempts to stir disturbances. But Asad realizes that a stable regime depends not only on thwarting attempts at overthrowing the regime, but by positive actions to improve conditions and carry out reforms. Asad's regime has inherited the legacy of lethargy and tra-

---

[44]See Asad's *Speeches*, Vol. V, (1975), pp. 55 ff.

ditional practices harmful to progress which only time and education can eventually overcome. Indeed, in party meetings and congresses, these issues have been raised and measures to deal with them were seriously considered. But actions will have to follow promises.

No less important for the stability of the regime is the need for enlisting an increasing number of the public to participate in the political processes not only through the mechanism of the ruling party but through a multiple party system in which differing views can be publically discussed. True, the Ba'th has allowed political participation through such organizations as the National Progressive Front and the People's Assembly, composed of elected representatives of progressive parties and corporate groups, but parties and groups advocating differing views can hardly be considered to enjoy free expression of political opinion. Asad himself has shown tolerance to differing views, but his example has not been followed by other leaders in official and unofficial circles.

Above all, the problem of military intervention in politics has yet to be resolved. To overcome possible military uprisings the Ba'th Party has enlisted the participation of top military leaders in the Party's activities and entrusted the supervision of military affairs to a Military Committee composed of high-ranking members of the Party. Perhaps no less important is the fact that President Asad, a former General of the Army in his own right, serves today as a link between the Army and the regime. No important decision is made without prior consultation with top military leaders. This working relationship between the Ba'th Party and the military has saved the country from recurrent

military coups. But if the top civil and military
leaders should disagree and the link between them
passed to lesser hands, the existing relationship
might no longer work harmoniously and the danger of military intervention might recur. Thus, the
correlation between civil and military leaderships
through the mechanism of the Ba'th Party is only a
step in the right direction; the ultimate goal would
be to achieve full subordination of the Army to the
political processes.

In accordance with its teachings, freedom is one
of the fundamental principles which the Ba'th
Party advocates; but since Syria had long been
struggling against foreign domination, freedom
meant liberation from foreign control and had to
take precedence over individual freedom until independence from foreign control was achieved.
However, no sooner had Syria achieved national
freedom than it passed under military rule. No individual liberty, regardless of how limited it existed
under foreign rule, was expected to survive under
military surveillance. Indeed, the problem of individual liberty has become not only a Syrian but an
Arab problem. Apart from Lebanon before the
Civil War, liberty passed through a period of serious crisis from which no Arab land has yet recovered. Restrictions on liberty in Syria reached the
high water-mark during the latter part of the fifties
and early sixties. Since he came to power, Asad
promised to relax restrictions and martial law has
been abolished; but full freedom and free expression of political opinion are not expected to flour-
ish overnight. Under the present regime, self-criticism inside the Ba'th Party, especially during the
meetings of National and Regional Congresses, has
been permitted—indeed, it has even been encour-

aged, as the experiences of the Seventh Regional
Congress (1979) demonstrated—but no such privilege has yet been granted to individuals outside official circles. Asad himself seems to be disposed toward public criticism and has shown tolerance to
differing views. In his speech at the final meeting
of the Seventh Regional Congress, he told his countrymen to communicate their grievances and differing views directly to him.[45] Perhaps no Arab regime under military rule has been prepared to
tolerate dissent, and yet no regime can be expected
to survive if it indefinitely denies legitimate expression of free opinion. Asad is not unaware of the
fact that the survival of his regime would depend
on the acceptance of the principle of dissent and
toleration of public criticism outside official circles. But his sense of toleration and acceptance of
the principle of dissent has yet to be shared by
party members.

---

[45]See *al-Thawra*, Damascus, January 6, 1980.

Part Three

CENTRALIZING LEADERSHIP

A folk that hath no chiefs must soon decay,
And chiefs it hath not when the vulgar sway.
Only with poles the tent is reared at last,
But when the pegs and poles are once combined,
Then stands accomplished that which was designed.

Abu Tammam, al-Hamasa (d. 850 A.D.)

CHAPTER VI

SULTAN QABUS OF 'UMAN

> I have undertaken the action against
> my father in an effort to place the
> country along the path of reconstruc-
> tion and development.
>
> Sultan Qabus

Becoming known to the outside world only in the age of exploration, 'Uman (Oman) has long maintained an independent existence despite foreign invasions, and the European Powers have recognized its independence since the mid-nineteenth century. After a major oil strike in 1963, the people of 'Uman, long suffering from deprivation and neglect, expected a sudden leap along the path of progress and development as soon as the country began to receive an income from oil. However, the policy of isolation which 'Uman's rulers had followed since World War I kept the country out of touch with the world and prevented her from adopting a program of national reconstruction which has become an overriding national demand in Arab lands.

In July 1970, Sultan Sa'id Bin Taymur, the ruling Monarch, was suddenly overthrown by his son Qabus and went into exile. Outwardly the event was reported in the press as merely a Palace uprising—the son, virtually under house arrest and prohibited from contact with the people, resorted to violence in order to put an end to his predicament by a short cut to the throne. Below the surface, however, the social forces that brought up the change were much more intricate and reveal how deeply these forces were rooted in the country's history, culture and traditions. A study of Sultan Qabus, heir of a dynasty that provided the country with an impressive leadership for almost two centuries, will throw light not only on the structure and dynamics of 'Umani politics, but, perhaps more important, on the nature and direction of change in a fragmented society struggling to achieve unity and modernization.

II

The Sultanate of 'Uman, as the country is officially called, comprises an area of 120,000 square miles and a population of nearly a million people, mostly still tribal or semi-tribal in their ways of life. Though virtually all of the people are Muslims, perhaps over two-thirds of them belong to the Ibadi community, a variant of—if not completely different from—the Khariji sect which is considered the earliest dissident group that had arisen in Islam.[1]

Apart from purely doctrinal differences, the Kharijis (and subsequently the Ibadis) developed their own theory of the Caliphate (or Imamate) of

[1]The Khariji sect began to develop following a conflict between the Caliph 'Ali and some of his followers over the question of arbitration as a means to settle the dispute between him and his rival Mu'awiya, the Governor of Syria and the future founder of the Umayyad dynasty. The Ibadi sect sprang from the Kharijis shortly afterwards when 'Abd-Allah B. Ibad, originally from 'Uman, began to advocate

the community of believers. The Imam, the supreme head of the community, is elected from among the "worthiest" of the believers without the claim of possessing legitimate rights or other attributes, as the Shi'i sect prescribes, or belonging to a special tribe as the Sunni sect maintains. He can also be deposed if he proves unworthy of the position. If no suitable candidate for the office were available it was preferable to leave the Ibadi community without an Imam than to elect an unworthy one. The period in which the community fails to elect an Imam is called the *kitman* (concealed or restrained) and consequently leadership would be excrcised temporarily by laymen or secular chiefs. In 'Uman, as in other tribal communities, the Imams were always elected by Shaykhs and tribal chiefs who, after consultation with their tribesmen, made binding decisions on their behalf. The tribal community of 'Uman is made up of innumerable tribes and clans; the two major divisions, which control the country's social and political affairs, are the Hinawi and Ghafiri confederations.[2]

Ibadi teachings, rejected by other Islamic communities, provided the rationale for 'Umani rulers to assert the country's traditional independence and to secede from Islamic unity as early as the eleventh century A.D. Apart from doctrinal justifi-

---

a different set of ideas from the original Khariji creed in Basra. From there Ibadi teachings gradually spread into 'Uman and other parts of the Islamic world. For a brief study of the history and doctrines of this sect, see T. Lewicki, "al-Ibadiyya," *Encyclopedia of Islam*, 2nd ed., Vol. III, pp. 648-60; and Elie A. Salem, *Political Theory and Institutions of the Khawarij* (Baltimore, 1956).

[2]For a discussion of the tribal structure of 'Uman and its significance, see John E. Peterson, *Oman in the Twentieth Century* (London, 1978), chaps. 4 and 6.

cation, however, 'Umani independence has to a large extent been made possible by the location of the country at the remote southeast corner of Arabia. Separated by desert, her rulers were able to assert their freedom of action from the centers of power in other Islamic lands. But the country's long coastline, consisting of almost 1000 miles, exposed her to foreign pressures which often compromised her independence; for, if the vast desert shielded her from Muslim conquerors, the high seas proved no important barrier to non-Muslim conquerors who were able to overrun and dominate the coastal areas. From antiquity, many conquerors—Babylonian, Persian, Greek, Portuguese, French and British—have made their descent upon the country by sea; but foreign invasions, though repeatedly asserted, invariably proved transitory and native rulers, despite conflicts and perennial tribal warfares, always succeeded in reducing and eventually bringing to an end foreign ascendancy.

After long European domination since the discovery of the sea route around Africa foreign influence was reduced by the middle of the seventeenth century and the country, under the rule of Imams belonging to the Ghafiri tribes, enjoyed unity and independence for over a century. But internal division and rivalry between the Hinawi and Ghafiri tribal factions prevented the Imams from holding the country together and invited foreign intervention. The Ya'rubi clan, supported by the Ghafiri tribes, monopolized the office of Imam during the seventeenth and early eighteenth centuries and no other candidate was able to contest it. The last of the Ya'rubi Imams (1739), in an effort to put an end to inter-tribal warfare, called upon the Persian Shah to assist him in pacifying the country. Nadir Shah, who had extended his rule from Iraq to India, seized upon the opportunity to extend his control to the Persian Gulf. The ensuing Persian domination of the northern 'Umani coast of al-Batina lasted from 1732 to 1749. Persian intervention, however, created a reaction to Ya'rubi rule, which gave an opportunity to the rise of a new dynasty—later known as the Al Bu Sa'id line—which gradually restored order and provided the country with a new leadership. Not only did power pass from Ghafiri to Hinawi tribes, but its locus shifted from the interior to the coast and opened a new horizon for the country's progress and development.[3]

The new dynasty was established by Ahmad Bin Sa'id who assumed power in 1739. Ahmad grew up in the port of Suhar where he rose to prominence as governor of that town. When the Persian army established its control over the coastal area of al-Batina, he refused to surrender Suhar and organized a force, supported by tribesmen, which eventually expelled the Persians in 1749. For this service he was rewarded by his elevation to the post of Imam by both Hinawi and Ghafiri tribes. Under his rule, the country was united, though tribal conflict never really stopped.

This unity, however, was short-lived. Ahmad's successors, in an effort to maintain unity, tried in vain to obtain the title of Imam but the tribal chiefs were opposed to any agreement with the Sultanate. In 1793, they even failed to agree among

---

[3]For an account of the events leading up to the downfall of the Ya'rubi dynasty and the rise of Al Bu Sa'id, see Nur al-Din 'Abd-Allah Bin Humayd al-Salimi, *Tuhfat al-A'yan Bi Sirat Ahl 'Uman* (Cairo, 1966), Vol. II, pp. 198ff. For an excellent survey of the modern history of 'Uman, see Robert G. Landen, *Oman Since 1850* (Princeton, 1967).

themselves on any single candidate to the office. This was the beginning of a long period of *kit-man*[4]; it lasted nominally to 1913, and power ultimately passed to temporal or secular rulers, though shorn of the spiritual attributes of the Imam. Failing to obtain recognition of their rule over the interior, the Sultans asserted their control over the coastal area and transferred the seat of government from Rustaq to Masqat. In 1789, the British East India Company signed a treaty which implied recognition of the Sultanate by Great Britain.[5] One of the most able members of the dynasty—Sa'id Bin Sultan (1804-1856)—adopted the title of Sayyid (later the family assumed the title of Sultan) and embarked upon a maritime policy in collaboration with British traders which extended his rule to Zanzibar in 1832. He even transferred his residence from Masqat to that remote African outpost, paying little or no attention to tribal affairs, and virtually became the ruler of a vast and prosperous empire.[6] Owing to adverse circumstances, his successors could not maintain the same power and ascendancy and the empire was divided between Masqat and Zanzibar. In Zanzibar, the dynasty lasted until 1964, when it was overthrown by a revolution originating in the mainland of Africa, but in 'Uman it continued without inter-

---

[4]Only 'Azzan B. Qays was acknowledged for a short period (1868-71) as Imam.
[5]This recognition was confirmed by Great Britain and France in 1862.
[6]For his life and achievements, see Rudolph Said-Ruete, *Said Bin Sultan* (London, 1929). For a history of Al Bu Sa'id dynasty, see Hamid Bin Muhammad Bin Ruzayq, *al-Fath al-Mubin Fi Sirat al-Sada Al Bu Sa'idiyyin*, ed. 'Abd al-Muni'm Amir and Muhammad Mursi (Cairo, 1977).

ruption to the present.[7] The title of Imam, over-shadowed by the office of Sultan, remained virtually vacant until it was temporarily revived early in the twentieth century.

Under the rule of the Al Bu Sa'id dynasty, the center of power shifted from the interior to the coast—from the predominantly tribal community to the semi-tribal merchant class, whose wealth and source of income depended primarily on overseas trade and collaboration with foreign mercantile houses. True, they continued to profess the Ibadi creed and remained loyal to the country's traditions and moral values; however they gradually began to adopt new values and practices and became more tolerant to foreign customs and practices and abandoned the medieval and traditional outlook to life. These trends, alienating the conservative community of the interior, prompted the tribal chiefs to refuse recognition of the Sultanate as the supreme authority and to claim their own authority, including the spiritual powers of the Imam (even though it existed in the state of *kitman*), was supreme over the land. For this reason, the power of the Sultanate, though in full control of the coast, remained devoid of the *de jure* sanction that stems from the office of Imam. The problem of the legitimacy of power was compounded when the caliphate was abolished in Turkey after World War I and no action to revive it in the Arab World was taken. Instead, secular rulers were entrusted with power either by artificial electoral processes or by sheer force devoid of popular consent. Despite attempts to revive the Imamate in

---

[7]For a study of the origins and development of the revolution in Zanzibar, see Michael F. Lofchie, *Zanzibar: Background to Revolution* (Princeton, 1965).

the interior of 'Uman, the country as a whole showed no great interest in it and seems to prefer a secular form of government.

The initial shift of power from the interior to the coast did not necessarily mean the ascendancy of the coast over the interior. It rather meant the split of the country into two major divisions, though leadership of the inland became a bone of contention among rival factions for the office of Imam. After World War I, when the Arab countries were able to establish new political systems, 'Uman had yet to grapple with the problem of internal unity before it could embark on a thorough reorganization of its regime.

Apart from the spiritual and social forces that separated the coast from the inland community, the power and prestige of the Sultans of Masqat began to decline after Sultan Sa'id's empire was divided by his successors. Though territorially the larger part, the interior of 'Uman was separated by desert and torn by tribal conflicts. For this reason, it became exceedingly difficult for the Sultans of Masqat to extend their control to the interior without a strong army that could restrain the power of tribal chiefs. By 1913, when Taymur Bin Sultan, a great grandson of Sultan Bin Sa'id, came to the throne, his authority hardly extended beyond the city of Masqat. This situation prompted the tribal chiefs to declare that the time to end the period of *kitman* had come. They called for the reactivation of the Imamate as a means to challenge the authority of the Sultans of Masqat and assert their independence from the coast. Salim Bin Rashid al-Kharusi, one of their number, was elected to the office of Imam. During World War I, when Masqat passed under British military occupation, the

Imam had occasion to proclaim his authority over the whole country.

After the war, concerned about the deterioration in the internal conditions of Masqat, the British tried to work out an arrangement which would reconcile the Sultanate with the Imamate in an effort to save the Masqat regime from falling apart, but the initial negotiations led to no agreement. In 1920, when Imam al-Kharusi was assassinated, a new Imam, Shaykh Muhammad Bin 'Abd-Allah al-Khalili, personally disposed to come to an agreement with the Sultan of Masqat, was elected to succeed him. The new Imam accepted the terms offered by the British and a treaty was finally signed at al-Sib (a suburb of Masqat) on September 25, 1920, between the representatives of the Imam and the Sultan. The treaty provided for the co-existence of the Sultanate and Imamate in peace, and the tribal Shaykhs agreed not to attack the coastal towns, presumably considered to be under the control of the Sultan of Masqat. By this arrangement, the Sultan, who was indeed in a weak position, seized the opportunity to control the country's foreign affairs as a whole, as the treaty made no mention of who would exercise those powers. Though authority was not formally divided, it was, however, understood that while the spiritual powers were reserved for the Imam, the exercise of temporal powers was in practice divided between Sultan and Imam.[8]

For over a decade, from 1921 to 1931, Taymur Bin Sultan, aware that his regime was dependent on British support, without which the dynasty

---

[8]For text of the Treaty of al-Sib, see Robert G. Landen, *Oman Since 1856*, pp. 403-404; and "Muscat and Oman," *The Middle East Journal*, Vol. II (Summer 1957), pp. 282-284.

would have been overthrown by powerful inland tribal chiefs, lost interest in the rule over a country torn by tribal rivalry and whose authority was restricted by foreign advisors. He often absented himself by travel abroad—to India, Europe and the United States—and finally decided to abdicate in 1931. He was succeeded by his son, Sa'id Bin Taymur, in 1932.

III

Sultan Sa'id's rule might be divided into two periods. The first, in which he proved to be a great statesman, endured over a quarter of a century and ended in 1958, when he took up permanent residence in Salala (the capital of the southern province of Dhufar) and never returned to Masqat. The second, lasting about twelve years, ended in his downfall and exile from the country in 1970. He died two years later.

Ascending to the throne at the age of 21, he had just returned from his studies in India. He was sent first to Baghdad where he received primary education in Arabic at a private school. Witnessing the nationalist agitation in Baghdad against British control when Iraq had not yet achieved independence, young Sa'id must have pondered on the plight of his country and was perhaps inspired with the idea of reducing foreign influences and pressures whenever the time would come when he would be entrusted with its destiny. From Baghdad Sa'id was sent to India where he attended a school for princes and received modern European education in English, which he learned to speak fluently. Far from being an introvert, he was not inclined to adopt the Indian princely habits, least of all their personal display of extravagance, as he was essentially a religious person and preferred to live a simple life. Before returning to his country, he made a tour around the world. Although he seems to have been impressed with Western material progress, he was concerned about its possible adverse effect on the traditions and moral values of his country. This concern became uppermost in his mind in later years.

Though Sultan Sa'id inherited a throne far from being secure, he proved equal to the task as a ruler. At first, his authority, which his father had relinquished to him, hardly extended beyond the principal coastal towns and was contested by the rival powers of the Imam and Shaykhs and restricted by foreign advisors. By his vigilance and close supervision of a corrupt administration, he was able to inspire a measure of efficiency and reduce the powers of foreign advisors. Perhaps even more important was his policy of austerity, both for himself and the country, which enabled him to reduce expenditure and balance the budget. Shortly after his assumption of power, he eliminated the debt which his father had incurred and was able to save a surplus which he wisely spent on organizing an army deemed necessary for internal security and defense. It was indeed that small force which later enabled him, with British support, to extend his control over the interior and unify the country.

Aware of financial limitations, Sa'id Bin Taymur realized that unless oil was discovered, he would never be able to provide adequate income to maintain order and hold the country together. For this reason, he invited oil companies to explore the country shortly after he came to the throne, hoping that the income from oil might provide the necessary means to achieve his goals.

However, oil exploration, which was intended to increase the country's income and bring about prosperity, brought him into conflict with the tribal chiefs of the inland community as it was conducted in areas considered to fall under their control. In an effort to assist the oil companies to do their work, Sultan Sa'id tried by peaceful methods to achieve his objective, but when the tribal chiefs resorted to violence and the disturbances led to foreign intervention, he was bound to use force in order to maintain order and achieve national unity. This unity, however, was achieved step-by-step.

From 1920, when the treaty of al-Sib was signed, to 1954, when Imam al-Khalili died, the Sib compromise—the co-existence in peace between Imam and Sultan—worked fairly satisfactorily. So long as the Imam al-Khalili was alive, relations between the Sultan and the Imam were on the whole friendly. But, after Imam al-Khalili's death in 1954, relations took a turn for the worse.[9]

There were several contenders, including Sultan Sa'id, for the office of Imam after al-Khalili's death. The Ibadi Shaykhs, reluctant to hand over

---

[9]Sulayman al-Baruni, the Tripolitanian leader, often acted as a link between the Sultan and the Imam to promote friendly relations. After he left Tripolitania, following the Italian occupation of his country, al-Baruni went into exile to Turkey, Iraq and finally to 'Uman. As an Ibadi follower, he tried in vain to impress upon the Imam the need to open the inland to foreign trade and reconcile his office with the Sultanate. He offered his services to both the Sultan and the Imam. He died shortly before the liberation of his country from Italian control, having vowed he would not return until the departure of the Italians. For a brief account of his career in 'Uman, see Muhammad Shayba b. Nur al-Din 'Abd-Allah B. Humayad al-Salimi, *Nahdat al-A'yan Bi Huriyat 'Uman* (Cairo, n.d.), pp. 379-92.

control of the interior to the Sultan of Masqat, elected Ghalib Bin 'Ali al-Hina'i (of the Hinawi tribes) as Imam in 1954. There were many reasons that led to the deterioration of relations between the Sultan and the new Imam, not only because Sultan Sa'id failed to obtain the title of Imam. Saudi Arabia, in an effort to obtain control of the eastern region of Arabia, considered rich in oil resources, seems to have cultivated friendly relations with Imam Ghalib—a move which aroused the suspicion of Sultan Sa'id who feared possible Saudi encroachments on his country. After World War II, when Western oil companies reactivated their exploration, the unsettled frontier questions aroused rivalry and intrigues among competing groups in 'Uman and elsewhere to control areas likely to be rich in oil resources.

The most notable area of dispute was the Buraymi oasis, claimed by Saudi Arabia to have been part of its territory, though at the time of the dispute it was jointly administered by 'Uman and Abu Dhabi. Since Abu Dhabi, then part of the Trucial Coast, had been under British protection, Britain became directly involved in the dispute with Saudi Arabia. British and American companies, active in oil exploration since the mid-thirties, prompted the British and Saudi governments to assert their conflicting claims over Buraymi and the adjacent area. In 1949, when the Arabian American Oil Company (ARAMCO) was exploring an area considered to fall within Abu Dhabi's boundaries, the British authorities prevented the exploration by force. The Saudi Government, in an effort to protect its rights in a territory where ARAMCO was conducting the exploration, protested the British action. This was the first step that raised the so-called Buraymi dispute. Negotiations between Britain and Saudi Arabia led to no agreement and the Saudi Government, perhaps trying to confront the British Government with a *fait accompli*, dispatched a force to occupy Buraymi in 1952.[10]

Sultan Sa'id, threatened by Saudi incursions into his territory, invited Imam al-Khalili, with whom he was on relatively good terms, to urge the tribal chiefs to mobilize their tribal forces (estimated at some 80,000 tribesmen) to take action against the Saudi force before it marched on Buraymi. Persuaded by the British Government to avoid confrontation with Saudi Arabia, presumably on the grounds that the dispute was to be settled peacefully, Sultan Sa'id ordered the tribal chiefs against their wishes to withdraw their tribesmen (thus giving the false impression that he acted under British pressure). Since the dispute was not settled by peaceful methods, despite an agreement to refer the dispute to arbitration in 1954, Sultan Sa'id was encouraged by the British Government to occupy Buraymi in a joint attack with Abu Dhabi in 1955. The joint attack gave further evidence that Sultan Sa'id was prompted to take Buraymi under British pressure, while the tribal chiefs of the inland had now been persuaded by Imam Ghalib to turn against Sultan Sa'id. To counteract the Imam's alignment with Saudi Arabia, Sultan Sa'id dispatched a small force which took the town of Ibri in October, 1954. Imam Ghalib, supported by Saudi Arabia, retorted by declaring the independence of

---

[10]For the conflicting Saudi and British viewpoints on the sovereignty of Buraymi, see Government of Saudi Arabia, *Memorial of the Government of Saudi Arabia*, 3 vols., (Cairo, 1955); and Great Britain, *Memorial Submitted by the Government of the United Kingdom of Great Britain and Northern Ireland*, (London, 1955), 2 vols.

the State of 'Uman, consisting of the area under his control, and applied for membership in the Arab League. Imam Ghalib's collaboration with Saudi Arabia, construed as leading to a possible Saudi incursion into the interior of 'Uman, prompted Sultan Sa'id to move his army, supported by a British force, and occupy Nazwa, seat of the Imamate, where he declared his complete control over the interior of the country. The Imam and his brother, Governor of Rustaq, fled to Saudi Arabia and established a government-in-exile at Dammam, on the eastern coast of Saudi Arabia.[11] Sultan Sa'id, denouncing the Imam for his collaboration with Saudi Arabia to establish a separate sovereign Imamate in violation of the treaty of Sib, seized the opportunity to bring the interior under his control and declared the supremacy of his authority over the whole country.[12] Thus, 'Uman became at last united under one supreme ruler—the Sultan. Though in theory the Imamate, like the Caliphate, is still in existence, it has to all intents and purposes come to an end. Sultan Sa'id, now without a rival to his authority, was no longer interested in putting forth a claim to the title of Imam. In

---

[11]While his petition for 'Uman's membership in the Arab League was still pending, Imam Ghalib petitioned the Secretary General of the United Nations to place the 'Umani question on the General Assembly's agenda. The Imam's application to the Arab League's membership raised the question of interpretation of the treaty of Sib, as both the Imam and the Sultan claimed to be the Head of the State of 'Uman. The League, uncertain about the validity of the conflicting claims of the Sultan and the Imam to supreme authority, postponed action. The whole matter, however, was dropped when Sultan Sa'id was overthrown and the Arab League recognized Sultan Qabus as head of the new regime in 'Uman.

[12]Before the country was fully pacified, Sultan Sa'id had to face a revolt inspired by the exiled leaders in 1957. British military support was needed before the revolt was completely suppressed in 1959.

achieving unity of these countries, he demonstrated that he was a man of great ability and statesmanship.

In the second period of his rule, from 1958 to 1970, Sultan Sa'id became increasingly unpopular and gradually lost control over areas that went into open rebellion against him. It may seem strange indeed that Sultan Sa'id, who succeeded in achieving the unity of the country, should fail in holding the country together just at the crucial time when the prospect of receiving an income from oil was realized. What went wrong with Sultan Sa'id?

IV

Unity and order having been achieved, Sultan Sa'id became concerned about security and defense against possible foreign attacks. For long protected by desert, 'Uman felt secure from neighboring Muslim rulers; but Saudi encroachments on the northwestern frontiers demonstrated that 'Uman could no longer remain secure from that direction. Sultan Sa'id felt that only the future prospect of an income from oil might provide the means to organize an army strong enough to defend the country. For this reason, he encouraged the oil companies to speed up the oil exploration in order to insure his country's security.

Ironically, however, the oil exploration that Sultan Sa'id expected to enhance his position itself became the issue between him and the inland tribal chiefs. They objected to the oil explorations not only because of interferences in the lands in which they resided, but, perhaps more important, because they were conducted in areas considered to fall under their control. Sultan Sa'id, ignoring tribal

complaints, issued orders to provincial governors
calling to their attention that all matters connected
with oil exploration should be left to him. When he
was still alive, Imam al-Khalili supported the position of Sultan Sa'id; after Khalili's death in 1954,
the situation began to change.

For two years, from 1955 to 1957, Sultan Sa'id
was still able to control the tribes and the new
Imam, Ghalib Bin 'Ali, made no move against him.
After 1957, when Saudi Arabia provided economic
and military support for the Imam, the tribal
chiefs began to renounce the Sultan's authority.
Sultan Sa'id, supported by a British force, as noted
earlier, moved to impose his authority on the interior and occupied Nazwa. Imam Ghalib and his
followers fled to the Jabal al-Akhdar and waged
tribal warfare that kept Sultan Sa'id's forces on the
defensive for over two years. Only with British
military support could the Sultan reduce Imam
Ghalib's forces and put an end to the war.

In order to control tribal warfare, Sultan Sa'id
declared military rule in the northern province and
issued orders to restrict the movement of individuals from town to town. Resenting these restrictions, representations were almost daily made to
the Sultan. Sultan Sa'id, partly to avoid complaints
but mainly to consolidate his position, moved his
seat of government from Masqat to Salala, the capital of the southern province of Dhufar.[13]

A similar situation developed in the Dhufar province. Annoyed by interferences in their lands, the
tribal chiefs made representations to the Sultan. Not

---

[13]Although the capital was Masqat, Sultan Sa'id spent most of his
time in Salala; thus the two provinces were united under him personally. Sultan Qabus integrated the two provinces under his regime.

heeding the complaints, the Sultan tried to silence them by force. The tribes counteracted by force and their resistance, supported by the poverty-stricken inhabitants of the province, led to open rebellion in 1965 which started at first for purely local reasons, but later, under ideological influences, it was transformed into a war of liberation against "imperialism" and "foreign influence."

When income from oil was first received in 1967, four years after it was discovered to exist in commercial quantities, Sultan Sa'id began to consider plans for development—plans which would meet essential needs, such as roads, schools and hospitals, but not those which he considered to be luxuries. In 1968, when the people began to wonder what the Sultan was going to do with the income, he made a public statement of policy in which he first described the financial position of the country and gave an apologia for the policy he pursued since he came to the throne. He then set forth a program for reconstruction and development and said optimistically that the year 1968 would open a new era for the country. As evidence that he was contemplating reforms, he proposed the following projects:

1. Building of new government offices for various departments;

2. Houses to accommodate expatriate personnel who would be engaged in the building of hospitals, schools, roads and other projects as the requirement for them arose, and also who would run the new hospitals and devise ways to improve the financial and administrative system;

3. Providing Masqat and Matrah with piped water which should be completed within 21 months of the agreement that had been signed;

4. Completion of the new power station which should provide Masqat and Matrah with electricity in the summer of 1968;

5. Assisting business in Matrah by the development of its port facilities. Suitable anchorages for cargo ships will be made, the customs house will be moved and more warehouses will be built;

6. A new Sultanate currency will be introduced in due course consisting of Sa'idi riyals of the following denominations: one riyal, half riyal and quarter riyal.

The Sultan also proposed to establish a Development Council which would carry out the development projects and a special council to execute the water and electricity projects. "Other plans," he added, "will be left to follow on later, putting the most important before the unimportant and asking help from Almighty God." However, he warned that as the country would develop and advance:

> We must keep before our eyes our true religion on which we place our reliance and the traditions which we have inherited. There are customs which are inviolable forever and there are customs which are alterable without infringing the basic traditions of the country which are considered to be among the glories of our worthy ancestors, of which we are proud and which protect us in our existence.[14]

---

[14]For full text of Sultan Sa'id's statement, see Kalimat al-Sultan Sa'id Bin Taymur, *Sultan Masqat wa 'Uman, 'An Ta'rikh al-Wad' al-Mali Fi al-Madi Wa Ma Ya'mal An Yakun 'Alayhi al-Hal Fi al-Mustqbal Ba'd Tasdir al-Naft* [The Words of Sultan Sa'id Bin Taymur, Sultan of Masqat and 'Uman, About the History of the Financial Position of the Sultanate in the Past and What it is Hoped it Will be in the Future, After the Export of Oil] (Masąt, Shawwal 1387/January 1968).

Written meticulously by himself, Sultan Sa'id's statement dwelt more on the past and the difficulties he had encountered than on future development. His proposals were modest, barely meeting the most pressing needs, and made no future promises. "Other plans," he said, "will be left to follow on later."

The Sultan's proposals, devoid of commitments, were very disappointing to both old and new generations. The people, long deprived of the bare necessities of life, were expecting that the opening of a "new era" should lead to the launching of a more ambitious program than was set forth in the public statement. Known for his shrewd and thrifty methods, the people may have suspected that the Sultan was more keen on keeping the income from oil in the treasury—virtually considered as the Sultan's private purse—than on its being spent on public reconstruction and development. Indeed, the people were disappointed with the Sultan's reluctance to earmark funds for reconstruction, for during the three or four years after the income from oil was received, a very modest beginning to construct roads was made, and only one new school and one hospital were built.[15] Improvement of the port of Matrah began shortly before Sultan Sa'id was overthrown and completed after his son Qabus succeeded him. Since income from oil was very limited at the beginning, not many projects were expected to be carried out. Nor did the Sultan give any indication that he was prepared to change his attitude once the income from oil should increase. Thus, the people lost confidence in him as a reformer.

---

[15]Previously only one school, called the Sa'idiya School, was in existence and one clinic was established.

However, the Sultan, who took pride in achieving internal order and national unity, became more concerned about the country's security than about reform. He watched the events in northern Arab lands with concern. In 1958, the establishment of the United Arab Republic and the subsequent downfall of the Iraqi Monarchy by Nasir's instigators, disturbed Sultan Sa'id. Indeed, Nasir's ambition to establish an empire extending from the Atlantic to the Gulf in the guise of Pan-Arabism alarmed many Arab rulers who feared that subversive activities and the appeal of Nasir's ideology might not only undermine but also overthrow their own regimes. More directly threatening Sultan Sa'id's regime was the outbreak of the revolution in Yaman in 1962 and the spread of the revolutionary movement first to Adan and then to South Arabia as a whole. While some of the Arab rulers tried to accommodate to the rising tide of the revolutionary movement either by the partial incorporation of the revolutionary ideology or by adopting other variants of Arab nationalism, Sultan Sa'id closed the doors of his country and followed an isolationist policy which he thought would keep his countrymen immune from foreign influences. As he grew older, he was convinced that isolationism was the right policy to protect his people from corruption and immoral influences. It was from this perspective that he formulated his views about development, stressing nonmaterial values and limiting the material projects to essentials. In an attempt to spare the country's surplus income from oil for security and defense against possible foreign attacks, he lost sight about possible internal uprising against him.

Opposition to Sultan Sa'id came from two directions—the new and old generations. The old, though sharing his conservative views about moral and religious values, were opposed to him because of interference in provincial affairs, while the new, under the influence of Arab nationalist stirrings, demanded the abandonment of his policy of isolationism and the launching of an extensive program of reconstruction. When the Dhufar rebellion first broke out in 1965, it was not supported by the new generation until it turned into an ideological struggle against deprivation, backwardness and foreign influence. Sultan Sa'id, opposed to both camps, made no attempt to compromise with either one. He had no sympathy with the aspirations of young men who were denied even the elementary requirements for education and considered their demands as a sign of corruption and moral decadence. He tried to prevail over the opposition of older men by his personal influence over tribal chiefs, but when tribesmen persisted in their demands, he tried to crush them by force.

From the mid-fifties, long before the tribes began to turn against him, many young men who had been denied the opportunity of entering school (as no schools save one or two for only favored families had existed) began to leave the country despite the Sultan's ban on foreign travel in order to study in other Arab countries. Some used to listen to Radio Cairo—the *Sawt al-Arab* (Voice of the Arabs)—which propagated Pan-Arab slogans, and aspired to identify themselves with the Arab nationalist movement that had been in progress in northern Arab lands. Since restrictions made it almost impossible to engage in political activities in 'Uman, they fled the country to join Arab political organizations abroad, hoping that under their in-

fluence a revolutionary movement might be insti-
gated in 'Uman to replace the Sultan's regime by
another congenial to them.

There had already been in the Gulf—Kuwayt,
Qatar, Bahrayn and the Trucial Coast—and in
Saudi Arabia many 'Umanis who had left their
country during and after World War II in search
of livelihood. The number of these emigrés began
to increase after the mid-fifties for political as well
as for economic reasons. They sought the support
of Arab political organizations in order to bring
pressure to bear on their ruler to open the country
to the outside world and perhaps to change his regime. Some joined the *Harakat al-Qawmiyyin al-
Arab* (the Arab Nationalists' Movement), whose
headquarters were in Bayrut, and others in Egypt,
Syria and Iraq worked to obtain support for their
objective. The Dhufari emigrés in particular became very active and organized a Dhufari unit to
promote their interests. The Arab Nationalists,
seeking unity of all Arab lands, were naturally interested in the activities of the 'Umani emigrés as
prospective supporters of the Pan-Arab union. On
the other hand, the 'Umani emigrés hoped that by
joining a Pan-Arab union, their country might be
saved from oppression and foreign influence. In
preparation for the revolutionary task, some went
to China for military training and others received
their training in the Arab World.[16]

Because of differences, both on procedural and
ideological grounds, with the local Arab Nationalists' unit in Kuwayt, the emigrés in Kuwayt organized a nationalist society called *al-Jam'iya al-*

---

[16]The writer's interview with Salim al-Ghazali, himself one of the
emigrés who went to China for military training (Masqat, October
15, 1978).

Khayriya (the Fraternal Society), whose members were drawn mainly from Dhufar. The immediate goal of the society was to raise funds for compatriots who could not work, especially young men who went to school, but the ultimate goal was to engage in political activities and to seek the support of organizations engaged in Arab revolutionary activities that had been spreading into the Gulf area from other Arab lands and aiming at the liberation of the Gulf countries from oppression and foreign influence. They were supported by other young men who shared their views and were opposed to repression and foreign rule in their own countries.[17]

The outbreak of the Yaman revolution in 1962, which received Egyptian support, was hailed as an important landmark in the Arab revolutionary movement and gave an impetus to groups in the Gulf to become active. Some went to Egypt and others to Syria and Iraq to seek military support in order to start similar revolutionary activities in their lands against what they considered as reactionary regimes and foreign influence. More specifically the Dhufari émigrés, whose province seemed to have been ripe for an uprising, organized a Dhufari group which became the nucleus for the Dhufari Liberation Front that came into existence in 1964. The aim of the Front was to set up a separate regime in Dhufar and secede from 'Umani unity. Though this objective may have appeared too narrow and inconsistent with the general goal of Pan-

---

[17]The writer's interviews with 'Abd al-'Aziz al-Ruwas, Minister of Information; Yusuf al-'Alawi, Deputy Foreign Minister, and others, who participated in the establishment of the society (Masqat, October, 1978). Yusuf al 'Alawi and Muslim Bin Nafal seem to have been the leading members (see 'Abd-Allah al-Nafisi, *Tathmin al-Sira' Fi Dhufar* [Evaluation of the Struggle in Dhufar] (Kuwayt, 1975), p. 53).

Arabism, the support it had received from the Arab Nationalists' Movement and from Egypt indicates that Dhufar was considered the ideal place to start the revolution from which it would spread into other parts of South and East Arabia.[18] Nevertheless, when the uprising began in Dhufar in 1965, the Shaykhs and local leaders supported it for purely local rather than for ideological reasons. Only two or three years later, when the leaders of the Front met at a conference in Humrayn (in the middle of Dhufar) to review the progress of the Dhufar war in 1968, did the Front alter its goals from a nationalist to a Marxist outlook. In the meantime, the name of the Front was changed from the Dhufar Liberation Front to the Arab Popular Liberation Front. Muhammad Ahmad al-Ghassani, leader of the Front, continued to act as the official head of the organization, but other perhaps more influential men from other radical organizations joined to reinforce it.[19]

When it was first formed under the impact of Nasirite and Arab Nationalist teachings, the Front accepted the hybrid platform of nationalism and socialism, with a stress on Arab nationalism and Arab unity. But the resolutions at Humrayn, embodying Marxist and other radical doctrines, created a rift between the principal leaders. The split into the North and South Yaman groups, especially after the British declaration to withdraw from Adan in 1968, accentuated the conflict between them. The domination of the South Yaman Revo-

---

[18]Cf. Nafisi, *Ibid.*, pp. 53-54.

[19]In 1980 Ghassani left the Liberation Front and returned to 'Uman in protest against Soviet domination of the Front's activities. He came to terms with Sultan Qabus and announced his loyalty to his regime.

lutionary Movement by Soviet and Maoist influences (and later by the Hawatima faction of the
Palestinian Liberation Movement), prompted the
leading members—'Alawi, Bin Nafal, Ruwas and
others—first to dissociate themselves from the
Front and later, when Qabus seized power in Salala, to join his camp against the Dhufar Front which
had become identified with the Popular Democratic Republic of South Yaman.

Most of the 'Umani leaders who participated in
political activities, belonging to an essentially conservative religious community, were prepared to
identify themselves with national but not with socialist symbols. For this reason, when they joined
the National Liberation Movement they were primarily interested in putting an end to repression
rather than in trading traditional for radical left
wing regimes. Therefore, when the Dhufar conflict
was transformed by the National Liberation Front
from a national into an ideological war and became identified with Soviet and Chinese symbols,
most Dhufari leaders began to dissociate themselves from it. Sultan Sa'id, as noted earlier, failed
to take advantage of the ideological conflict between the two camps and continued to denounce
them with equal vehemence because he was opposed to both national and Marxist ideologies.
When Sultan Qabus moved to replace his father's
regime and offered to cooperate with the nationalist camp, the Marxists became seriously in danger
and the tide began to turn against them.[20]

---

[20]For the events leading up to the Dhufar conflict and its develop-
ment, see John E. Peterson, "Britain and 'The Oman War,'" *Asian
Affairs*, Vol. 63 (October, 1976), pp. 285-98; and Idem, "Guerilla
Warfare and Ideological Confrontation In the Arabian Peninsula:
The Rebellion in Dhufar," *World Affairs*, Vol. 139 (Spring, 1977), pp.
278-95.

Sultan Sa'id, not entirely unaware of these developments, reacted negatively and seems to have thought that his policy of isolationism and repression could keep the country immune from outside influences. He was horrified by the events that took place in Iraq in 1958 which led to the downfall of the Monarchy and was deeply suspicious of Nasir's ambition to achieve Pan-Arab union. He therefore tried to keep his country out of the stream of Pan-Arabism and prevented his countrymen from travel abroad even if they were to leave the country for reasons that had nothing to do with political activities. It was indeed the Sultan's repressive measures that alienated his countrymen and set in motion the tribal uprising in the Dhufar province. These events opened an opportunity for Qabus, already frustrated with his father's policy, to identify himself with the opposition and he came to the conclusion that, if his country were ever to be saved from dangers, his father's rule should come to an end. Since Qabus' name was fully associated with the events that brought his father's rule to an end and provided leadership for the country after his assumption of power, an inquiry into his upbringing and character might be useful.

V

Qabus was born in Masqat on November 17, 1940, eight years after his father had come to the throne. Very little is known about his early life and upbringing save that his father had kept him long within the walls of his Royal Palace and he had little or no contact with children outside the family. Overprotected, he grew up as a shy and withdrawn child under the guidance of a domineering father. He received his early education at home under his private tutor Hafiz al-Ghassani, who taught him the Arabic language, religion and elementary English. Nor did Qabus have access to literature for young men of his age, except perhaps the classics of Ibadi teachings, as his father was distrustful of the corrupting influences of the outside world.

At the insistence of his English advisors, Sultan Sa'id agreed to send his son to study in England at the age of 18. He was enrolled in a private school in Suffolk where a very small group, hardly exceeding a dozen students, was studying. Had he been enrolled in a larger school, or in one of the reputable public schools where some other children of Arab royalty had gone for study, Qabus might have found it exceedingly difficult to adjust. And yet it was not easy for any young man to be taken from the secluded world of his family to an entirely new social environment. "Were you shocked by the very different way of life in Suffolk from your home?" I asked Sultan Qabus. "Everything was different—the weather, the houses, the manners and customs, and the whole way of life," he replied. Despite the initial cultural shock, Qabus very soon began to like his new social environment. Mr. Roman, teacher and headmaster of the school, and Mrs. Roman took a special interest in Qabus and made him feel at home and mix with other students. Almost from the beginning, Qabus seems to have liked the school and became so appreciative of the attention given him by the Romans that he kept in touch with them after leaving the school. He spent two years in Suffolk, concentrating in the main on mastery of the English language.[21]

From Suffolk Qabus went to Sandhurst in 1960. He received his training in the infantry, though he was interested in military affairs as a whole. After a two-year course of study, he went to West Germany where he joined a regiment for further training with the British Army. He passed seven months in several units, as he wished to acquaint himself with all aspects of military training in the field. He also visited various parts of West Germany and was impressed with its institutions and industrial development. He seems to have liked social life in Germany; he mixed with a number of families and developed in particular an interest in classical music.

After seven months of training, Qabus embarked on a world tour for the next four months. He traveled to several European countries—France, Switzerland, Italy, Turkey and others—and then visited the United States and returned to England via the Far East and South Asia. He passed the next six months in the study of government and public administration, and visited various institutions and government departments to supplement his studies with apprenticeship and personal experiences. While he was in London, he visited other cities and the countryside and became more intimately acquainted with English society. He made friendships with a number of Englishmen, some of whom were later to work with him in his country either before or after he came to the throne.

---

[21]Sultan Qabus told the present writer that he read no other than English books while he was in Suffolk, not even listening to Arabic broadcasts, in order to have mastery of the English language.

His studies having been completed, Qabus returned to his country in December 1964. During a
six-year period of formal studies—Suffolk, Sandhurst and special programs in London—he received a rounded education, augmented by personal experiences, conversations with a number of
public men, and social contacts. He also devoted
some time to reading, and paid attention to the arts
and theater. Asked by the writer about the book in
which he was most interested, Sultan Qabus replied: "In Suffolk, I read English literature and became interested in the writings of Bernard Shaw—
they are witty and critical—but at Sandhurst and
London, I read books on military and political subjects, and on history in general." Inspired by these
studies and exciting experiences, Qabus returned
with high hopes of playing a constructive role in
the development of his country.

Qabus returned to live in Salala where his father
had moved his official residence shortly after he
had gone for study abroad. He was anxious to enter into service of the state after he attended to
personal affairs. Very soon, however, he found his
time was wasted, not knowing what to do. In a
conversation with his father, Qabus requested to
be entrusted with an official function. The father,
who had not yet decided what Qabus should do,
suggested that before Qabus should undertake any
official responsibility, he first had to acquaint himself with Islamic teachings which he had missed
while he was studying in Europe. Thereupon, Qabus passed the first year after his return home in
reading Ibadi texts dealing with religion and law
under private tutors. He was kept in his mother's
house virtually as a prisoner.

In another conversation with his father, Qabus

inquired whether the time had come to make use of his knowledge and experiences abroad in the service of the country. Suspecting that he might have fallen under foreign (corrupt) influences, his father rebuked him for his inquiry. The staff of the Army in the northern province suggested that perhaps Qabus might benefit from training if he were to join the Army, and his residence with the staff in the north might give him the opportunity to acquaint himself with the country and the people.[22] Sultan Sa'id, still undecided what his son should do, was not inclined to let him leave Salala. He might have intended to protect him from the intrigues and personal influence of corrupt elements before he had matured under his guidance. In order to keep him busy, his father urged him to get married and suggested one of the ladies of loyal families, but Qabus showed no interest in that lady. As a result Qabus became restless and a tense relationship developed between father and son.

"How did you pass your time in the Palace?" I asked Sultan Qabus. "During the first year," he replied, "I read text-books on religion and law that were made available to me, but later—until 1970—I had absolutely nothing to do but to recline on the sofa and meditate: I began to reflect on my present condition and contemplate on what might happen to the country in consequence to my father's policy." [23] Needless to say, Qabus was bored and uncomfortable but he harbored no resentfulness toward his father. However, a sense of despair that his father had unnecessarily ignored him inevitably

---

[22]The writer's interview with Brigadier Colin C. Maxwell, Military Advisor to the Army (Masqat, October 21, 1978).

[23]The writer's interview in an audience with Sutan Qabus (Masqat, October 23, 1978).

developed and he began to contemplate how to escape from that prison-like way of life which had
been imposed on him through no fault of his own.

In his solitude, Qabus often reflected on the possibilities of ending his confinement. There were
only two alternatives open to him—either he had
to wait until his father had died, or his father must
be removed whether by peaceful or violent methods. Though his father was not in the best of
health,[24] he was still in his mid-fifties and therefore
might live for another decade or two. The prospect
of rising to the throne by peaceful methods seemed
remote, and Qabus became very impatient to wait
any longer. There was only the possibility of an
uprising, military or otherwise, with which he
might overthrow his father's regime. But how
could he contact the leaders of an uprising when
he was virtually a prisoner and carefully watched?

While he was preoccupied with gloomy thoughts
and out of touch with the outside world, rumors
began to reach Qabus' ears that his father, as he
grew older, had become increasingly unpopular in
the country. A popular uprising inspired by 'Umani
young men in exile would succeed only if supported either by the Army or by the intervention
of one of the revolutionary Arab governments that
might bring about the fall of his father's regime.
But if his father's regime were overthrown by
such an uprising as in the Yaman, the monarchical
regime itself would be swept away and Qabus
would have no role to play in the future reconstruction of the country in which he was indeed
keenly interested. Therefore, an uprising by loyal
elements in the Army would be the only way to

---

[24]He was suffering from sinus, a mild heart condition and possible
diabetic symptoms, according to some of my informants.

make room for him to rise to the throne. Yet his father's hold over the Army through expatriates might render such an uprising unlikely. Nor was the Sultan unaware of the impending danger of the Arab revolutionary movement on his country, but he was satisfied that such a movement would be resisted by the tribal chiefs and the conservative elements who were opposed to it. He also held that his British advisors, with whom he had full confidence, would not allow foreign intervention. He, accordingly, discounted the possibility of an uprising and continued to rely on his method of holding the country by repressive measures with consequent exposure of the country to danger.

What was that danger? It was the Dhufar rebellion, which began as a local uprising against the Sultan's repressive measures, but later, supported by the Arab National Liberation Movement, was transformed into a nationalist war against "oppression" and "foreign influence." Sultan Sa'id failed to appreciate the delicate position in which Britain found herself if she were to give him military support contrary to her declared policy of withdrawal from the region as a means to come to terms with the people on the basis of respect of their freedom and independence. Britain may have sympathized with the Sultan as a reliable ally, but she was not expected to come to his rescue by full participation in the military operation against the Dhufar rebellion, which had gained the reputation of a nationalist uprising, even though Sultan Sa'id's military defeat might lead to further reduction of British influence in the region. It was Sultan Sa'id's inability to grasp the significance of the Dhufar rebellion that sealed his fate and prompted his son to put an end to his policy by a Palace revolt.

VI

The person who was the first to broach the idea of initiating a military uprising whose banner would be raised in the name of the Sultan's son might never be known—perhaps it was envisioned by more than one person—but the plan was master-minded by a few able men close to Qabus who kept it in utmost secrecy. It is no longer a secret that Qabus had been in touch with a number of expatriates in the Army of the southern province—some he had met while he was studying in England—who were concerned with the trends of events in the south. In a meeting with one of them, Qabus seems to have encouraged the expatriate to proceed with the plan of a military uprising and secret messages for its execution were carried by one of Qabus' own personal servants. The principal expatriates involved in the plan were Brigadier John Graham, Intelligence Officer of the Army at Dhufar (then senior officer of the Army in the south) and Colonel Oldman, Military (later Defense) Secretary and Supreme Commander of the Army in Masqat. Another expatriate, then an intelligence officer in Dhufar, acted as a link between Qabus and his collaborators. But before they could proceed with the plan they had to obtain the approval of the principal political officers of the region. These were the British Consul General in Masqat and the Political Resident in Bahrayn. Aware of the gravity of the Dhufar war, no great effort was called for to obtain their assent, though prior approval of the home government was deemed necessary. The case in favor of a change in the highest position of the State of 'Uman was so forcefully presented to London that prompt reply of approval did not take very long.

Why did the British Government approve of the change?

Sultan Sa'id, it is true, was a great friend of England; indeed, the whole line of Al Bu Sa'id dynasty was bound in a traditional friendship with Great Britain. But the British Government did not look at the matter from a purely personal angle. What was at stake was not the protection of Sultan Sa'id's regime but the survival of the Monarchy itself and the security of the State. The lesson of the overthrow of the Hashimi House in Iraq must have been at the back of the minds of British policy makers. In giving its approval to let Sultan Sa'id fall, the British Government had indeed tried to protect the throne for his successors. Notwithstanding his personal discomfort, Qabus himself had become concerned about the consequences of his father's policy if he remained on the throne. It was this meeting of the minds between Qabus and his expatriate advisors that made the transfer of powers possible in an almost bloodless Palace revolt.

The plan was worked out in detail by the staff of the Army and carried out by a few officers in Dhufar. A group of half a dozen reliable soldiers under the command of an able 'Umani officer were instructed to break into the Sultan's private chamber and force him to abdicate. The officer chosen to undertake the delicate task of breaking into the Sultan's chamber was Shaykh Burayq, who was on good terms with the Sultan and considered to be equal to the occasion. Meanwhile, a unit of the Army was provided to surround the Palace and prevent the Sultan from either escaping or contacting loyal forces that might come to his rescue.

The date for the assault on the Palace was set on

July 23, 1970, some time in the afternoon when all servants except the guard were expected to have retired for the siesta. Shaykh Burayq, in collaboration with a number of Palace personnel, came to an agreement with the Palace guard to allow his men to enter on the day of the attack.

On July 23, at 4:00 p.m., Shaykh Burayq, armed with a gun, sallied forth to the Palace with a few hand-picked men. It was agreed that the front door was to be left unlocked and Shaykh Burayq entered the central hall unnoticed.

While the Sultan was expected to be resting in his private chamber, he was on that day quite busy, dealing with a number of official matters with a secretary. Suddenly, the secretary, listening to a conversation that was going on down the hall, alerted the Sultan about the matter. The conversation was between Burayq and one of the servants in the course of which Burayq was inquiring about the chamber in which the Sultan was sitting. He was told that the Sultan was in his study on the second floor.

The Sultan, suspecting that something unusual must have been happening, at once picked up an old pistol laid down on an end table. He must have been prepared for such events; for, as it transpired later, he had left in each Palace chamber some weapons for defense. Upon hearing that someone was drawing near to the study, he and his secretary began to shoot in the direction of the door. When Burayq arrived, one of his men who rushed into the study was shot and Burayq himself was hit in the upper part of the chest. While the Sultan was refilling, one of the bullets of his own pistol hit his foot by mistake and it was injured. By this time Burayq had come face to face with the Sultan and with a gun in his hand, he asked the Sultan to surrender. Realizing the futility of resistance, the Sultan at once agreed to surrender. He was told that if he abdicated in favor of Qabus, his life would be spared and he would be allowed to go into exile outside the country. The Sultan demanded that his abdication should be made to the Commander of the Army. Shaykh Burayq replied that his wish would be communicated to his son Qabus.

Meanwhile, Qabus and his advisors were busy in the preparation of the abdication text which was to be presented to the Sultan for his signature. The text having been duly signed, the ex-Sultan was flown in a private aircraft to Bahrayn where he was given quick medical attention to stop the bleeding of a vessel. The whole affair from beginning to end hardly lasted more than a couple of hours. From Bahrayn, the ex-Sultan was flown to London, where he received further treatment. In exile, father and son exchanged letters but the father did not see his son before he died two years later.[25]

From the moment Sa'id Bin Taymur left the country, the son, assuming the powers relinquished by his father, was proclaimed the new Sultan. The news of the transfer of powers was broadcast to the nation which elicited spontaneous celebrations in the streets both in the southern and northern provinces, as the people had already been aware by word of mouth that the son was opposed to his father's rule. To dispel any doubt that the ex-Sul-

---

[25]In an interview with Brigadier Colin C. Maxwell, the writer learned that the ex-Sultan blamed the British Government for its support of the movement that led to his fall, but he made no public statement against the new regime.

tan's repressive measures were no longer to continue, a proclamation in the name of Sultan Qabus
was broadcast in which all exiles and enemies of
the former regime were pardoned and the country's doors thrown open to all to return unmo-
lested.

Apart from Dhufar, where the conflict continued for the next four years, the people as a whole
welcomed the change of regime. Even those who
did not at once return from exile were prepared to
wait and give Sultan Qabus an opportunity to demonstrate his readiness to open a new era of tolerance and reform.[26]

Since propaganda against Sa'id Bin Taymur had
spread into other Arab lands by 'Umani exiles and
reflected on the country as a whole, Qabus embarked on an active foreign policy in an effort to
explain the reform program of the new regime and
to solicit support for it. Syria was the first Arab
country to recognize the Qabus regime, but the
other Arab governments wished to know more
about a country that was almost completely isolated from the outside world. It was, therefore,
deemed necessary that a good will mission should
visit Arab capitals and explain the policy of the
new regime. The mission, headed by Sa'ud al-Khalili, Minister of Education, left 'Uman two or three
months after the new regime had been set up and
visited the Arab Gulf states, Iraq, Syria, Jordan and
later Egypt and other North African countries. The
only country that refused to recognize the new re-

---

[26]Some of the young 'Umani leaders who were out of the country
agitating against the Sa'id Bin Taymur regime, advised their supporters to halt their activities against the new regime and to give
Sultan Qabus time to demonstrate by actions his new policy (the
writer's interview with Salim al-Ghazali, Masqat, October 15, 1978).

gime or receive the goodwill mission was South Yaman, because its leaders had been deeply involved in the Dhufar rebellion and had demanded not only the overthrow of Sultan Sa'id but the abolition of the monarchical system itself. The dispute between 'Uman and South Yaman was submitted to the Arab League, but no final decision was taken because of the differences of opinion among the members about the Dhufar conflict despite the visit of the League's Commission, headed by a Tunisian, to the area of dispute and its recommendations for a peaceful settlement.[27] In the same year, Sultan Qabus paid a state visit to Saudi Arabia, which had also withheld recognition because of a pending frontier dispute and its prior support of Imam Ghalib who had established a government-in-exile at Dammam. Negotiations between King Faysal and Sultan Qabus, in which the two Monarchs came to an understanding, resulted not only in Saudi recognition of Sultan Qabus' regime but also, perhaps more important, in its support for 'Uman in the Dhufar conflict.[28] Since the South Yaman regime was looked upon as a potential threat to the Saudi Monarchy as much as it was to the 'Umani Monarchy, King Faysal saw in Sultan

---

[27]The Arab League Commission visited 'Uman in 1971 and went to Dhufar but was unable to visit the part under the control of the National Liberation Front, called the "liberated part," on the grounds of security. The proposal of a peaceful settlement, though acceptable to 'Uman, was rejected by South Yaman and the National Liberation Front.

[28]Since Saudi recognition of Qabus would be construed by Imam Ghalib, who had been given prior Saudi encouragement, as a let down, King Faysal seems to have urged Sultan Qabus to discuss with Imam Ghalib the difference that separated the Sultanate from the Imamate. Imam Ghalib met with Sultan Qabus, but before the two could even begin the discussion of the subject the Imam failed to address Qabus as Sultan and the meeting came to an abrupt end.

Qabus an ally and not an enemy, and both agreed to cooperate in their opposition to Soviet penetration through such radical movements as the National Liberation Front in South Yaman and elsewhere. Upon the recommendation of Saudi Arabia, 'Uman was first admitted to membership of the Arab League in 1971 and, a year later, supported by other Arab countries, admitted to membership of the United Nations. In the conduct of foreign affairs, Sultan Qabus has been assisted by his able Foreign Minister Qays al-Zuwawi.

While soliciting Arab and foreign support, Sultan Qabus was in the meantime engaged in the erection of a new political structure for the country. His father's regime was indeed very simple. It was based on the assumption that he alone held power—he appointed his First Minister (of Interior), the governors of provinces and all other personnel. He made almost all decisions and expected his subordinates to carry them out. When Sultan Sa'id was deposed, and his secretaries and advisors disbanded, the power structure collapsed. Sultan Qabus stepped in to find that there was no regime which he could keep going—he had to begin not only to fill vacancies but to construct a new system of government.

Shortly before the abdication of his father, Sultan Qabus seems to have given some thought to the future. As noted before, he told me that in his long idle hours, he had been thinking about the future of the country and how to remodel the regime. From his studies and travel abroad, he became aware that the country cannot be adequately put on the path of development and progress by a single head without consultation with its leaders and that some delegation of power was necessary. He was, however, aware that his countrymen, who had long been governed by despotic rulers and deprived of representative institutions, were not expected to accommodate overnight to democratic institutions. If democracy were to succeed, he said, he had to proceed step-by-step.

From the beginning, Qabus was assisted by a number of able men; some were native compatriots and others a few military expatriates who cooperated in the execution of the plan to transfer power from his father. It was natural that if Sultan Qabus were to abandon the pattern of his father's individual rule and share power with his countrymen, a form of Cabinet Government, presided over by a First Minister, should be established. Since Tariq Bin Taymur (Sultan Qabus' uncle and a younger brother of the ex-Sultan) who had left the country because of a disagreement with his brother and was known for his progressive ideas, was invited to become Prime Minister of the newly created post as Head of the Government.[29]

The newly established Cabinet consisted of the already existing Ministry of the Interior, and the new Ministries of Defense, Economy, Justice, Education, Health and Labor. These were filled with men who had either received their education abroad or had an acquaintance with public affairs. Despite lack of experienced civil servants, the de-

---

[29]Tariq Bin Taymur was educated in Germany and was living there with his German wife when he was invited to return to 'Uman. He was well known in Arab political circles as he travelled often in Arab lands as a representative of a German firm and was in close touch with 'Umani opposition leaders in exile. His call to office implied an endorsement for Sultan Qabus' invitation to opposition groups to return and assist in the development of the country under the new regime (see John Townsend, *Oman: The Making of a Modern State*, p. 79).

partment heads, assisted by a few expatriates, applied themselves with vigor and enthusiasm to carry out hurried plans of development under the pressure of immediate needs and expectations. Perhaps it was not unexpected that the plans were not all correlated nor adequately prepared for implementation, but each department tried its utmost to achieve in quantity more than was perhaps expected in the short span that followed the establishment of the new regime.

Premier Tariq, though a brilliant man, had no patience with administrative details. He often discussed matters with his Ministers individually, but rarely met with his Ministers in regular Cabinet sessions. He disapproved of direct advice rendered to the Sultan by expatriates on matters concerning which he should have been first consulted. Jurisdictional conflicts necessarily developed which reflected on the relationship between the Sultan as Head of State and Tariq as the Head of Government, especially on defense and financial affairs, though the Dhufar war was a matter concerning which Sultan Qabus tried personally to handle in consultation with British advisors in the Finance and Defense departments. Since Tariq took the position that 'Uman was an independent country, he tried to reduce foreign influence, as the Arab press often hinted at the lingering British influence under the new regime.[30]

Matters came to a head when both the Sultan and the Premier made decisions before the Premier had first consulted with the Sultan, especially on financial and foreign affairs. Tariq seems to

[30]See Townsend, *op. cit.*, p. 125.

have blamed the expatriates for the ensuing jurisdictional conflicts, but it also became clear that the
Premier's actions often impeded the administrative
process and the implementation of projects. To resolve the conflict Tariq resigned and was succeeded by the Minister of Health, in an acting capacity.[31] Because of the Dhufar war, Sultan Qabus
decided that it would be more expedient to become
his own Prime Minister and retain control over defense and financial affairs as the war required
prompt decisions.

As both the Head of State and Government, Sultan Qabus began to preside over the Cabinet and to
discuss with his Ministers all matters that needed
decisions on the Cabinet level. Even when he did
not attend a meeting, the decisions were formally
issued in his name, presumably on the grounds
that prior approval had already been obtained. Before the Cabinet could develop its own rules of
procedure, there was some confusion about how
to carry out decisions, but very soon the Sultan began to delegate power to his Ministers, reserving
control over defense and security affairs.[32] No political system is expected to emerge overnight; in
'Uman the emerging political system will have to
draw on several sources—the Islamic and cultural
heritage, the experiences of Arab neighbors, and
the country's own experience following the establishment of a new regime.

---

[31]After his resignation, Tariq became first personal advisor to Sultan
Qabus and then Governor of the Central Bank in Masqat. He died in
1980 and was buried in Masqat with full honors.

[32]It is beyond the scope of this essay to discuss administrative problems, since it is essentially a study of the Sultan's role as a leader.
For a critical study of administrative problems, see Townsend, *op.
cit.*, chaps. 4, 7 and 8.

VII

What would be the shape of the emerging system? During more than a decade since Qabus came to the throne there are signs that the traditional patterns of authority have already begun to change. Sultan Qabus has not only delegated power to his Ministers but also urged them to take responsibility. He has no desire to control all departments nor to go into the details of the administrative system. Indeed, the increasing functions of the regime and the Sultan's commitment to development have made it exceedingly difficult to cope with all the problems in accordance with the traditional personal rule.

Second only to the delegation of power has been the establishment of a Cabinet to meet regularly and take decisions on specific matters concerning development and larger issues. The Sultan has not yet appointed a Prime Minister to preside over the Cabinet, but he intends to do so once the lingering effect of the past experience with the former Head of the Government has vanished. Cabinet Government seems to be the logical step in the development of the regime from a traditional to a modern system.

The third step in the evolving political system should be the participation of the public in political decisions. "When will such participation be expected to take place?" I asked Sultan Qabus. "At the present we are preparing the way by an emphasis on modern education; the next step would be to invite an enlightened public to participate in the political process," he replied. Since illiteracy is so widespread and the tribal traditions form the basis of society, the political system is bound to reflect these social forces. "At the present all the provinces, tribes and classes," the Sultan added, "are represented in the Government on all levels; but participation through representative institutions will have to be preceded by popular education." The Sultan, however, expressed his concern about the impact of rapid social changes without the people having been prepared for them. Since quick changes are likely to produce social and political upheavals, the Sultan said, slow changes would be more suitable and reassuring than revolutionary changes. Though there are some people, especially young men, who are anxious to see the country achieve a higher level of progress, they are not unaware of the dangers that follow social upheavals, as the experiences of some Arab neighbors have demonstrated.

What will be the pace of change which 'Uman can safely follow in achieving progress and development? In countries that have at their disposal abundant resources, like Saudi Arabia and some of the Gulf countries, the temptations for sweeping changes are so great that policy makers often find it exceedingly difficult to keep a balance between the advocates of rapid and slow changes. However, 'Uman has relatively limited income from oil and cannot afford the luxury of laying down ambitious reform programs. Thereupon, slow progress is not only the deliberate choice of her rulers; it is also dictated by the country's limited resources. Witnessing the impact of development in Iran, many social thinkers might well ponder on the wisdom of excessive expenditure without self-restraints in the process of the country's transformation from a "traditional" to a "modern" society. Above all, Qabus came to the throne not with an intention to introduce an ideological "revolution," but to carry out a constructive reform program. His regime may be said to rest on several legitimate claims.

First, Qabus did not come to the throne as an outsider who rose to the throne by overthrowing an old regime and establishing a new "revolutionary" regime. He had already been an heir apparent and was expected to succeed in his own right. His accession to the throne by forcing the father to abdicate was not a military revolution on the model of the revolutions that took place in some Arab countries and claiming to derive their legitimacy from ideologies representing revolutionary movements. Nor does Qabus approve of calling the action taken to force his father to abdicate revolutionary. Ever since he came to the throne, no one has questioned the legitimacy of his accession any more than his ancestors' right to the throne had ever been questioned.[33]

Second, since Sultan Sa'id had incurred widespread dissatisfaction in the country—indeed the Dhufar uprising began as a protest to his oppressive rule—the people were potentially prepared to support a movement in favor of his abdication. Indeed, the Ibadi creed justifies the deposition of rulers if they prove to be unworthy or undesirable. Qabus' rise to the throne had indeed been received with public acclaim which indicated a tacit approval of the abdication of his father in favor of him in accordance with popular demand.

Third, Qabus has shown readiness to delegate

---

[33]According to several informants, though Sultan Sa'id had not appointed his son as an heir apparent, there was no doubt in his mind that his son was to be his successor in accordance with the country's traditions and practices.

authority to the country's leaders and has taken
initial steps to give practical expression for his intent to share authority with them. These steps are
indications that his regime is in the process of developing eventually into a democratic system, derived from the Islamic heritage and from Western
models. In order to survive, the emerging system
must satisfy the needs and aspirations of all sections of the country—a goal which the Sultanate
has sought to achieve as the embodiment of its
leadership. Sultan Qabus, having opened a new
chapter in the history of his country, enjoys the es-
teem and loyalty of his people; he may well be
considered—at the age of 40—as the country's
best hope for its development and leadership.

CHAPTER VII

SHAYKH ZAYID OF THE
UNITED ARAB AMIRATES

> It is in the nature of states that author-
> ity should be concentrated in one per-
> son. (In Arab lands) states are founded
> on solidarity and solidarity is formed
> by the union of groups, one of which,
> being more powerful than the rest,
> dominates and directs the other.
> Ibn Khaldun (d. 1405 A.D.)

For over a century and a half, in pursuit of trade and the control of the Indian Subcontinent, Great Britain played the predominant role in the maintenance of peace and security in the Gulf area at relatively small cost. Before she was drawn to this police role early in the nineteenth century, the Gulf was very active in privateering (personal gain was perhaps the immediate objective, but privateering as a movement may be said to have been on the whole an expression of resentment against foreign intrusion) and torn by dynastic rivalries which invited foreign intervention. Earlier the Portuguese first made their appearance in this area and were followed in turn by the Dutch, the French and finally the British.

Although Britain succeeded in keeping the area as a whole in peace by inducing the rulers of the Gulf principalities (often called Shaykhdoms) to stop their support of pirates and making war with one another, especially in the lower Gulf (known as the Coast of Piracy and later renamed the Trucial Coast) by signing a series of agreements prohibiting privateering and warfare, she kept out of domestic affairs and jurisdictional conflicts save insofar as they might affect the peace and tranquility of the region as a whole. Except perhaps in the coastal areas belonging to Turkey, Persia and 'Uman, Britain gradually extended her formal protection to all the Gulf principalities and controlled their foreign relations. In the latter part of the nineteenth century, even some of the autonomous or semi-autonomous provinces of the sovereign states passed under one form of British control or another before they finally regained their full sovereign attributes, some after World War I and the others after World War II.[1]

The discovery of oil in the Gulf and the increasing dependence of the industrialized countries on these (and other Middle Eastern) oil resources have rendered peace and security in the Gulf region even more important to maintain than did the trade and strategic interests which induced Great Britain in the past to defend this region. However, because the position of Britain in the world has become so weakened after World War II she no

---

[1]Persia (Iran) recovered control over her coastal area after World War I, but one of the successor states of the Ottoman Empire (Iraq), which is a Gulf state, passed under British control and formally became independent in 1932. Other Gulf principalities—Kuwayt, Bahrayn, Qatar, and the Trucial Coast—already under British protection before World War I, became independent after World War II. Under international law, only control of foreign relations is surrendered to the protecting Power; in the case of her protection over the Gulf principalities, Britain exercised control not only over foreign affairs but also over some domestic affairs. For this reason some jurists have made a distinction between regular protectorates and the special category of Asiatic and African protectorates. See W.E. Hall, *A Treatise on the Foreign Powers and Jurisdiction of the British Crown* (Oxford, 1894), Chap. 3.

longer possessed sufficient power or prestige to defend the Gulf. Nor could she control the rising tide of nationalism, whose advocates aspired to have the benefits of the newly discovered riches for their own welfare as well as to assume responsibility for self-government and the maintenance of peace and security.

In 1969, in the face of mounting internal economic difficulties and other pressures, the British Government announced its intent to withdraw its military presence from the Gulf by the end of 1971, presumably on the understanding among the Great Powers that to avoid international rivalry and conflict, responsibility for the maintenance of peace and security should fall on the Gulf states themselves. From the regional viewpoint, there were two possible approaches for the maintenance of peace and security—either one of the two major Gulf states, Iran and Saudi Arabia, would assume responsibility singly or jointly, or all the Gulf states might cooperate collectively in the achievement of the task by the creation of a regional organization entrusted with security matters.[2]

Before such a Gulf organization—indeed, any security system—could be set up, it was generally felt that the tiny principalities of the southern Arab coast of the Gulf should form some sort of union, federal or otherwise, to coordinate their relationship more closely and reduce, if not completely eliminate, their traditional inter-dynastic (and tribal) rivalries. No Great Power has more fully understood the significance of such a step than Britain, having known from past experience how dis-

---

[2]For a discussion of the Gulf security from a global perspective, see Hermann F. Eilts, "Security Considerations in the Persian Gulf," *International Security* (1980), Vol. V, pp. 79-113.

turbing those rivalries had been to the tranquility
of the region, and she sought to bring them under
control by encouraging the rulers of her erstwhile
dependencies to subordinate narrow local interests
to a higher level of national existence before they
achieved independence. Aware of the threat of foreign intervention, the nine Shaykhs of the lower
Gulf initially rose to the occasion and began to explore the possibilities of unity soon after Britain
had made public her intention to withdraw from
the Gulf, although only seven, consisting essentially
of the principalities of the Trucial Coast, the hot
bed of past privateering activities and inter-tribal
feuds, succeeded in forming a federal union
known as the United Arab Amirates (UAA).[3] The
other two—Bahrayn and Qatar—opted for separate statehood, although initially they did seriously
consider joining the proposed federal union and
conceivably would be persuaded to join it in the
future.

Before first we discuss the creation of the United
Arab Amirates, a little background about the
coastal area as a whole is necessary for an understanding of the leadership of the newly created
Gulf federal union.

II

While the Gulf's eastern seaboard is controlled
by one non-Arab state, its western coast is divided
among a dozen Arab states—Iraq, Kuwayt, Saudi
Arabia, Bahrayn, Qatar and the seven Trucial principalities (now called the United Arab Amirates)—
not to mention the southeastern corner of Arabia

---

[3]The official spelling is the United Arab Emirates (UAE).

which forms another political entity, the Sultanate of 'Uman, to which the territory of the Musandam Peninsula, crest of the Trucial Coast, belongs. Some of the major Gulf states—Iran, Iraq and Saudi Arabia—have claimed sovereignty over large portions of the Gulf's western seaboard, which might have reduced territorial division; but since their claims did not materialize, local assertion of sovereignty prevailed and the attempts at reducing the number of the Gulf's entities failed.[4]

Local resistance to unity stems essentially from the demographic and social (tribal) structure of society rather than from the geographical configuration of the territory. As in Central Arabia, where the tribal structure of society kept the region in almost permanent warfare and anarchy, the migration of the tribes from the interior of Arabia to the eastern coast carried with it a pattern of life marked by tribal rivalry and conflict and absence of a central authority and laid a foundation of social disorganization which made it exceedingly difficult to create political unity out of a society

---

[4]First Iran, which had occupied Bahrayn long before it passed under British protection, claimed its sovereignty on more than one occasion before it finally recognized it as an independent state in 1969. For the Iranian viewpoint, see Gholam-Reza Tadjbakhche, *La Question des Iles Bahrein* (Paris, 1960); for the argument against the Iranian claim, see M. Khadduri, "Iran's Claim to the Sovereignty of Bahrayn," *American Journal of International Law*, Vol. 45 (1951), pp. 631-647. Second, Iraq claimed sovereignty over Kuwayt on historical and administrative grounds, but failed to carry out its annexation despite initial favorable response before Kuwayt achieved independence (see my *Republican Iraq* [London, 1969], pp. 166-173; and *Socialist Iraq* [Washington, D.C., 1978], pp. 153-159). Third, Saudi Arabia, which had occupied the Buraymi oasis and laid claim to a vast portion of Abu Dhabi in the mid-fifties, renounced later her claim and recognized the newly established United Arab Amirates (in which Abu Dhabi was included) as an independent state (for the Saudi claim to Buraymi, see pp. 253-54, above).

which lacked cohesiveness and social solidarity. By its very nature, each tribe—indeed, often each clan—constitutes an independent unit having its own tribal chief who owes allegiance to no one and acknowledges no law save the Shari'a and tribal (customary) laws.[5]

The tribes of Al Bu Falah, traditionally associated with the larger confederacy of Banu Yas, began to move from the interior of Arabia to the eastern coast in the mid-eighteenth century. They settled in the area known today as Abu Dhabi[6] and established a town known by that name in 1761 on a small island where fresh water was found. Other tribes—Al Bu Falasa, al-Mazari', al-Sudan and others—which were associated with Banu Yas spread along the coastal region beyond Abu Dhabi and then were split by internal rivalries and feuds into several clans and factions. Still others, especially the Qawasim, spread to the north and settled in al-Sharqa and Ra's al-Khayma. Early in the nineteenth century, the Wahhabi tribes of Najd, in an attempt to spread their puritanical creed along the eastern coast, invaded the region and persuaded some of the tribes, especially the Qawasim, to accept their creed and pay the *zakat* (legal alms) as a symbol of loyalty to the Wahhabi authorities.[7]

[5]These laws constitute self-limitations on the chief's authority in such cases as vendetta, compensation for unintentional killings, exchange of prisoners of war and other rules governing inter-tribal warfare (see my *War and Peace in The Law of Islam*, pp. 19-22).

[6]This is the official spelling, though technically it should be Abu Zabi (see George Rentz, "Abu Zabi," *Encyclopedia of Islam*, Vol. I, 2nd ed., p. 166).

[7]The tribal distribution in the United Arab Amirates is as follows: The Banu Yas tribes, consists of the clan of Al Bu Falah, al-Mazari', al-Sudan, al-Qubaysat, Al al-Rumaythi and others have spread along the coastal region. Al al-Nahayan, the ruling family of Abu Dhabi, Al al-Suwaydi and Al al-Mahdi, are clans belonging to the Banu Yas.

Although the tribes had for centuries depended on raids as the time-honored mode of livelihood, they began to learn some new methods for the acquisition of property from their neighbors in the area. In their new homeland they naturally learned, among other things, how to catch fish and in time they began to dive and bring to the coast pearls which they sold to foreign agents in the Gulf markets. They also began to learn how to construct wooden boats and to engage in trade with settlers and in piracy against ships of rival settlers across the Gulf. Meanwhile, they continued their traditional methods of raising sheep and cattle which they carried from the interior of Arabia.

Despite preoccupation in their new homeland with new trades, which improved conditions and raised their standard of living, they seem never to have forgotten their customary tribal feuds and rivalries which they inherited from fathers and forefathers. Only when the tribes were united under a strong leader did they enjoy momentary peace and tranquility. However, once the unifying leadership disappeared, tribal rivalries were resumed and the region relapsed into natural chaos and disorder which disrupted daily activities and kept the region in poverty and backwardness.

In 1855 the coastal tribes, under the able leadership of Shaykh Zayid Bin Khalifa—known as Zayid

The Banu Yas have also spread into Dubayy. Al Bu Falasa, to whom the ruling family of Dubayy belongs (known as Al al-Maktum), and al-Rawashid and others are the principal clans. Al-Qawasim spread into 'Ajman; Al 'Ali resided in Umm al-Quwayn; and al-Sharqiyun in Fujayra (The writer acknowledges the assistance of 'Umran Bin Salim al-'Uways, an authority on tribal genealogy, for information on tribal distribution). See also Arabian American Oil Co., *Oman and The Southern Shore of The Persian Gulf* (Cairo, 1952), pp. 174-176; and Clarence C. Mann, *Abu Dhabi: Birth of an Oil Shaikhdom* (Beirut, 1969), pp. 14-18.

the Great—were united and rivalry and warfare were brought under control. Relative tranquility and order reigned during his rule which lasted over half a century (53 years). Indeed his control extended all over the coast and deep into the desert and his influence was felt throughout the entire coast of 'Uman. His power and prestige, especially his ability to maintain peace, seem to have impressed the British and they cooperated with him in the supression of privateering. Under his rule, tribes lived in peace and security and enjoyed relative prosperity by attending to their daily preoccupations. Shaykh Zayid died in 1908 at about the age of ninety.[8]

Rivalry and disunity, almost always the rule rather than the exception, followed Shaykh Zayid's firm control. It was not easy for his successors to maintain tribal unity, as they themselves fell victims to rivalry and personal ambition. Shaykh Zayid was succeeded first by his son Tahnun, who ruled until 1912, when he was assassinated by his brother Shaykh Saqr. Saqr, suspecting that his younger brothers (who had gone to al-'Ayn pretending to deal with family affairs) might intrigue against him, invited them to Abu Dhabi and offered to attend to their comfort and welfare, but in reality he sought to bring them under his control. Suspecting that Shaykh Saqr might hurt them, if he indeed did not intend to liquidate them, they sought refuge in the house of a powerful tribal chief and refused to return. In 1928, Shaykh Saqr was assassinated by a tribesman of a hostile house, whose motives and identity remained unknown, but the event gave an occasion for the restoration

---

[8]See Mann, *op. cit.*, pp. 48-65; Rentz, *op. cit.*, p. 166.

of power to legitimate hands in accordance with the tribal rule of primogeniture.

Shaykh Shakhbut, though only twenty-five years old, succeeded Shaykh Saqr, in accordance with tradition, as oldest male member of the family. Although young and inexperienced, he ruled the country to the satisfaction of other tribal chiefs for over three decades because he well understood how to deal with them, exercising minimum control and leaving internal affairs to them. His correct and congenial manners helped him maintain friendly and conciliatory relations with them.

Before the discovery of oil, when the country's resources were meager, Shaykh Shakhbut's policy of conservatism and careful spending was considered prudent and highly commendable. Above all, his integrity and straightforwardness compelled all foreign (as well as British) agents, with whom he had a special relationship, to respect him. But after the discovery of oil, when both foreign agents and native leaders began to expect a change in policy, Shaykh Shakhbut refused to change. For long in poverty and deprivation, the people considered the new source of income an opportunity to improve conditions but Shaykh Shakhbut failed, in their eyes, to rise to the occasion. Should the country look for a new leadership?

III

In the mid-fifties and early sixties conditions in the Gulf region—indeed, in the Arab World as a whole—had already begun to change in favor of modernization and progress, and inevitably affected the movement of opinion in Abu Dhabi. The progress achieved by Kuwayt—its rise to statehood and its social and economic developments—set an example for what other Gulf states could do to achieve like progress. Of the Trucial states, only Dubayy seems to have followed Kuwayt's open-door policy before achieving independence. The tribal Shaykhs of Abu Dhabi were not slow to reproach Shaykh Shakhbut for failure to follow the example of his neighbors and change the pattern of his rule. But Shaykh Shakhbut was insensitive to warnings and paid little or no attention to their appeal to improve conditions.

When oil was discovered in Abu Dhabi, Britain had already decided to withdraw from the Gulf and to bring to an end her protection over Abu Dhabi and the other Gulf principalities. Before relinquishing her responsibility, Britain naturally tried to insure that the course of political development would not take a turn adverse to her interests. She sought to achieve at least two important objectives, each closely connected with the other: first, after her departure, the country should not fall into hostile hands; second, the country's new leadership should pursue a policy of development and throw open its doors to foreign goods and services so as to insure the recycling of oil income to Britain and other industrialized countries.

Shaykh Shakhbut, however, long accustomed to a simple way of economic life—he was, among other things his own Minister of Finance—was mentally unprepared to embark on an open-door policy leading to heavy expenditures which in his opinion might expose the country to dangers. Like Sultan Sa'id Bin Taymur, who was adverse to the expenditure of public monies, Shakhbut contended that oil income should be saved for the future, when the country would need it, notwithstanding

that Abu Dhabi's proven oil resources far sur-
passed 'Uman's relatively limited ones. When foreign experts were invited to report on projects for
reconstruction, he was reported to have complained that all that foreign experts would advise
was to spend rather than save the country's income. At heart a conservative, he was convinced
that his country did not really need rapid social
change, which he sincerely thought would corrupt
the people and squander its resources on unnecessary Western luxuries.

For almost four years after oil was discovered,
from 1962 to 1966, Shaykh Shakhbut remained dubious about the wisdom of using the oil royalties
for development. He appeared at first uncertain
about the need for change and then, under pressure, began to argue against it, because he suspected that foreign advisors were more concerned
with spending money under the guise of "social
change" than with the harmful impact that change
might have on the country. His motives seem to
have been misunderstood, as he was considered
opposed to dealings with Westerners, though his
relations with British and other Western diplomats
were well-known to have been agreeable and cooperative. He may have been at times irritated by
Colonel Hugh Bousted, the Political Agent in Abu
Dhabi, and William Clark, the Economic Advisor,
because they offered advice he was unprepared to
accept. As he failed to accommodate, rumors began to circulate that Shaykh Shakhbut was opposed to foreign firms, and his refusal to deposit
money in foreign banks, preferring to hoard it, tarnished his image in the public eye. He was depicted in the foreign press as a ruler unfit to govern his people, who were anxious to achieve

progress and cross the threshold of the modern world. These rumors, unchecked by a ruler who tried to keep his dignity by silence, created a feeling of uneasiness in the ruling family and disarray in the country.

Although Shaykh Shakhbut was not unaware that agitation and the demand for change were spreading in the country, he perhaps thought that if he kept calm and ignored the agitation, the crisis would eventually pass and the commotion disappear. However, the pressure was increasing and he stubbornly closed his ears not only to warnings from the British advisors, but also to those from his brothers and other tribal chiefs within his own establishment. Since Shakhbut refused to bend, his countrymen began to talk openly about the money they had heard was pouring into the country, but concerning which they saw no sign that he would be willing to share it with them—they only heard that he was hoarding it and that he had no intention of using it to improve the country's conditions. Some had already begun to talk about development and progress in neighboring lands, Dubayy in particular, and expressed hope that similar progress might be achieved in their own country. Shakhbut, however, was not convinced that Abu Dhabi should follow the path of its neighbors since in his view these had fallen under foreign influence and departed from the traditional way of life, though some members of his family called his attention to certain deficiencies that had already become apparent in his regime and argued that new methods of administration had become necessary to overhaul or replace the old system.

Before Britain formally terminated her protection over the Trucial states, her proconsuls in the

Gulf began to warn their Government that unless
some pressure was brought to bear on Shaykh
Shakhbut to change his policies, the country might
eventually fall under radical influences and be
swept by revolutionary winds from South Arabia.
The British press, in dispatches from correspon-
dents in the Gulf, began to hint that perhaps Abu
Dhabi's ruler might be persuaded to open his country to foreign trade. When Shakhbut paid no attention to such hints, the press began to criticize him
and to call openly for a change in the regime in the
interest of stability and progress not only in Abu
Dhabi, but also in the Trucial Coast as a whole.[9] No
less concerned were the neighboring Arab states—
Saudi Arabia, Kuwayt, Bahrayn and others—
whose press began to publish statements made by
public figures in which it was suggested that the
Trucial Coast might benefit from the oil royalties
by following the path of progress and development
which the neighboring countries had chosen when
they began to receive oil royalties. Although such
statements had no direct effect on Shakhbut himself, they prepared the public for the idea of his
possible removal, since he failed to heed to the call
for reform.

Unable to influence Shaykh Shakhbut, Britain's
agents in the Gulf began to approach members of
his House, first to influence him to change his
mind and then, after he resisted family pressures,
to replace him by one of them—Shaykh Zayid. At
the outset Shaykh Shakhbut listened to family en-

---

[9]"If the revenues from oil at Abu Dhabi," wrote the *Financial Times*
correspondent (February 9, 1962), "are not to be used for the benefit
of the people, it will be *reductio absurdia* for the whole Sheikhly system." For further citations from the British press, see Claud Morris,
The Desert Falcon (London, 1974), pp. 51-53.

treaties; he even admitted that some changes might be made, but he was exceedingly reluctant to carry them out himself. He went so far as to invite his brothers to participate in the administration and carry out the changes themselves; but they were hesitant to accept, perhaps because they suspected that Shakhbut might allow them to accept responsibility, but would not permit them to carry out reforms. Further talks within the family made no impression on him; in moments of weakness, he often appeared tired and hinted that he was prepared to relinquish responsibility in favor of another member of the family. But such hints were not taken very seriously, as no one thought that he really meant to step down.

Very soon talks within the family became rather serious. Shaykh Shakhbut's brothers, Zayid, Hazza' and Sultan, either individually or collectively began to urge him and even to put pressure on him to accept change and to heed the calls for reform. But Shakhbut was not convinced of the need for change; he began to suspect that Zayid, the second in line of succession, was behind the drive to influence him in pursuit of personal ambition. Even when some of his brothers went to talk with him in almost pleading words, he suspected the hidden hand of Zayid behind the move and warned them against Zayid's intrigues. Nor was Shaykh Shakhbut prepared to listen to advice or tolerate family pressure, and his brothers realized that nothing could be done to change his mind.[10]

---

[10]In an interview with the writer, Shaykh Zayid said that in one of his talks with Shakhbut words of recrimination passed between them. Though Shakhbut reproached him for personal ambition, Zayid simply pointed out that other members of the family were all agreed that he should change his policy (the writer's interview with Shaykh Zayid, March 20, 1979).

In Britain—indeed in all Gulf political circles—it became clear that no change was expected in Abu Dhabi as long as Shaykh Shakhbut remained in power. Britain's agents in the Gulf, concerned about Abu Dhabi's future, gradually came to the conclusion that Shakhbut, though still on good terms with the British authorities, must be replaced by another ruler. Such an action was considered to be not only in Britain's interest but also in Abu Dhabi's own interests. Events in South Arabia had already convinced the British Government that it could not afford to stand indifferent to the call for change in an area so vital to Britain and other Western countries.

Once the rumors had begun to circulate about an impending change in the regime, the eyes of those who desired a change turned to Shaykh Zayid as the natural successor to Shaykh Shakhbut. Open-minded and prudent, Shaykh Zayid had impressed all who knew him as a reformer and an ingenious public servant ever since he had become Governor of al-'Ayn. He won a reputation as a statesman of integrity and high dedication whose ability had already been tested; he was, therefore, considered the right man to succeed Shakhbut as Ruler. Although he was hesitant at first to turn against his brother, Shaykh Zayid agreed to undertake such a step as a matter of duty. Before an account of how he came to the throne, a little background about his life and character is perhaps in order at this stage.

IV

Zayid Bin Sultan was born sometime toward the end of World War I; his birth date, either because it is not really known or not yet officially disclosed, is still in obscurity.[11] Nor do we know much about his early life. As a boy, he seems to have had little or no education; but later, when he realized the need for literacy, he began to learn the art of reading and writing in order to attend to public functions and to keep up with world affairs. Endowed with keen observation and good memory, he learned from personal experiences and from the experience of others with whom he had personal contacts more than from classrooms.

He was brought up in the desert and liked its way of life. He also participated in tribal raids and became familiar with tribal warfare. Above all, he enjoyed hunting and he seems to have excelled in this sport. Though most of his pastime was in the desert, he often visited the town of Abu Dhabi, the seat of Government, and stayed in the Palace of his oldest brother and listened to the conversations of tribal chiefs who attended his *majlis* (public audience) almost every day. From these conversations, as well as from personal contacts and experiences, he learned the style and traditions of tribal politics in which he became, as a tribal chief and Governor of al-'Ayn, a master.[12] While still young, Shaykh Zayid had already become fairly well-informed about public affairs and his horizon was widened by travel and personal contacts with foreign statesmen.

---

[11]In conversations with a number of men who have known Shaykh Zayid from childhood, they seem to disagree on his birth date. Some were inclined to think that he was probably born in 1917; others thought he was born earlier. Still others said that today he is either in his late fifties or in his early sixties, i.e., that he was born after World War I.

[12]For the rules and traditions which Shaykh Zayid had learned about tribal affairs as he stated them in an interview with Claud Morris, see Morris, *op. cit.*, pp. 17-18.

"What was the first official assignment entrusted to you," I asked Shaykh Zayid. "When I was 18 years old," he replied, "my brother, Shaykh Shakhbut, sent me on a mission to al-'Ayn province to settle a dispute between the ruler of Dubayy and the tribes of al-Awamid and Abu Shams." Peace having been achieved, he went on to say, he returned to report to his brother on the matter. Because of his ability to deal with tribal affairs, his brother appointed him first as a personal representative at al-'Ayn and then, after the death of the Wali (Governor) of al-'Ayn, he succeeded him.[13] No record seems to exist to determine the date of Shaykh Zayid's appointment at al-'Ayn. If he were born in 1917 or 1918, as noted earlier, the date of the assignment must be in the mid-thirties, on the strength of the statement of Shaykh Zayid earlier that he was only 18 years of age when he went to al-'Ayn.[14]

Upon his appointment as Governor, Shaykh Zayid began at once to attend to domestic affairs. Because of the availability of fresh water, al-'Ayn enjoyed the reputation of having been a relatively prosperous province. However, the underground canal system (al-Aflaj) had long been neglected and water became scarce, causing a decline in the quality and quantity of the crops. In turn, the decline in the region's economy affected social conditions and aggravated feuds and tension among the

---

[13]The province of al-'Ayn was considered the most important agricultural center in Abu Dhabi.

[14]According to one of my informers, Edward Henderson, former British Ambassador to Abu Dhabi, Shaykh Zayid's assignment was almost a decade later, perhaps in 1945 or 1946. But it is probably a littler earlier, as when Ambassador Henderson met him in 1948, Shaykh Zayid had already become well-known in the area and enjoyed high prestige resulting from a relatively long residence.

tribes. So concerned was Shaykh Shakhbut about the situation that he dispatched his brother, Shaykh Zayid, with a mission to ease the tension and improve conditions in the area as a whole.

After consultation with men well acquainted with local affairs, Shaykh Zayid immediately realized that repair of the *Aflaj* and proper working of the irrigation system were absolutely necessary, if the landowners were to resume cultivation of the lands. Previously, landowners had abandoned their farms because of the scarcity of water, and consequently their value dropped. Now, new canals were constructed and agricultural production began gradually to increase. Shaykh Zayid also paid attention to transportation as a means to promote trade. He raised the dues on irrigation, to which landowners seemed to have had no objection, in order to provide funds earmarked for improvement of the transportation and irrigation systems as well as for other services.

When economic conditions showed signs of improvement, Shaykh Zayid was able in a relatively short time to ease tension by settling disputes arising from vendettas. Blood feuds were part of the way of life in the desert, but they had been increased partly by tribal raids from 'Uman and partly by deterioration in economic conditions. Although his resources were relatively limited, Shaykh Zayid showed generosity to tribesmen and his shrewdness and subtle manners proved instrumental in restoring peaceful relations among feuding tribes. Even the tribes from 'Uman that had infiltrated into the area and settled near Buraymi became loyal to him because of tranquility and improvement in their conditions. He also induced other tribes in neighboring areas to settle and become engaged in agriculture, such as the cultivation of fruit trees, vegetables and other ways which helped to establish peace and security in the region and contributed in no small measures to the improvement of economic conditions as a whole.

No less significant was Shaykh Zayid's diplomacy and personal relationships with the tribal chiefs of the area. Not only did his generosity (though he was not a rich man) and concern about their welfare endear him to them, but he also enhanced his position by marital relationships—he married three wives from different tribes in the al-'Ayn province and came to be regarded as one of them. He demonstrated his loyalty to the country by his opposition to the Saudi claim to Buraymi in the mid-fifties and turned down pecuniary remuneration which the Saudi authorities seem to have offered to win him to their side.[15] His graciousness and dedication to local affairs of the province enhanced his prestige and turned all eyes to him when Shaykh Shakhbut's ability to govern was in question. He remained at al-'Ayn as Governor until he went to Abu Dhabi to become ruler.

While he was still Governor of al-'Ayn, Shaykh Zayid paid his first visit to England in 1953 and later visited the United States and Arab countries. He made his visit to Paris with his brother Shaykh Shakhbut. Though both were impressed with Western material progress, Shakhbut is reported to have said that "in the obscurity of a cautious feudalism, Islam could find its best defence against the twentieth century."[16] More optimistic than his brother's remark, Shaykh Zayid, in answer to a

---

[15]See Clarence C. Mann, *op. cit.*, p. 85.
[16]*Ibid.*, p. 45.

question about his impression of England, said: "al-though the English way of life in general is differ-ent from ours, economic development is what we need for the reconstruction of our country."[17] Nothing along the path of such development, Shaykh Zayid added, is contrary to Islamic teach-ings. These and other casual remarks about the need for reform and development, in contrast with his brother's aversion to change, attracted atten-tion to him, and other tribal leaders seem to have become impatient for him to succeed Shakhbut, without waiting for Shakhbut's death (Shakhbut was only 62 in 1966).

V

In the past, rulers who were engaged in a strug-gle for power with other tribal chiefs or who came into conflict with other members of the family were eliminated by violence—rarely had they been deposed by peaceful methods. In the modern age, especially after the Trucial Coast passed under for-eign protection, that crude method seems to have become unacceptable to most people and a more humane, though not necessarily more congenial, method came into vogue. Since Britain was still the protecting Power, a change in the country's ruler-ship must necessarily meet approval not only of native leaders but also of Her Majesty's Govern-ment. Although Shaykh Zayid was next in the line of succession should Shaykh Shakhbut relinquish the seals of office in accordance with the country's traditions, British approval had first to be obtained.

In July 1966, Shaykh Zayid paid a visit to Eng-

---

[17]The writer's interview with Shaykh Zayid.

land. It was conveniently arranged that he would
be the guest of the Ottoman Bank. Once he was in
London, however, he moved in high political circles and talked with responsible leaders. No less
significant was an invitation to an official party to
meet the Royal Family. The future of his country
was often the subject of discussion, and the need
for a change in its leadership hinted. Before he left
England, it was tacitly agreed that he should take
responsibility, but the method of change was
deemed unnecessary to be discussed at that stage.
It was probably felt that the matter should be left
to Britain's proconsuls in the Gulf to work out the
details.

After his return, Shaykh Zayid tried in vain to
persuade his brother on more than one occasion to
step down in an honorable way without pressure,
but Shaykh Shakhbut refused. Zayid felt that some
form of pressure had become necessary to compel
him to abdicate. A plan was laid down by the British authorities of which Shaykh Zayid seems to
have approved, to be carried out in successive
steps.

On August 6, 1966, Hugh Balfour Paul, Deputy
Political Resident in Abu Dhabi, went to see
Shaykh Shakhbut in his office to inform him that
dissatisfaction in the country required that he
should step down in favor of his brother Zayid.
Shakhbut, unyielding, asked to see Zayid. In the
course of their talk, Zayid suggested that Shakhbut
should abdicate. Considering this an affront,
Shakhbut rejected the suggestion and said bluntly
that he would never abdicate.

Returning to his other brothers to report on the
conversation, Zayid suggested dispatching Shaykh
Hamdan Bin Muhammad, an uncle held in high re-

spect by Shakhbut, to persuade him to step down. Shaykh Hamdan saw Shaykh Shakhbut shortly before noon, but Shakhbut would not yield. At this stage, Shaykh Zayid suggested that more pressure had become necessary. In a telephone conversation with Shakhbut, Zayid warned that if he (Shakhbut) did not "abdicate honorably," pressure would be used to force him to. Shakhbut defiantly refused.[18] Thereupon it was decided as a last resort to use force.

In order to prevent him from outside contact, first the Palace was surrounded by a detachment of a few soldiers from Dhufar.[19] Meanwhile, Balfour Paul went to the Palace to warn Shakhbut that he had no choice but to abdicate. The siege lasted almost five hours—until 4:30 p.m.—but Shakhbut refused to surrender. Thereupon, a handful of soldiers were ordered to enter the Palace and force him to leave. Shakhbut rebuked them for their action. But, paying no attention to his resistance, they managed to maneuver him out of the Palace. A car, waiting at the front door, carried him to the airport where a special plane was ready to take him directly to London.[20]

Shaykh Zayid, who seems to have been restive during the siege of his brother's Palace, was relieved when the operation was over. He went directly to the Palace and declared the abdication of

[18]The writer's interview with Shaykh Zayid.

[19]It was deemed necessary to spare the tribesmen of Abu Dhabi the embarrassment of playing the role of rebels, if they were to participate in a military action against the ruler.

[20]Shaykh Shakhbut lived in a suburb of London for a couple of years before he returned to live in retirement in a special palace at al-'Ayn. He seemed to be content, visited occasionally by members of his family, and not infrequently returns to the capital for short visits.

Shahkbut. His supporters and well-wishers went immediately to offer congratulations and acknowledge him as the new Ruler. The next morning he began his official work promptly and declared the end of his country's isolation by following an open-door policy. From that moment plans of reconstruction and development were laid down and have subsequently been carried out.

VI

Abu Dhabi is not the only Trucial state to show readiness to enter the modern age and pursue the path of progress and development. Almost all other members of this family of states have displayed like readiness in varying degrees. Of these Dubayy has the longest record of liberal policy and its Ruler, Shaykh Rashid Bin Sa'id Bin Maktum, opened the doors of his country to foreign trade before all others. Since this essay is essentially a study of the leadership of the federating (or the centralizing) state, the role of the other states will be discussed only as members of the union rather than separately. Dubayy, however, whose ruler is the Prime Minister of the federation, was second only to Abu Dhabi in laying the foundation of the federal union. Before we turn to a discussion of the formation of the Union, a little background about Dubayy and Shaykh Rashid is necessary.

Dubayy, like Abu Dhabi, is the name of both State and Capital—the latter is a port on the Trucial Coast—with a population roughly estimated at about 100,000. Though essentially Arab in language and culture, the population is a mixture of Arabs, Persians, Indians and Pakistanis. As in Abu Dhabi, the tribesmen came originally from

Central Arabia and were traditionally considered components of Banu Yas. As a political entity, it became independent in 1833 when the tribesmen of Al Bu Falasa, under the leadership of Maktum Bin Bati Bin Suhayl, entered Dubayy and took control of it. It became the bone of contention between the rulers of Abu Dhabi and Sharqa, but on the whole it preserved its internal independence, especially when the entire Trucial Coast passed under British protection toward the end of the nineteenth century.

Shaykh Rashid (b. 1912), great grandson of Shaykh Maktum (who founded the ruling House), became ruler of Dubayy in 1958. Before he became ruler, he had already demonstrated an ability in management and statecraft. When his father, Sa'id Bin Maktum (1912–1958), became the target of attack by his cousins and almost capitulated by relinquishing power to one of them in 1934, Shaykh Rashid and his mother rose to the occasion and saved the throne from slipping into the hands of their opponents.[21]

In 1938, Shaykh Sa'id's opponents made another attempt to snatch power by urging the Municipal Council of Dubayy to control the expenditure of public money. Shaykh Rashid, in league with tribal Shaykhs unfriendly to his father's opponents, seized the opportunity of an incident occurring during a marriage ceremony and, under the guise of reestablishing order, opened fire which caused

---

[21]It is said that Shaykh Rashid and his mother Hissa sent word to the Admiral of the British navy then stationed in the Gulf and appealed to him to act as an arbiter in the dispute between Shaykh Sa'id and his cousins. British intervention, intended to insure stability and peace in the country, saved the throne for the house of Shaykh Sa'id.

the death, among others, of some of Shaykh Sa'id's opponents, including their leader. Until his death in 1958, Shaykh Sa'id's authority was no longer challenged by his cousins. When Shaykh Rashid succeeded his father, there was no question that Dubayy had passed under the control of an efficient and powerful ruler.[22]

Ever since he came to the throne, Shaykh Rashid has followed a liberal policy of opening the country's doors to foreign trade. He improved the port of Dubayy and encouraged foreign traders to use his country as a transit center. As a result of his open-door policy and his encouragement of trade with other commercial centers of the Gulf and the Indian Ocean, his country became one of the most prosperous in the Gulf. He also consolidated his position by cementing friendly relations with his neighbors, especially with the Shaykh of Qatar.[23]

The discovery of oil provided another source of wealth which enabled the ruler of this small state—much smaller in area and more limited in natural resources than Abu Dhabi—to play almost as important a political role as that of Abu Dhabi's Ruler. Shaykh Rashid, a highly competent administrator and an experienced diplomat, at once realized the advantages of unity and came to a quick understanding with Shaykh Zayid on coordinating their activities as a preliminary step to creating a union with other lower Gulf states. This cooperation between the Rulers of Abu Dhabi and Dubayy

---

[22]Shaykh Rashid is also credited with certain adjustment of the frontiers between Dubayy and Abu Dhabi in favor of Dubayy in the dispute over Ghannada in 1947.

[23]The former ruler of Qatar, Shaykh Ahmad Bin 'Ali, was married to Shaykh Rashid's daughter in 1959.

proved instrumental in setting in motion the movement that eventually led to the establishment of
the United Arab Amirates.[24]

VII

The achievement of independence in northern
Arab lands, first in Iraq and Egypt in the thirties
and then Syria, Lebanon and Jordan after World
War II—had a profound impact on the Gulf countries, arousing the political consciousness of their
people and inducing them to embark on the liberation of their lands from foreign control. The discovery of oil in some of these countries triggered
this liberation and enabled their leaders to assert
the principles of both independence and unity. The
new generation, falling under radical doctrines that
swept the Arab world in the mid-fifties and early
sixties, did not call only for independence and
unity but also for liberation from local rulers
whom they denounced as authoritarian and reactionary. In South Arabia, local opposition took a
violent turn and resulted in the establishment of a
radical regime in Adan which later provoked the
Dhufar rebellion, leading eventually to the fall of
the Sultan of 'Uman. Some of the younger tribal
Shaykhs of the Gulf who aspired to become rulers
or play a political role in their countries after independence took an active part in the nationalist
movement, but the moderate elements preferred to

---

[24]For a brief account of the geography and history of Dubayy, see
Phebe Marr, "Dubayy," *Encyclopedia of Islam*, Vol. II, pp. 618-619;
for its social and political structure, see J.D. Anthony, *Arab States of
the Lower Gulf* (Washington, D.C., 1975), pp. 153-171; and E.M.
Khoury, *The United Arab Emirates: Its Political System and Politics*
(Hyattsville, Md., 1980).

move cautiously and achieve nationalist goals by slow and peaceful methods.

Under these circumstances the tribal Shaykhs of the Trucial Coast, though relatively secure under British protection, were bound to respond to the call for independence and unity, and some, especially the potentially rich Amirates, realized that their future security and survival would be dependent on the achievement of liberal nationalist goals. In the early sixties, Kuwayt was the first shaykhdom to achieve independence and set the precedent for other Gulf principalities. Great Britain, in an effort to prevent her erstwhile protectorates (officially referred to as "under protection") from falling in the hands of radical elements, urged the Gulf rulers to identify themselves with the unity movement and to provide it with leadership before it fell into rival hands. Some of the rulers, especially the Shaykhs of Qatar and Bahrayn, displayed greater enthusiasm for unity than others and went so far as to propose an elaborate unification scheme capable of including the entire lower Gulf coast.

The first practical step toward unity, however, was undertaken by Shaykh Zayid, the Ruler of Abu Dhabi, and Shaykh Rashid, Ruler of Dubayy. After preliminary talks on February 18, 1968, they came to a quick agreement that laid down the foundation of the federal union of the Trucial Coast. The two Shaykhs invited the other Gulf rulers to join, and they agreed to meet in a general conference to be held at Dubayy on February 25-27, 1968. Before the delegations of the nine amirates convened, the Shaykh of Qatar circulated a draft convention of a federal union, presumably based on the general terms acceptable to them, as a basis for discussion in the forthcoming meeting at Dubayy.[25] No sooner had they met, than the representatives declared their approval of the federal system, as its underlying principles had already been agreed upon in the preliminary talks.[26] In a communiqué issued on the final day of the conference (February 27, 1968) it was declared that the rulers of the nine Amirates had signed an agreement to establish a federal union in principle and that steps would be undertaken to carry it out. The purpose of the union, as stated in the communiqué, was as follows:

> ... to cement the relations among the member-Amirates, promote cooperation among them in all fields, correlate their progress and welfare, support and respect the independence and sovereignty of each one by the others, coordinate foreign policy and unify diplomatic representation, organize collective defense to maintain their security and peace, and examine generally all their affairs and common interests in order to realize their hopes and achieve the aspirations of the larger Arab homeland.[27]

The Dubayy agreement provided for the establishment of a *Majlis A'la* (Supreme Council), composed of the nine rulers of the Gulf Amirates, and

---

[25]For text of the relevant documents, see Wahid Rai'fat, *Dirasa wa Watha'iq Hawl al-Imarat al-'Arabiya fi al-Khalij* [A Study and Documents Relating to the Arab Amirates of the Gulf] (Cairo, 1971), pp. 161, 167-170); Center of Documents and Studies, *The Arab Emirates: Historical Study and Documents* (Bayrut, 1972), pp. 29-31.

[26]Not only the rulers of the Arab Gulf states but also the heads of some other Arab countries, incuding King Husayn of Jordan and President Nasir of Egypt, declared themselves in favor of the movement of unity among the Arab Gulf countries, as they were in favor of Arab unity among all Arab countries in principle. Only in Iran was the movement denounced in the press as having been inspired by Western imperialism, presumably on the grounds that Bahrayn, still considered part of Iranian territory, was involved in that movement.

[27]For text of the communique, see Rai'fat, *Ibid.*, pp. 172-74.

an executive organ, called *Majlis al-Ittihad* (Federal Council), to assist the Supreme Council in the discharge of its functions. The agreement also provided for setting up a Supreme Court whose structure and functions were to be defined in a special law. The Supreme Council was entrusted with the functions of preparing a draft pact of the federal union and the laws necessary for its implementation.

The Supreme Council held four meetings. The first, convened in Abu Dhabi (May 25-26, 1968), proved inconclusive and was suspended mainly because of differences on procedural matters. When the meetings were resumed on July 6-7, 1968, the Council passed a number of resolutions, including the election of Shaykh Zayid, Ruler of Abu Dhabi, as President of the first session. The second and third sessions were held at Dawha, Capital of Qatar, during October 20-22, 1968, and May 10-14, 1969. In the course of these meetings, the members were not unnaturally divided into two schools of thought: one was in favor of a strong federal government and the other in favor of states rights. Moreover, the larger Amirates—Bahrayn, Qatar and Abu Dhabi—pressed for the strengthening of the federal authorities, and the smaller Amirates, especially the tiny ones—al-Sharqa, Fujayra and others—stressed states rights. Bahrayn, whose population is larger than all the other Amirates, demanded that the seat of the Union should be in its territory and that representation in the Union Assembly should be based on the strength of the population of each member-state. There was also disagreement on the mode of the distribution of federal departments and representation in the Union Assembly. Though there was at the beginning a tendency to compromise on these issues, the small Amirates, recognizing their weak position, continued to stress states rights.

The fourth session, held at Abu Dhabi, took place on October 21-25, 1969. Disagreement on fundamental questions of federal and states rights were overshadowed by procedural issues and no reconciliation was in sight. In one of the meetings (October 25, 1969) the Deputy British Resident in Abu Dhabi, at the instance of the British Resident in Bahrayn, asked to deliver a message in which Her Majesty's Government urged cooperation among the Amirates and expressed hope for their success to establish the federal union.[28] This message, misinterpreted as an attempt to interfere in domestic affairs, seems to have served as a convenient pretext for some to withdraw from the unity talks. The Shaykh of Qatar, the first to withdraw from the meeting, was followed by the Shaykh of Ra's al-Khayma and the meeting was temporarily suspended. Attempts to resume the talks were to no avail, as there was a hardening on conflicting demands. Even before the meeting was convened there were rumors of sharp disagreement between the small and the large Amirates on the question of states rights, despite assurances that each state was to have full control over domestic affairs and that all would enjoy equal status within the union. In an effort to reach a compromise, Bahrayn and Qatar, though still competing on the location of the federal capital, declared their readiness to accept the principle of equal representation in the Union Assembly. However, Qatar, whose chief delegate served as Premier of the temporary Federal Cabi-

---

[28]*Ibid.*, pp. 119-120.

net, expressed the desire to have the Premiership
of the Union reserved to it and the Ruler of Ra's
al-Khayma demanded that the portfolio of defense
should be the share of his state. These and other
matters rendered agreement among the Amirates
exceedingly difficult and the prospect of resuming
the meetings of the Supreme Council was uncertain.

Meanwhile, Bahrayn and Qatar, separated by sea
from the Trucial Coast, felt that each could proceed to achieve its independence without participation in a federal union with their neighbors. Indeed, the Ruler of Bahrayn had already begun to
take steps designed to reorganize the internal regime of his country as an independent state. These
steps had been undertaken in anticipation of the
negotiations that were going on between Britain
and Iran which subsequently led to the recognition
of Bahrayn's independene by Iran on the grounds
that its people had exercised their right of self-determination by a plebiscite held under the supervision of the United Nations. On May 12, 1970, Britain and Iran recognized Bahrayn's independence.
As a result, Bahrayn's Ruler became exceedingly
reluctant to subordinate the newly won sovereignty of his country to a federal union with his
neighbors. Similarly, the Ruler of Qatar promulgated a Constitution (April 27, 1970) in which it
was stated that his country was an independent
sovereign state. Some of the provisions in the Constitution of Qatar were considered contrary to the
spirit, if not to the letter, of the Constitution of the
federal union which was under preparation by a
Committee of Jurists appointed by the Supreme
Council. Since all efforts to reconcile the differences among the Amirates did not materialize, the

meetings of the Supreme Council were prorogued *sine die.*

Informal conversations were resumed among the Trucial Amirates without the participation of Qatar and Bahrayn. After a year and a half of negotiations, in which Sir William Luce, personal representative of the British Foreign Secretary, made a tour in the Gulf to narrow some of the differences, the rulers of Abu Dhabi, Dubayy, al-Sharqa, 'Ajman, Umm al-Quwayn and Fujayra declared that they had agreed to establish the United Arab Amirates (UAA) on July 18, 1971. Thereupon, Bahrayn formally declared its independence on August 14, 1971, and Qatar followed suit on September 3, 1971. The rulers of the remaining six Amirates adopted with minor modifications the draft Constitution which the Committee of Jurists had prepared under the authority of the Supreme Council as a Provisional Constitution and it came into effect in December 1971.[29] Ra's al-Khayma, prevailed upon to join the UAA, agreed to become its seventh member-state in 1972.[30]

VIII

The Provisional Constitution provided for the establishment of a Federal Union, composed of federal and states authorities. The latter, retaining residual powers, exercise full control over state-affairs, and the former, though entrusted with the sovereignty of the union as a whole, exercises au-

---

[29]See text in the *Official Gazette*, Vol. I (December 1971), pp. 2-39.

[30]For text of the adhesion of Ra's al-Khayma, see *Ibid.*, Vol. II (March 30, 1972), pp. 6-7. For a background of the establishment of the union, see Rosemarie S. Zahlan, *The Origins of the United Arab Emirates* (New York, 1978).

thority over internal affairs as specified in the Constitution. The Federal Union of the UAA is perhaps nearer to the Canadian than with the American system.[31] The Federal Government of the UAA consists of a Federal Supreme Council, in which the federated states are equally represented;[32] a Federal National Assembly, in which each state is represented in accordance with its size and demography;[33] and a Cabinet, composed of an unspecified number of Ministers selected on the basis of competence and experience.[34] The Presidency of the Union has in practice become the privilege of Abu Dhabi, the largest and in resources the richest state in the Union; the vice-presidency and Premiership have become the privilege of Dubayy, second in stature to Abu Dhabi, and the Cabinet posts have ordinarily been chosen by agreement between President and Premier from among representatives of the states with a view to enlisting their participation in federal affairs and share collective responsibility.

Except Abu Dahbi, the other federated states are tiny in size and population. Small wonder that when Britain suddenly announced its intention to withdraw her protection, it was immediately realized that the seven entities should unite into one

[31]This comparison is strickly confined to the structure of the federal authority.

[32]Each state, represented by its Ruler, enjoys equal voting rights. In order to be binding, decisions must be carried by a majority of five including the votes of Abu Dhabi and Dubayy in all substantive matters. Decisions on procedural matters are carried by a simple majority (Article 49).

[33]Abu Dhabi and Dubayy are assigned 8 seats each; Sharqa and Ra's al-Khayma 6 seats each; 'Ajman, Umm al-Quwayn and Fujayra 4 seats each.

[34]It is taken for granted that the states are represented in a manner that would maintain a balance among them.

larger state in order to protect their own common interests. However, when they met to discuss unity, local and centrifugal forces came immediately into play to prevent full unity. The federal system, though somewhat loose in structure, proved a convenient compromise between the conflicting interests of the large and the small states. But the centrifugal forces were not confined to the tiny entities; there were forces working against full unity even in the larger states. What were the sources of the centrifugal forces?

In a relatively small area such as the Trucial Coast, essentially a flat desert land with little fresh water and natural resources (except oil, which became known only in recent years), physical conditions were not expected to raise essential barriers to political unity. It was not geography but demography—the distribution of the population in accordance with descent, real or fictitious, and the traditional method of exercising authority—that stood in the way of achieving unity.

The political division of the Trucial Coast into seven political entities was the product of the history, traditions and social habits of a tribal society. Before they entered the Trucial Coast, the tribal polity had already been molded in Central Arabia. Each tribe, with its chief (the Shaykh) as a supreme ruler, was an independent political entity no matter where the tribe had chosen to reside. When the tribes of Banu Yas had taken residence along the eastern coast of Arabia, the area was necessarily divided among the ruling tribal families, though well-defined boundaries could not be established and the jurisdiction of each tribal Shaykh expanded and retracted on the basis of the power and prestige he could muster over the expanse of the desert land that came under his control. Even after the tribes had accepted territorial division under British protection, tribal feuds and raids prevented the establishment of fixed frontiers. Since the British authorities were more interested in the maintenance of peace and control of piracy than in altering the social habits of the tribes, the essential character of the tribal community continued virtually unchanged until Britain finally decided to terminate her protection over the Trucial Coast. Before she withdrew from the Gulf, Britain urged unity among the ruling tribal chiefs, who realized that the political and economic realities of the region required cooperation and coordination of their efforts rather than separation and conflicts. The upshot of the centripetal forces that came into operation was the establishment of a federal union —the United Arab Amirates.

Previous Arab experiences with the federal system demonstrated, however, as in Syria and Libya, that the system was adopted only as a temporary measure to prevent separate political entities from drifting apart rather than as a continuing regime which would bring about harmony and social cohesion in a fragmented society. When the Syro-Egyptian union (the United Arab Republic) was founded in 1958, several Arab leaders urged that it be organized on a federal basis; but the opinion of extreme Pan-Arabs prevailed in favor of a unitary state. Arab low regard for federalism, reflecting a concern about disintegration, often led Arab leaders to take the short-cut of creating a unitary state system. When an Arab federal union was occasionally created, as between Iraq and Jordan in 1958, it was very soon dissolved before achieving the harmony and social cohesion needed to achieve integration. For this reason, political and military pressures were often used to keep political entities together because the federal system under which those entities were brought together was prematurely abolished before the objectives of the federation had been achieved.[35]

Of the seven rulers who joined to establish the Federal Union, two of them—Shaykh Zayid, Ruler of Abu Dhabi, and Shaykh Rashid, Ruler of Dubayy—proved instrumental not only in taking the lead to persuade the other rulers to join the Union, but also in providing leadership and in sharing the wealth of their relatively prosperous lands with the others. Because Abu Dhabi is greater in population, size and economic resources, Shaykh Zayid enjoys greater power and prestige than other rulers. But Shaykh Rashid, supported by Shaykh Saqr, Ruler of Ra's al-Khayma—a traditional ally of Dubayy and rival of Abu Dhabi—has been able to keep a balance by championing the cause of states rights. Unlike the European federal processes, especially in Germany and Italy, where a powerful federating state was necessary, the UAA followed the American pattern where two major states—Massachusetts and Virginia—cooperated to maintain balance and harmony in the federating process. But competition and rivalry among federating states often breed discord and friction which, if not resolved by peaceful means, may eventually lead to violence

---

[35]After the break-up of the United Arab Republic, President Nasir seems to have realized that the Syro-Egyptian union should have been created on a federal foundation as a nucleus for the future United Arab States to which other Arab countries might be drawn; but when Syrian and Iraqi leaders met in Cairo in 1963 to discuss unity, Nasir was not convinced that even a federal regime could bring about unity.

as the American experience has demonstrated.
Competition between Abu Dhabi and Dubayy has
so far been confined to a relatively few jurisdictional issues which Shaykh Zayid has been able to
resolve by caution and the private talks in which
he excells. But the drive for social and economic
development and the increasing influence of the
UAA in inter-Arab affairs prompted the nationalist
elements, especially among the new generation, to
urge Shaykh Zayid to champion the cause of the
Union's process toward further unity which came
to be know as "the Union's Procession" (*al-Masira
al-Wihdawiya*). Shaykh Rashid, supported by elements opposed to the increasing influence of Abu
Dhabi, has counselled moderation and slow process in the drive for unity. Shaykh Zayid, although
prudent and prepared to wait, has often found his
powers as head of the Federal Union restricted by
statutes considered to be temporary. He has, indeed, taken actions which appeared to encroach
on states rights.

Matters came to a head over the preparation of
a draft Permanent Constitution which the National
Assembly and the Cabinet had jointly prepared for
submission to the Federal Supreme Council in
1979. The Provisional Constitution, which came
into force in 1971, provided a transitional period of
five years before it could be revised or replaced. In
1976, a slight revision was introduced to enable the
federal authorities to establish a unified military
command and united judiciary. Before the second
five-year transitional period was due to expire, the
preparation of a draft Permanent Constitution was
in order to supersede the Provisional Constitution.
A Constitutional Committee, composed of members
of the Federal National Assembly and the Cabinet,

began to prepare a draft Constitution in consultation with experts on constitutional law. The draft, approved by both the National Assembly and the Cabinet, was in favor of enhancing the powers of the Federal Government and considered a step in the right direction in the Union's progress. Before the draft was submitted to the Supreme Council, it was circulated among the rulers of the seven states for scrutiny. Two of the rulers, Shaykh Rashid and Shaykh Saqr, had some reservations, but all seem to have agreed on the need for the preservation and the strengthening of the union in principle. It is indeed not unnatural that some of the provisions were to be the subject of criticism, but it was hoped that a final text would be approved to the satisfaction of all.

When the Supreme Council met on March 27, 1979, however, Shaykh Rashid and Shaykh Saqr failed to attend, presumably on the grounds that their objections to the draft were so extensive that further preliminary talks were necessary to narrow the differences before formal discussion should take place. Rumors, set on foot by the advocates of a strong federal authority, reflected unfavorably on the two Shaykhs, who were denounced as opposed to change and to the pursuit of the Union's progress. Stirred by these rumors, the students of al-'Ayn University, joined by high school teachers and students, began to demonstrate in the streets of Abu Dhabi a week before the Supreme Council was to assemble. On the day of its opening session (March 27), the students submitted a petition to Shaykh Zayid, President of the Union, in which they urged pursuance of the Union's procession and approval of the permanent Constitution which the National Assembly and the Council of Ministers had prepared.[36]

Since the matter had become a public concern and the press published unfavorable remarks about him, Shaykh Rashid felt obliged to release to the press a memorandum (March 26, 1979) which he had prepared for the Supreme Council in order to defend himself and put his views about constitutional changes before the public.[37] In his memorandum, Shaykh Rashid declared that he was not opposed to, but rather in favor of, the preservation of the federal system and that the agreement of the seven Trucial states to form a union had in fact created a "true modern concept of the State." In order to preserve it, its basic law—the Constitution—must govern the acts of its institutions, allowing no violation or suspension of its provisions. But, he added, the Provisional Constitution had often been violated and the new move to prepare a new Constitution seems to imply that the present Constitution would be suspended. In a statement to the press two days later (March 28, 1979), he declared that in his opinion:

> Matters developed to the degree of demanding that the provisional constitution be held in abeyance until the permanent constitution was prepared.

> Many parts of the joint memorandum prepared by the Federal National (Assembly) and the Cabinet showed a disregard of the constitution's provisions.[38]

---

[36]For text of the petition, and the student's demonstrations, see *al-Fajr*, Abu Dhabi, March 28, 1979.
[37]For text of Shaykh Rashid's Memorandum of March 26, 1979, see *Khaleej Times*, Dubayy, March 28, 1979.
[38]See the *Khaleej Times*, Dubayy, March 29, 1979.

As a result, Shaykh Rashid went on to say, a constitutional crisis had developed, to which he referred as a "real crisis." The reason, he added, was that "the joint memorandum . . . indicates that those who drafted [it] . . . have totally ignored the provisions of the constitution, thus aiming in an unconstitutional manner to shake the foundations of which the federation of the United Arab Amirates stand." He cited as a case in point the attempts to unify the command of the armed forces and the judiciary which he held would undermine the federal system. He also indicated that the draft Permanent Constitution made no reference to Islam; he urged that any new draft should be based on Islamic principles and on the country's traditions.

In his reply to Shaykh Rashid, Shaykh Zayid stated in a memorandum published in the press four days later (March 30, 1979) that the draft Permanent Constitution was submitted only as a set of proposals for discussion at the Supreme Council. Had Shaykh Rashid attended the meeting on March 27 he would have had the opportunity to present his views and propose changes in the draft. At any rate, Shaykh Zayid said, the new Constitution could not have been adopted without Shaykh Rashid's approval, as all decisions at the Supreme Council on substantive matters require a majority of five including the votes of Dubayy and Abu Dhabi. Nor were the changes to which Shaykh Rashid had objected unconstitutional or violations of the Provisional Constitution, as they were carried out in accordance with the proper procedure to which Abu Dhabi had given its approval. Indeed, Shaykh Zayid added, if violations of the Constitution had ever been perpetrated, Dubayy itself should share responsibility for the prior approval of acts that he considered contrary to the Constitution.[39]

Some of the points which Shaykh Rashid raised in his memorandum, like the unification of the armed forces and the judiciary, were important substantive matters that touched on security and basic states rights, but others were essentially procedural. By unification of the armed forces under the command of the federal authorities, Shaykh Zayid's own position as Head of State would be enhanced at the expense of states rights. Not only Shaykh Rashid, but others, were opposed to the unification of the armed forces partly on the grounds of internal security, but, perhaps more important, for the reason that the concentration of the armed forces under unified federal command might induce some officers to use the Army as an instrument to effect changes in the regime, as the experiences of northern Arab countries have demonstrated. Shaykh Zayid, conceding that Army officers might be tempted to interfere in politics, held that such a possibility should not stand in the way of creating efficient federal organizations. As to the possibility of military uprisings, he felt that the problem should be dealt with by other methods and not by allowing the states to organize separate forces. Nor did Shaykh Zayid advocate the dismantling of all state forces at once; he seems to have merely called for the unification of some forces and the creation of a relatively large federal force as a means to strengthen the Federal Union as a whole.

---

[39]For text of the Memorandum, see *al-Ittihad*, Abu Dhabi, March 30, 1979; and *al-Fajr*, Abu Dhabi, March 31, 1979.

IX

For almost six months, the deadlock between the two schools of thought over the federal vs. states rights issue prevented the Supreme Council from resuming its meetings and the very existence of the federal system seemed in jeopardy. But in reality, though the Supreme Council did not meet, private conversations among top rulers of the member-states were never interrupted and the good offices of neighbors, Saudi Arabia and Kuwayt in particular, provided all the necessary rapport between Shaykh Zayid and Shaykh Rashid to iron out their differences. Private talks between the two Shaykhs reduced the differences to two substantive issues— the unification of the armed forces and the preservation of the Provisional Constitution until a Permanent Constitution was laid down and approved by the Federal Supreme Council. During these informal talks, time and again Shaykh Rashid and his supporters stated that the drive toward the Union's progress should not be pushed too soon and too fast, in order to consolidate the federal system and overcome obstacles which might impede the achievement of national goals. Shaykh Zayid went on to say that his aim had always been to pursue the progress and development of the Union as a whole through the mechanism of the federal system; but, he pointed out, that the deficiencies and perplexities of the system itself, which nearly a decade of experiences had shown, must be first attended to. Otherwise, the national goals would be impossible to achieve. Shaykh Rashid conceded that certain procedural defects in the federal system did exist, leading to constitutional violations, but he warned against quick changes in the federal system before full scrutiny of an alternative plan—or plans—and adequate preparations for carrying them out were laid down.

In the course of their conversations, whether carried out directly between Shaykh Zayid and Shaykh Rashid or through an intermediary, it was agreed that there was no question about the need for the preservation of the federal system, because it provided a working framework within which the seven member-states could cooperate and serve their best interests. But the two Shaykhs also realized that its working to the satisfaction of all fell short of expectations and that the need for overhauling and strengthening the system had become necessary.

How could the two Shaykhs, one fully involved with domestic and the other with federal affairs, reconcile their differences? Though Shaykh Rashid was nominally the Vice-President of the Federal Union, the two Shaykhs had scarcely met alone to discuss federal problems save when the seven rulers of the member-states assembled in the Supreme Federal Council. When the two Shaykhs finally met to discuss their differences in 1979, Shaykh Zayid pointed out that it was indeed easy and perhaps quite natural for the Ruler of a member-state to assert states rights. In order to have a balanced view of the relationship between federal and states rights, Shaykh Rashid was invited to undertake the Premiership of the Federal Union in order to participate more actively in federal affairs. Perhaps in an effort to avoid being involved in federal affairs, Shaykh Rashid pointed out that his son was the Prime Minister of the Federal Union. He was told, however, that if the problem of federal vs. states rights were ever to be resolved, he should himself become the Prime Minister. Shaykh Rashid, at that point, conceded that he was indeed duty bound to share federal responsibility.[40]

Shaykh Rashid's agreement to serve as Premier under the Presidency of Shaykh Zayid proved a victory of the advocates of the Union's procession, as Shaykh Rashid would be bound to support acts undertaken at the federal level, even if they were to affect matters considered within state jurisdiction. Although Shaykh Rashid might not be inclined to encroach on states rights, his participation in the exercise of federal authority is considered likely to consolidate and eventually to strengthen the federal authority.

Shaykh Zayid, Head of the Federal Union, was and still is the man who occupies the central position in the country. By leadership qualities and by experience, he has proved to be a statesman who could reconcile tribal chiefs, inspire confidence and command respect. His readiness to cooperate with Shaykh Rashid, the first Ruler to cooperate with him in the establishment of the Union (though later contesting his championship of the Union's procession), demonstrated that he was not merely in pursuit of personal power, but was trying to provide leadership for a country in need of social and political integration. His prudence, dedication and flexibility—qualifications for which he has been highly respected ever since he became a provincial governor—have eminently qualified him to play a centralizing role in Arab federal experiences.

---

[40]I have it on the authority of one of my informants that the suggestion to offer the Premiership to Shaykh Rashid had been made by one of the UAA's neighbors.

CHAPTER VIII

CONCLUSION

We were reproached that we were few
in numbers; So I said to her: Indeed,
noble men are few.

al-Samaw'al (d. circa mid-sixth century A.D.)

We have seen that the Arab personalities who form the subject matter of this study belong to what we called the realist school. They are realists in the sense that they hold moderate views and their actions have relevance to conditions. Although some may have been and still are committed to certain ideological premises, none seems to be inclined to subordinate the requirements of security or other immediate objectives to ideological goals. As I pointed out in the introductory chapter, the days of the idealist and radical leaders of the Nasir era are perhaps over and the type of leadership which is increasingly in demand and most highly respected in the Arab World today is that which belongs to the realist school.

Although the leaders scrutinized in this study tend to play the realist role, they have not all begun their careers as realists. Some, like the Saudi and Arab Gulf leaders—King Khalid, Crown Prince Fahd, Shaykh Zayid and Shaykh Rashid—owe their quality of realism to the social milieu in which they have grown up and to family traditions acquired from long experience. King Husayn and Sultan Qabus, though they have been brought up in houses that have had long dynastic traditions, rose to the throne rather young, before their sense of realism matured. In time, King Husayn's leadership proved to be one of the most balanced and pragmatic in the Arab World; and Sultan Qabus, after a decade of apprenticeship in the art of governance, seems to be pursuing the best traditions of his family's moderation and realism. By contrast, Presidents Sadat and Asad, who made their entry into the political scene on horseback and participated in military upheavals identified with the Pan-Arab ideology, naturally played at the outset the fashionable role of ideological leaders. Only after Nasir's departure did their propensity to play the realist role come into operation and rise to the occasion in the wake of a national crisis, by subordinating ideological claims to practical considerations.

II

In describing the Arab leaders of today as realists, we do not mean that they are devoid of principles or that they have no concern about ultimate national goals. Like the realists of the interwar years, they are in agreement in principle with the idealists—if not the ideologues—on essential national goals, but have made a distinction between immediate objectives which they intend to achieve and ultimate goals which provide guidelines rather than prescribed rules for action. What are these ultimate goals?

Today, all Arab leaders subscribe to Islam and Arab nationalism and consider them as fundamental principles binding on all. No one, not even Communist leaders who negate religion, denounce Islam or dismiss its cultural and moral values as irrelevant to Islamic society. Nor do Muslim fundamentalists, who consider Islam ecumenical in nature, reject nationalism as inconsistent with Islamic teachings. True, some, like the Saudi and the Arab Gulf leaders, profess their primary loyalty to Islam, while the leaders in northern Arab lands stress in varying degree nationalism as the idyllic symbol of identity. But all consider Islam and nationalism as complementary rather than as contradictory principles. No matter how important the call for secularism is, no Arab leader today is prepared to advocate secular nationalism devoid of religion or to call for separation between "church" and "state," as the Kamalist leaders did, though many Arab thinkers still insist on the need for it.

In professing loyalty to both nationalism and Islam, the realist leader in northern Arab lands has not yet formally indicated to which his primary loyalty belongs. It is true that the younger leaders have shown preference for nationalism as an overriding principle—indeed, the inclusion of Islam as an ingredient in nationalism is a tacit confirmation of the primacy of nationalism over religion—but the matter has by no means been made clear on the official level. In Arabia Islam is still the primary loyalty; but nationalism, spreading rapidly among the new generation, may ultimately become an overriding principle in these lands.

The trend of mixing religion with nationalism, however, although sound in principle, has raised serious problems to the realist leader. In countries where Muslims are divided into Sunnis and Shi'is (not to speak of the existence of other religious minorities), the adoption of religion as a component of nationalism tended to stimulate sectarian and confessional strife in domestic politics, mainly because nationalism, although intended to create cohesion and social solidarity in a fragmented society, has not yet penetrated to the masses to supersede confessional loyalties. For this reason Asad (a Shi'i) in Syria and Saddam Husayn (a Sunni) in Iraq have become the target of attacks on confessional grounds from communities considering themselves to form the majority in their respective countries, though both are leaders of an ardent nationalist party—the Ba'th Party—which claims to command allegiance on the grounds of Pan-Arab rather than Islamic identity.

In countries where important ethno-cultural groups exist, like the Kurds in Iraq, the emphasis by Arab leaders on nationalism to reduce confessionalism has accentuated ethnical tensions. Despite the fact that the Kurds share with the Sunnis the same confessional loyalty, the former are concerned about the undermining of their ethnic identity if Iraq should become part of a Pan-Arab union. Thus, the leaders of Iraq and Syria are caught between the two horns of the dilemma when religion is interwoven with nationalism. If Asad and Saddam Husayn were to assert secular nationalism, as some Arab thinkers suggest, nationalism might eventually supersede confessionalism. In Arab countries like Saudi Arabia, where ethnic or religious minorities are small or non-existent, religion may be a useful ingredient of nationalism, but in countries where confessional feeling is deeply rooted, secular nationalism is absolutely necessary to overcome indigenous counter-currents. Yet the Syrian and Iraqi leaders are not in a position today to assert secular principles, despite the need to meet confessional challenges. If confessionalism and the complex majority-minority problems are ever resolved, secularism would indeed be necessary to promote a higher level of loyalty.

No less significant are Arab aspirations to adopt democracy. All leaders subscribe to it in principle, but they have found it exceedingly difficult to achieve as an immediate objective. In northern Arab lands, where parliamentary democracy was established before independence, it was abolished by the revolutionary movement that swept the Arab World in the fifties because it was considered unsuitable in the form in which it was transplanted from Western countries. In Egypt and Syria, Sadat and Asad are trying to reestablish a form of democracy combining the principles of free-enterprise and collectivism. Such a system, seeking to achieve an equilibrium between free economy and distributive justice, is a form of social democracy based on principles which have become fashionable in northern Arab lands.

In Arabia, although social democracy is inherent in a tribal society, political democracy based on popular representation and free elections is an alien institution. In accordance with tribal traditions, the Shaykh, though he may tolerate differing opinions, makes his final decisions irrespective of the advice of counsellors. On the strength of the traditional principle of consultation (*shura*), the Saudi and the Arab Gulf leaders are seeking to evolve democratic institutions in which the public will participate in decision making. The Arabs hope

that this process may eventually lead to the emergence of a native form of democracy comprising
elements stemming from the national heritage as
well as from contemporary societies.

III

For almost a quarter of a century after World
War II, the Arab World experienced continuing social and political upheavals with consequent frequent changes of regimes that scarcely gave an opportunity to most leaders to stay long in power.
After Nasir's departure, although no Arab leader
has yet been able to acquire the image of a charismatic leader or assert grand Pan-Arab designs, almost all seem to enjoy longer terms in office than
their predecessors, despite the deep sense of
insecurity and occasional threats to their regimes
which continue to haunt them.

As an ideology, Pan-Arabism is still a dream
which continues to govern Arab political thinking
and influence the relationships of each Arab country with others in varying degree. But the realist
leaders are trying today to give Pan-Arabism a
more practical meaning by asserting Arab cooperation and solidarity to resist foreign and Israeli
pressures. True, disagreement on how to deal with
the Great Powers, and with Israel in particular, has
often divided the Arab World into two or more
camps; but they are in agreement on the premise
that Israel's existence is a threat to all even though
some Arab lands are remote from danger. No matter how long the disagreement may last, however,
the Arab leaders have always found it in the common interest to meet and iron out their differences. Despite Egypt's sudden break with the Arab

fold, the readiness of Arab leaders to meet and display solidarity has been more noticeable since the Six-Day War. Perhaps no single event has taught the Arabs a greater lesson than that war, as it brought home the military strength of Israel and demonstrated that Israeli power cannot be dismissed by empty rhetorical statements. Despite occasional discord, the Israeli challenge is likely to bring about further collaboration and unity—indeed, Israel may well prove eventually to be the greatest unifying factor among the Arabs, regardless of how long the process may take. Not only will its very existence keep alive the dream of Pan-Arab unity, but also its superiority in skills and other matters are bound to inspire them with the realization that unless they achieve reform and reconstruction they will never be able to stand up to the challenge.

The Arab retreat from the Pan-Arab ideal today has brought in its train the assertion of local and parochial propensities. The upsurge of local feeling is not new in the Arab World. It manifested itself in the rivalry for leadership between Iraq and Egypt in the past and now in the dissension between Egypt and other Arab countries. It is not unnatural that whenever the differences among Arab leaders have come up to the surface, a relapse into parochialism almost always followed, stemming primarily from geographical variations, diverse historical traditions accentuated by the human and material sacrifices that the confrontation countries—Egypt, Syria and Jordan (and more recently Lebanon)—have suffered during thirty years of almost continuous hostility and warfare with Israel. The non-confrontation countries, though richer in resources, have rightly been reproached for having contributed far smaller amounts than their share in the war efforts, partly because of an unconscious parochial feeling but mainly because they were not directly involved in hostile actions. Disparity in economic resources, especially between oil-producing countries and others which have endured sacrifices and are desperately in need of funds both for reform and development, is another cause of dissension. Saudi Arabia and Kuwayt are examples of generous contributors, but these examples have not been followed universally.

Concomitant with the changing character of leadership from idealist (and ideological) to realist, is the gradual transformation of Arab regimes from authoritarian to relatively liberal regimes. During the Nasir era, military authoritarianism prevailed in almost all northern Arab lands and personal rule was still fashionable in Saudi Arabia and the Gulf Shaykhdoms. Today, military authoritarianism is necessarily restricted by the re-emergence of political parties and other organizations seeking to play an increasingly participating role in the process toward political democracy. The Army, it is true, is still the power behind the throne, particularly in the countries that have experienced military rule, but civilian control over the Army in Egypt, Syria and Iraq has received public support and the man on horseback is perhaps unlikely to survive long, if he seized power by a military uprising. Nevertheless, the danger still exists, and the Army is vigilantly watched and treated with care in all Arab lands.

No less significant is the retreat from socialist and radical collectivist policies that dominated a number of Arab countries during the Nasir era.

Iraq and Syria may still claim to adhere to collectivist doctrines in principle, but Arab Socialism, which the Ba'th leaders consider as the basis of economy, is a departure from the nationalization policy which Syria and Iraq had pursued earlier. Egypt might still be considered a socialist country, but the growing private sector and the emergence of a new middle class (composed of entrepreneurs, engineers, physicians, lawyers and other professionals) are obvious manifestations of a shift from collectivism to free enterprise. However, the oscillation of the pendulum has not yet been completed.

Perhaps an even more important shift in economy is the retreat from an emphasis on industrialization to a reaffirmation of an agricultural policy. One of the major aims of the revolutionary movement that swept Arab lands in the fifties was to start industrial enterprises which the *ancien régimes* had been reluctant to initiate for various reasons under the influence of Western industrialized countries that tried to keep Arab lands dependent on Western industry. After a decade or two of industrial experimentation—some countries persisted in the experimentation longer than others—the Arab leaders have come to the conclusion that neither in quality nor in the cost of production can they compete with Western industry and that only certain specific industrial enterprises—oil production, if it exists in commercial quantities, and some industries that meet the needs of local markets—are justified economically. The income from oil and other minerals that exist in abundance, some Arab leaders maintain, should be used to improve agricultural production rather than wasted on uneconomical projects, as agriculture will remain for long—indeed, for an indefinite time—the backbone of Arab economy.

IV

Broadly speaking, all Arab leaders—not only those who form the subject matter of this work—are agreed on asserting their independence as a primary objective and in pursuing a foreign policy which would protect and enhance that independence by joining a regional alliance and cultivating the goodwill of, if not a formal alliance with, a Great Power. As noted earlier, there are two foreign policy objectives on which all are agreed—opposition to foreign intervention and to Zionist national claims. Beyond that, the Arab leaders can scarcely be said to have an agreement on foreign policy.

With regard to their attitude toward the East-West conflict, the Arab leaders are divided into two schools of thought. First, the Monarchical leaders, opposed to Communist ideology, have preferred to maintain friendly relationships with the Western Powers. Except perhaps for Jordan, the Arab countries governed by Monarchies are in possession of oil and other mineral resources which prompted them to seek the more profitable Western rather than Eastern markets. Jordan, a former ward and ally of Britain, had been the recipient of British and now American economic assistance. For these, and perhaps other reasons (cultural and otherwise), the Monarchical leaders have been well disposed toward the Western Powers and might have entered into a formal alliance with one or more had they not been liable to be reproached

by anti-Western critics who constantly reminded
them of American support for Israel against Arab
interests.

The military leaders, on the other hand, have advocated non-alignment in principle, presumably
because they rule over new regimes that replaced
older ones considered to have been the unequal allies (if they were not under the complete domination) of Western Powers. Because they never felt
an immediate Soviet threat, they resisted all Western attempts to solicit commitments and sought
economic and military assistance from the Soviet
Union without entering into a formal alliance with
it. Confrontation with Israel necessarily led to a
heavy dependence on Soviet support and eventually to formal commitments. In due time, all military leaders, whether in South Arabia or in northern Arab lands, have obtained at one time or
another Soviet economic and military assistance.
Soviet prestige in the Arab World reached its high-
water mark in the Six-Day War (1967). When the
Arabs failed to recover the territory lost in 1967 despite Soviet support, the military leaders began to
have second thoughts about the wisdom of Arab
dependence on Soviet assistance. Though some
military leaders began to diversify their sources of
foreign support, only Sadat went so far as to break
the Soviet alliance and seek American political and
economic assistance in an effort to recover Egyptian territory lost in 1967. Iraq and North Yaman,
not directly exposed to Israeli threats, have been
able to move away from heavy dependence on Soviet support; indeed, North Yaman, accepting both
Soviet and American assistance, may well be regarded as a truly non-aligned Arab country. Syria,
unable to receive adequate American backing to

recover its lost territory, felt bound to depend on Soviet support in the face of continuing Israeli pressures; but Asad, a cautious and prudent leader, even after he entered into a formal alliance with the Soviet Union has not been prepared to grant any special privilege to a Great Power. He may take pride in the fact that he can still consider Syria a non-aligned country and has maintained correct, if not always friendly, relationships with the United States and obtained both American economic and Soviet military assistance.

V

Compared with their idealist and ideological forerunners, the realist leaders of the Arab World today—at any rate the leaders scrutinized in this study—are perhaps the most constructive though not necessarily the most popular that have made their appearance since the early postwar years. Like the realists of the interwar years, who tried to compromise with the facts as they were, the realists of today are trying to maintain a balance between ultimate and immediate objectives. Consequently, they have not been accorded as great an enthusiasm as Nasir or Qasim in the fifties. Nor do the realists of today fall in the category of charismatic leaders. A leader endowed with charismatic or Napoleonic qualities is a man possessing not only a set of personal qualities—the ability to inspire and sway the public, moral courage and others—but also capable of achieving national goals which his contemporaries had been unable to achieve before. In Arab countries, such national goals have consisted of the achievement of independence (if independence were not complete), the recovery of Arab territory that may have passed under foreign domination, and putting an end to one form of foreign encroachments or another. Nasir and Qasim are cases in point: the former defied the Western Powers and obtained Soviet arms, nationalized the Suez Canal and achieved a momentary Syro-Egyptian unity as a step toward ultimate Arab union, although the dream remained unfulfilled; and the latter, though falling short of rising to the height of Nasir's prestige, provided leadership for the revolution that overthrew the Iraqi Monarchy and put an end to British (and Western) domination of the country by termination of the alliance with Britain and the Baghdad Pact. He also took the first drastic step in the nationalization of the oil industry.

Of the personalities scrutinized in this study, Sadat is the only leader who has shown the courage, in line with his predecessors, to defy a Great Power (the Soviet Union) on the grounds that it sought the domination of his country. Perhaps even more important was his highly successful collaboration with Asad in the planning and execution of the October War (1973) resulting in the partial rehabilitation of Arab pride by winning an initial victory for which Asad deserves almost equal credit. But neither Sadat nor Asad has yet acquired the image of a Nasir or Faysal in the public eye, because of their relative moderation and realism, which are not popular in extremist circles. Equally endowed with great moral courage and strong convictions is King Husayn, who deserves a greater appreciation than has yet been accorded to him, mainly because he pursued policies considered too friendly to the West and not always in accordance with Arab interests. Only in recent years did his countrymen begin to recognize the long-term advantages of his endeavors.

In the span of almost half a century since the Arabs began to have an independent national existence a plethora of political figures has risen to power and assumed responsibility—but how many realist leaders?

The symbols of "national goals" and "national aspirations" fashionable in Arab countries are embodied in the broad and collective terminology called in Western countries the "national interests," which may or may not always represent the common interests of the nation as a whole. Western political leaders claim to weigh the national interests on a scale of rational and objective criteria and to try by flexible but firm methods to pursue those interests whether in the saddle or in opposition. Leaders who have proved incapable of serving the national interest or appearing to serve it rarely survive to play the political game. By contrast, Arab leaders have often appeared to weigh the national interests in light of intemperate and subjective standards, because traditional and emotional factors out-weigh other considerations. What were those factors?

In the past, Arab leadership was in the hands of dynasts and military adventurers who seized power by violence or by political manipulation. In most cases, the religious leaders tended to support those in power on the strength of the principle that public quietude was in the best interest of the Muslim community even though often the beneficiaries of this rationale were the vested interests.

Foreign ideas and pressures, especially the rise of nationalism, caused a change in the traditional pattern of leadership, but these patterns have not

yet completely been superseded. Today, an increasing number of Arab leaders who are capable
of weighing the national interests on the scale of
rational and objective criteria are making head-
way, slow as the process may be, but have not yet
been able to command the public, because the traditional leaders who stress intemperate methods
are still capable of arousing the concern of important sections of the public. For this reason, no realist leader can completely disregard the lingering
traditional influences which extremists often exploit to sway audiences. Yet in most Arab lands the
trend seems unmistakably toward a greater appreciation of the realist rather than the extremist—
idealist or ideological—leadership. It is likely that
this trend will gain further ground if the process of
social change which is now underway is continued
by peaceful and constructive rather than by violent
methods.

INDEX